LACAN AND ROMANTICISM

SUNY series, Studies in the Long Nineteenth Century
—————————————————————————
Pamela K. Gilbert, editor

Lacan and Romanticism

Edited by Daniela Garofalo
and David Sigler

Cover image: Leonardo Alenza y Nieto (1807–1845), *Sátiras del suicidio romántico*, nineteenth century, painting, oil on canvas. Madrid, Museo del Romanticismo.

Published by State University of New York Press, Albany

© 2019 State University of New York

All rights reserved

No part of this book may be used or reproduced in any manner whatsoever without written permission. No part of this book may be stored in a retrieval system or transmitted in any form or by any means including electronic, electrostatic, magnetic tape, mechanical, photocopying, recording, or otherwise without the prior permission in writing of the publisher.

For information, contact State University of New York Press, Albany, NY
www.sunypress.edu

Library of Congress Cataloging-in-Publication Data

Names: Garofalo, Daniela, 1968- editor. | Sigler, David, 1977- editor.
Title: Lacan and Romanticism / edited by Daniela Garofalo and David Sigler.
Description: Albany : State University of New York Press, [2019] | Series: SUNY series, studies in the long nineteenth century | Includes bibliographical references and index.
Identifiers: LCCN 2018020087| ISBN 9781438473451 (hardcover) | ISBN 9781438473475 (ebook) | ISBN 9781438473468 (paperback)
Subjects: LCSH: Romanticism—Great Britain. | Lacan, Jacques, 1901-1981—Influence. | Psychoanalysis and literature. | English literature—19th century—History and criticism. | English literature—18th century—History and criticism. | Psychiatry in literature.
Classification: LCC PR457 .L35 2019 | DDC 820.9/145—dc23 LC record available at https://lccn.loc.gov/2018020087

10 9 8 7 6 5 4 3 2 1

CONTENTS

List of Illustrations,   vii

Acknowledgments,   ix

Introduction: Lacan and Romanticism,   xi
DANIELA GAROFALO AND DAVID SIGLER

1   The Gaze of *Frankenstein*,   1
PAUL A. VATALARO

2   Goya's Gaze: Seeing Non-relation in *Los Caprichos*,   21
RITHIKA RAMAMURTHY

3   Jacques Lacan and John Keats's "Noble Animal Man,"   37
COLIN CARMAN

4   Abandoned by Providence: Loss in Jane Austen's *Persuasion*,   61
DANIELA GAROFALO

5   Logical Time and the Romantic Sublime,   81
ZAK WATSON

6   The Eros of Thanatos: Eighteenth-Century Graveyard Poetry and Melancholic Sublimation,   99
ED CAMERON

7   Toric Tropes Are Stolen Boats: Reading Wordsworth's *The Prelude* Topologically, with Lacan,   119
DAVID SIGLER

8   Tyranny as Demand: Lacan Reading the Dreams of the Gothic Romance,   141
MATT FOLEY

9   Jouissance, Obscene Undersides, and Utopian/Dystopian Formations in Sarah Scott's *Millenium Hall* and Mary Shelley's *The Last Man*,   157
EVAN GOTTLIEB

Contributors,   177

Index,   179

ILLUSTRATIONS

Figure 2.1 Francisco Goya y Lucientes (1746–1828), *Nobody knows himself* (*Nadie se conoce*), *Los Caprichos*,   29

Figure 2.2 Francisco Goya y Lucientes (1746–1828), *Even thus he cannot make her out* (*Ni así la distingue*), *Los Caprichios*,   30

ACKNOWLEDGMENTS

The Editors gratefully acknowledge the support of our colleagues at the University of Oklahoma and University of Calgary. We offer thanks for the expert editorial work performed by Amanda Lane-Camilli and Chelsea Miller at SUNY Press, that of series editor Pamela K. Gilbert, and the immensely helpful and thoughtful advice of the anonymous readers. We thank Callie Craig for her timely research assistance and the office of the vice president for research at the University of Oklahoma for facilitating that assistance. We gratefully acknowledge the comradeship of our colleagues Anna Kornbluh, Joel Faflak, David Collings, and Anna Shajirat. We appreciate colleagues met and conversations had at the LACK conferences in 2016 and 2017, and especially Todd McGowan's work in building the LACK community. We thank The Rabbit Hole in Colorado Springs for its hospitality on several occasions as we, in league with Colin Carman, talked through our plans for this project and ideas-in-progress.

Daniela Garofalo would additionally like to thank her colleagues at the University of Oklahoma for their feedback on her work on Jane Austen and Lacan, as well as Molly Anne Rothenberg for her many insights on these two remarkable figures. Finally, she thanks Derek Hook for his wonderfully enlightening class on Lacan at Birkbeck College, University of London.

David Sigler would additionally like to thank Russell Grigg for generously welcoming him (me) into his seminar on "Psychoanalysis and Sexualities" in the spring of 2017, David L. Clark for his wise advice on a draft of chapter 7, and Dawn Hamilton for being thoroughly spectacular. His work on chapter 7 was supported by an Insight Grant from the Social Sciences and Humanities Research Council of Canada.

Introduction
Lacan and Romanticism

DANIELA GAROFALO AND DAVID SIGLER

Why *Lacan and Romanticism*? At a time, within Romantic studies, in which the turn to historicism has just begun to loosen its three-decades-long grasp on the field, and in which scholars have meanwhile been variously bemoaning or acclaiming the demise of theory, the study of Lacan with Romanticism might seem like a quixotic enterprise. Confronted by the juggernaut of historicism, theory, some might argue, is dead. Yet some of the richest and most interesting work in literary and cultural studies, all the while, has remained thoroughly informed by theory, and new theoretical praxes have emerged in the last decade or so. As Vincent Leitch writes: "[D]espite all the talk about posttheory and after theory that has been floating around for several decades, there is a theory renaissance underway."[1] Jacques Lacan—engine of the twentieth century's first theory renaissance with his ever-controversial "return to Freud"—has been an important part of that resurgence within the study of Romanticism and within literary studies more broadly.

In particular, Lacanian theory has experienced a wide-ranging revival since the 1990s, especially with the publication of Slavoj Žižek's groundbreaking work. It emphasized (and emphasizes) how and why Lacan matters for a politicized study of culture. Concomitantly, over the last ten years, beginning with Bruce Fink's translation of Lacan's complete *Écrits* and then with the publication of Lacan's other seminars and lectures, scholars have begun to move beyond Lacan's most familiar writings, such as the oft-anthologized essays on "The Mirror Stage" and "The Agency of the Letter in the Unconscious," to explore the many unfamiliar corners of Lacan's thought.

Several books published in the last few decades have been dedicated to the purpose of aligning Lacan with current literary and cultural studies.[2] They have raised the question of what Lacan brings to the study of literature in particular and culture more generally. Although the word "symptom" is often associated with Lacan and psychoanalysis, a Lacanian focus can offer an alternative to symptomatic readings of literary texts, or offer new ways to think about the symptomatic nature of texts. Lacanians are not alone in this effort, but are an important part of a turn away from primarily historicist and new historicist approaches. There was a time when Lacanian studies of Romanticism would face inevitable, and often just, accusations of peddling seemingly timeless myths—and thus ideology. To speak of a psychoanalysis *avant la lettre* was considered anachronistic and thus intolerable. Psychoanalytic work in Romanticism has, in recent decades, taken seriously these concerns, adapted its methodologies, and accordingly upended such conclusions: what is more obvious today is that psychoanalytic ideas emerged as a discursive development of the late eighteenth and nineteenth centuries, and that the Romantic focus on the psyche and the unconscious demanded new ways of reading and storytelling. Romanticism, in Britain and throughout Europe, was closely involved in the representation, analysis, and production of human desire—and, as Colin Carman's essay in this volume indicates, desire beyond the boundaries of the human—and thus in many ways inaugurated psychoanalytic discourses.

New historicist approaches to Romanticism, as pioneered by critics such as Jerome McGann and Marjorie Levinson, have tended to see literary texts as reactions to a cultural context that informs them even (or especially) when the writer represses or ignores their political and historical milieu.[3] Thus the critic reads the text suspiciously for what the author would occlude about politics, an evasion that nonetheless thoroughly informs the work. To a text shaped by an evasion of social realities, the critic returns a missing context that illuminates the symptomatic nature of the work. Even when historicist critics are less suspicious of the text and simply want to show the importance of material culture in a work (for example, Napoleon as subtext for Coleridge's "Kubla Khan"),[4] the critic tends to find that the context is more interesting than text. When read as symptoms of their culture, texts indicate aspects of a pervasive, if dynamic, context, which thoroughly shapes them.

Lacanian readings can be just as invested in historical particularity, but typically they focus on the text itself, finding that literature, painting, film, and other art forms importantly intervene in the symbolic order and do not merely reflect and react to it. Sharply breaking from traditions of psychoanalytic literary criticism focused on psychobiography, for Lacan "it is out of the question to analyze dead authors." Instead, he recommends:

> You must start from the text, start by treating it, as Freud does and as he recommends, as Holy Writ. The author, the scribe, is only a pen-pusher[.] . . . Please give more attention to the text than to the psychology of the author—the entire orientation of my teaching is that.[5]

Accordingly, Lacanians tend to see the literary and artistic text as a unique expression, as an intervention in the socio-symbolic network that the text interrogates, undermines, and alters. Far from asserting timeless truths of the unconscious, current iterations of Lacanian literary criticism, including the contributors to this volume, critically examine and even vastly destabilize the political uses to which texts might, or might have historically, been put. They do so by attending to, rather than displacing, the aesthetic aspects of texts. As Todd McGowan has written recently in defense of the masterpiece: "We must retain the category of the masterpiece despite the ideological uses that critics have made of it because it provides a name for the power of the literary work to change our symbolic coordinates."[6] Lacanian literary studies, as it is usually practiced now, tends to think about the artwork as an ideological network of signifying systems with potentially subversive implications. Thus we can retain the category of the masterpiece without merely reifying hegemonic structures of canonicity, given how "the majority of masterpieces are the crumbs of other unknown masterpieces."[7] Texts themselves, intentionally or not, have something to teach us, and can remake the world around them. This is a quintessentially Romantic assumption, admittedly. Thus psychoanalysis can be, and has been, an instrument of canon revision and renegotiation, as adaptable for the works of popular writers such as Joanna Southcott and Walter Scott as for masterpiece makers such as Jane Austen, John Keats, and Francisco Goya.

Because of an emphasis on the uniqueness of the text, the way a text works against its own seeming intentions or protrudes in unexpected directions, Lacanian approaches also offer an alternative to certain kinds of approaches in the Digital Humanities (DH). Franco Moretti's "distant reading," which emphasizes a study of archives instead of the single text, sees close reading as an outdated and overused technique.[8] Yet Lacanians tend to address questions of desire, social organization, language, and the unconscious, which manifest differently in each text. They depend on close textual analysis, their capacity for surprise, and a willingness to find what is unspoken—or what really was spoken, despite expectations. Lacan underscored how every patient speaks a different language, how every subject uses language and processes images in their own particular way. One of the ethical commitments of psychoanalysis is to remain true to those differences, not to collapse subjects into types or groups, which allows us to ignore individual uses of language, image, and narrative. In recent literary studies, much has been made of Moretti's "distant reading" and its emphasis on tools that allow the scholar to explore an archive of thousands of works. With its attention to quantity, to being able to extract data from a large number of texts, and the importance of finding patterns across the digital archive in a historical period, Moretti's version of DH has led to a de-emphasis on close reading, the individual text, and even the individual author. Lacanian readings indicate the merits of a different approach. A single text can construct a vision of the world and the mind that are irreducible to historical context or larger cultural tendencies. Lacanian readings emphasize how texts can offer new ways of seeing and knowing. They often focus on formal features of texts and on close readings, emphasizing the crucial differences and details that allow the text to continue to surprise and inform us. Lacanian literary and cultural scholarship, in other words, participates in a recent scholarly reaction against the assumptions of historicism, distant reading, and data collection. Our wager is that Lacanian theory offers a particularly rich and profound approach to textual scholarship that reveals the interactions among psyche, society, and history in ways that will reinvigorate textual study.

Lacanian psychoanalysis offers no roadmap for success, however, and cannot predict in advance the sorts of insights it will generate. In "Variations on the Standard Treatment," Lacan argued that psychoanalysis, if it were to be meaningful, would not concern itself with myth structures. Rather, given the specificity of each analysand and each analyst, and the open-ended, overdetermined contexts for any analysis, it "progresses essentially in non-knowledge." As we learn its techniques, he warns, "its foundations must be laid open to criticism."[9] The tension between this relentless questioning of first principles, and yet the radical fidelity to the text on the page, including Freud's, even when it says something improper or unexpected, represents a tension found everywhere in Lacanian literary criticism.

Certain kinds of texts lend themselves especially well to such approaches, and Romantic-era writing, which responded, often wildly, to a world in which absolutely everything seemed up for grabs or possible to reimagine, makes special demands of the theory, too. Pioneering for their innovative re-renderings of the mind, consciousness, and subjectivity, Romantic literature and art make possible especially innovative Lacanian readings. As Joel Faflak argues in *Romantic Psychoanalysis*, British Romantic writing anticipates the concerns that Freud would address a century later, and can even be said to have been "inventing psychoanalysis."[10] Romanticism was, it would seem, the incubation of psychoanalytic reason, and yet it had to articulate its psychoanalytic insights without recourse to its terminological apparatus, and thus without fixed expectations for what it was encountering. Lacanian approaches to the study of Romanticism tend to work so well because the texts in question have not anticipated the Freudian-Lacanian lexicon or epistemologies. This means that Romantic-era texts tend to be "wild" in the Freudian sense, too—the texts commit errors of psychoanalytic interpretation that challenge and distort psychoanalytic orthodoxies.[11]

Lacanian approaches to the study of Romanticism are too numerous and longstanding to recap here. One area that has been particularly indebted to psychoanalytic approaches has been the study of the Gothic, which makes sense given the intense psychic register of that genre.[12] But Lacanian literary scholars have undertaken the study of Romanticism more broadly, including studies of canonical writers such as Jane Austen, John Keats, Lord Byron, and William Wordsworth.[13] The current interest in Lacan among Romanticists brings the theory full circle, given Lacan's own investments in British and Spanish Romanticism. In *Seminar V*, Lacan spoke at some length about wit in English Romanticism, and then he identified Spanish Romanticism as "the main tradition," leaving it aside in his commentary only "because it's too important for us."[14] Two years later, Lacan described psychoanalysis as an elaboration of the idea, from Wordsworth's "Ode: Intimations of Immortality," that "the child is father of the man."[15] He variously commented on Romanticism's relation to love, childhood, and wit, supposing that British Romantic writers were "radically different from the poets who preceded them":

> [I]t is no accident that we discover it in that period with its fresh, shattering, and even breathtaking quality, bursting forth at the beginning of the nineteenth century with the industrial revolution, in the country that was most advanced in experiencing its effects, in England. English romanticism has its own special features, which include the value given to childhood memories, to the whole world of childhood, to the ideals and wishes of the child.[16]

British Romanticism was, for Lacan, a privileged literary corpus for understanding psychoanalytic ideas. Lacan tended to see Romantic poetry as the unspoken or hidden part of psychoanalysis, and an important precursor to, and interlocutor for, Freud. Knowledge of Romanticism was valued by Lacan: for instance, he admired the way that Freud was able to read the lacunae in Daniel Paul Schreber's *Memoir* through his familiarity with Byron's *Manfred*.[17] It was Lacan's opinion that true Freudians would need to be Romanticists, in the sense that the thematic preoccupations of the period's literature tend to address the gaps and silences in contemporary psychiatric and psychological discourse. Romantic-era writing makes possible psychoanalytic reason and can align psychoanalysis with "the true, solid backbone of Freud's thought," curbing the discipline's normativity and prescriptiveness.[18]

Yet Lacan, being neither literary scholar nor time traveler, had a typically narrow vision of what Romanticism was and could be. In the 1950s and '60s, it meant insightful male writers reacting to the industrial revolution through acts of imagination. Thus Lacan saw the imaginative encounter with one's childhood as the era's pervasive concern, rather than, say, the abolition of slavery, or rationalizations for empire, or patriarchal oppression. The purview of his British Romanticism extended only so far as Scott, Byron, Wordsworth, Coleridge, and Hazlitt. He lived in a world in which Austen was a strangely belated eighteenth-century novelist, Wollstonecraft's posthumous reputation had been obliterated, and Wordsworth had revived the sonnet tradition.

Romanticism as it appears today is more contradictory and multifarious than Lacan could have imagined, and far more Lacanian. The writers and topics that have come into view since Lacan's death in 1981 have vastly expanded our sense of what desire could mean in the period, where the gaze could wander, how the Real could interrupt but also anchor the era's commercial and imperial systems. Since Lacan's death, the period has more widely been acknowledged to have invented psychoanalysis, cognitive science, and the systematized study of perversion;[19] entire branches of psychoanalysis, following Wilfrid Bion, have organized themselves around Keats and negative capability.[20] It falls to today's scholars, then, to make the necessary introductions between Lacan and the multiform Romanticisms that we call Romanticism today.

The reverse is equally the case, however: scholarship on Romanticism has, until recently, had only a very partial and limited access to Lacan. Generally, we might say that Lacan loved Romanticism more than Romanticists have tended to love him back. In that sense, it really was love: he was giving something he didn't have—(i.e., expertise in the period and its literature)—to those who haven't generally wanted it.[21] Greater interest in Lacan within literary studies has tended to follow on the heels of new translations and new editions of his work: the previous big wave of Lacanian literary criticism, in the 1990s, for instance, relied upon the publication of several "new" Lacanian seminars in English: David Collings began analyzing *das Ding* in Wordsworth's poetry shortly after the 1992 publication of Lacan's *Seminar VII*, and Mark Lussier's 2002 analysis of Blake's *The Four Zoas* depended upon the 1998 English publication of *Seminar XX*.[22] Critics in the 1990s, as Laura Claridge explains, were discovering how "Lacan allows readers a certain freedom in letting the literary text speak of its own plurality to us."[23] Still, until as recently as 2006, Romanticists really had access to only six of Lacan's twenty-seven seminars, and only "A Selection" of the *Écrits*.[24] Things began to change significantly, though, with the publication that year of Bruce Fink's translation of the complete *Écrits*. That monumental work, activating concepts like "logical time" for English literary criticism, has instigated an unprecedented era of Lacan translation under the editorial eye of Jacques-Alain Miller. Since 2007, we have seen the English publication of six further seminars (four since 2016 alone!), along with translations of other

Lacanian texts such as *My Teaching* (2008) and *The Triumph of Religion* (2013).[25] This means that the number of pages of Lacan's thought available to English-language scholars has more than doubled in the last ten years, with the process still vastly accelerating. Given Lacan's tendency to think out loud, to improvise "live theory" as a kind of performance art, this new material opens the conversation in unexpected directions. To be a Lacanian literary critic today means something very different from what it meant in 1995, or 2006, or even 2015: we have seen Lacan's life's work on a fuller scale, and the available concepts and contexts are often significantly different. It will take some time for literary scholars to work through and learn this fresh material, but there is every reason to believe that it will summon a wave of Lacanian literary analyses in English, ones that will be unfamiliar in their methodologies and perceptions. Our contributors are beginning this process in these pages: Colin Carman and Matt Foley draw upon a range of newly published texts, including *Seminar X* ("Anxiety"), *Seminar XXIII* ("The Sinthome"), and *My Teaching*, and David Sigler draws upon *Seminar V* and other still unpublished materials. In engaging with and working through these ideas, we imagine that our volume might signal several ways forward for Lacanian studies in the field of Romanticism.

This book is significant because our contributors, many of whom have been leaders in this critical conversation so far, often employ concepts that may be less familiar to those who remember Lacan from the 1990s or from Žižek's work. This marks an important turn in the field. Although Romanticists, in recent years, have returned with greater frequency and open-mindedness to Lacan's ideas, they have most frequently done so indirectly, through engagement with Žižek's writings. Forest Pyle notes that "the Lacanian analysis of desire... has found its second coming of sorts in the work of Žižek,"[26] and Daniela Garofalo similarly observes that "Lacanian psychoanalysis, particularly as mediated by Slavoj Žižek's politicization of Lacan, has become increasingly interesting to Romanticists" recently.[27] Žižek's ideas have informed the work of a wide and diverse swath of Romanticists, including Mark Sandy, Guinn Batten, our contributor Evan Gottlieb, Neil Fraistat, George Haggerty, Orrin N. C. Wang, and Brian Cooney.[28] Žižek usefully "amplifies" Lacan, as our contributor Paul A. Vatalaro explains elsewhere, to reveal the political and ideological aspects of desire in the period.[29] Yet Lacan's oeuvre is vast and multifaceted, and Žižek's repertoire has tended to "amplify" only a few Lacanian concepts for Romanticism. The challenge today, as Sam Warren Miell has urged, is arguably "to reclaim Lacan on his own terms"—while not forgetting the insights that Žižek-inspired scholarship has developed so far.[30] The aim of our collection is thus to open the study of Romanticism to less familiar Lacanian ideas and methodologies, so they might gain a foothold in the field.

Our contributors thus stake out relatively unfamiliar Lacanian territory as a way of reimagining what Lacanian literary studies can mean. They explore topics from Lacan that have been underutilized in literary criticism, such as his interrogations of aesthetics, topology, logical time, and need and demand. Others develop innovative rereadings of Lacan's most familiar texts, such as "The Subversion of the Subject," "The Mirror Stage," or *Four Fundamental Concepts of Psychoanalysis*, transforming those texts in the process. In so doing they find themselves frequently contesting critical orthodoxies about the self-making of Frankenstein's Creature, the meaning of the marriage plot, or the political commentary encoded in Goya's dark visions. They artfully import Lacan into discussions in which Lacan has so far had only limited impact, or had seemed *persona non grata*, such as nonhuman animal studies, the politics of aesthetics, the ethics of sublimity, or literature and the environment, and in doing so they invent a contemporary Lacan better adapted for the critical and social preoccupations of the late 2010s. Carman traces in Keats, for instance, a queer critical ecology that resists oppressive models of political sovereignty. Rikitha Ramamurthy sharpens the political edge of Lacan's theory of the gaze even as she finds ways of reading Goya that aren't reducible to political allegory. She reveals how Lacanian models of analysis can, when given the right materials, get beyond the impasses of Foucauldian methodologies—offering, implicitly, a bold challenge to work in Romantic and Gothic studies that has sought to reconcile psychoanalysis with Foucault.[31] Evan Gottlieb even somehow finds a glimmer of utopianism in Lacan, with ramifications for the way that we understand the relation between social justice and science fiction. Our contributors ask political questions such as, What is tyranny? and, What does utopia want?; they trace the sacrifices demanded by global capitalism onto sex and love; they rescue, through their studies of eroticism, alternative ways of political world-building. They resist attempts "to squeeze profits from the Real," as Zak Watson thoughtfully says, as he situates logical time within the unconscious. They show us the forgotten temporal element of the sublime. They show how the quintessentially Romantic project of subject-formation tends to get caught up, irredeemably, in its impasses. They ask aesthetic questions such as, How does writing generate meaning through rupture?, What shapes can literary language take?, What is a genre?, or, How can a fetish lend itself to representation? They theorize the bases of perception. They ask questions of rights, such as, What qualifies as merit?, Why would utopia want to retain oppression?, or, Where does sexual difference appear? They ask questions of affect, such as, What happens when mourning becomes sublime? and, Why go on? How does a psychic economy of profit and loss respond to the capitalist economy, and, knowing that, might we discover how the fusion of love with commodity capitalism could serve a binary system of sexual difference?

The questions provoking our contributors, then, are not ones that we would typically associate with Lacan. They are questions much more familiar to Romanticists—and in this sense the collection seeks to bring Romanticism to Lacan rather than the other way around. Yet in pursuing these questions through Lacan, our contributors frequently push against the boundaries of what might be considered Romanticism, opening the conversation to include eighteenth-century predecessors of Romanticism such as Elizabeth Carter, Edward Young, Robert Blair, William Collins, and Sarah Scott. Even Austen, a writer who has seemed, at times, "immune to psychoanalysis" and for whom "the volume and quality of psychological studies . . . lags significantly behind work done from other perspectives," is here shown to be thinking about loss and recovery in a hauntingly psychoanalytic way, as Garofalo reveals in her analysis of *Persuasion*.[32] But our contributors are also returning to authors such as Wordsworth, Horace Walpole, Keats, and Mary Shelley with long and remarkable histories of Lacanian interpretation, using new Lacanian methodologies to rethink desire, subjectivity, and politics in some foundational Romantic texts.

While each of the essays explores different areas of Lacanian theory, they are all concerned, in various ways, with the problem of lack. Lack becomes in these pages the guiding thread that unites the work of these Lacanian Romanticists, who are informed not only by Lacan's emphasis but also by Romanticism's abiding concern with the topic. The first essay in *Lacan and Romanticism*, Paul Vatalaro's "The Gaze of *Frankenstein*," takes up a novel that has frequently been given the Lacanian treatment in influential readings by Mladen Dolar, David Collings, and Denise Gigante. Vatalaro's essay in this collection highlights the significance of the gaze in Mary Shelley's novel and how it compels an encounter with traumatic lack. Rithika Ramamurthy's "Goya's Gaze: Seeing Non-relation in *Los Caprichos*" extends the focus on the gaze but connects it to the problem of sexuation and the lack of the sexual relation in an unexpected political register. Daniela Garofalo's "Abandoned by Providence: Loss in Jane Austen's *Persuasion*" further develops the Lacanian theme of sexuation in order to examine, as do Ramamurthy and Vatalaro, the encounter with a traumatic lack, finding in the novel's discourses of sexual difference a meditation on personal finance and loss in every sense. Colin Carman's "Jacques Lacan and John Keats's 'Noble Animal Man' " analyzes Keats's *Endymion* through the topics of sexuation and lack, but in connection with environmental disaster and questions of political sovereignty. In so doing he finds an ambivalent place for Lacan in ongoing studies of nonhuman subjectivity—a conversation in which Lacan has been presumed, thanks to deconstructive criticism, to be unhelpful. Zak Watson's "Logical Time and the Romantic Sublime" pursues the aesthetic strands of that analysis in relation to William Collins's "Ode on the Poetical Character," a poem which enables Watson to theorize, *contra* dominant models of the sublime from Immanuel Kant and Thomas Weiskel, how the sublime leads to a realization not only of subjective lack but also of the lack in the Other. Ed Cameron, in "The Eros of Thanatos: Eighteenth-Century Graveyard Poetry and Melancholic Sublimation," extends Watson's analysis of the sublime and Garofalo's analysis of loss by considering how a generation of graveyard poets turn to sublimation in order to bring poetry, dwelling in affective loss and the failures of representation, to the dignity of the presymbolic primordial Thing. David Sigler, in "Toric Tropes Are Stolen Boats: Reading Wordsworth's *The Prelude* Topologically, with Lacan," studies *The Prelude*'s stolen boat scene as an encounter with the problem of subjective lack, in order to show how literary language can be a form of topology. Matt Foley's "Tyranny as Demand: Lacan Reading the Dreams of the Gothic Romance," returns us to the Gothic, and especially Walpole's *The Castle of Otranto*, to consider the lack in tyrannical power, which conflates the levels of need, demand, and desire in destabilizing ways—attempting to fill in the gap in the Other and disavowing symbolic structures. Finally, Evan Gottlieb, in "Jouissance, Obscene Undersides and Utopian/Dystopian Formations in Sarah Scott's *Millenium Hall* and Mary Shelley's *The Last Man*, discusses how these utopian/dystopian novels, representing opposite ends of a long Romantic century, reveal a lack in the utopian ideal. Gottlieb examines this lack through the Lacanian concepts of ego ideal and ideal ego—and in doing so highlights an invisible, even seemingly utopian aspect in Lacan's thought and in psychoanalysis more broadly.

 We are hopeful that our collection might update Lacan for Romantic studies at a moment when the next surge in Lacanian Romantic scholarship is just beginning, even as it allows Lacan to make contact with a wider range of Romantic-era texts and writers than has yet been attempted. It is the wager of this book that Romantic studies and Lacanian theory share similar preoccupations and concerns; as fellow travelers, navigating the effects of lack both in the subject and in the big Other, these fields are made better, richer, by engagement and interchange. It is our hope, furthermore, that the essays collected here will go a long way to dispel the notion that Lacan is inaccessible because of his notoriously obscure and elliptical style. That fear has perhaps limited the engagement by Romantic scholars with the work of Jacques Lacan. Focused on fundamental Lacanian ideas, the essays here clarify complex terms and model their application, enabling Lacan to make sense for and of Romanticism. Accessible in both style and subject matter, they can speak to the scholar or student coming to Lacan for the first time, as well as the more practiced reader of Lacanian theory.

Notes

1. Vincent B. Leitch, *Literary Criticism in the 21st Century: Theory Renaissance* (London: Bloomsbury, 2014), 8.

2. *Lacan and Literature: Purloined Pretexts*, Ben Stoltzfus, ed. (New York: SUNY Press, 1996); Jeremy Tambling, *Literature and Psychoanalysis* (Manchester: Manchester University Press, 2012) and *The Cambridge Introduction to Literature and Psychoanalysis*, edited by Jean-Michel Rabaté (New York: Cambridge, 2014) focus on Lacan as well as other psychoanalytic theorists. Also, monographs focused primarily on Lacan, which address a variety of literary fields, have appeared. Some examples among many: Shoshana Felman, *Jacques Lacan and the Adventure of Insight: Psychoanalysis in Contemporary Culture* (Cambridge: Harvard University Press, 1987); James Mellard, *Using Lacan, Reading Fiction* (Bloomington: University of Illinois Press, 1991); Sheldon Brivic, *Joyce through Lacan and Žižek: Explorations* (New York: Palgrave, 2008); Sheldon George, *Trauma and Race: A Lacanian Study of African American Racial Identity* (Waco: Baylor University Press, 2016).

3. Jerome McGann, *The Romantic Ideology: A Critical Investigation* (Chicago: University of Chicago Press, 1985); Marjorie Levinson, "Insight and Oversight: Reading 'Tintern Abbey,'" in *Wordsworth's Great Period Poems: Four Essays* (Cambridge: Cambridge University Press, 1986), 14–57; Marjorie Levinson, "The New Historicism: Back to the Future," in *Rethinking Historicism: Critical Readings in Romantic History*, ed. Marjorie Levinson (Oxford: Blackwell Publishing, 1989), 18–63.

4. Simon Bainridge, *Napoleon and English Romanticism* (Cambridge: Cambridge University Press, 1995), 25.

5. Jacques Lacan, *The Seminar of Jacques Lacan, Book II: The Ego in Freud's Theory and in the Technique of Psychoanalysis, 1954–1955*, ed. Jacques-Alain Miller, trans. Sylvana Tomaselli (New York: Norton, 1988), 152–53.

6. Todd McGowan, "The Bankruptcy of Historicism: Introducing Disruption into Literary Studies," in *Everything You Always Wanted to Know about Literature but Were Afraid to Ask Žižek*, ed. Russell Sbriglia (Durham: Duke University Press, 2017), 101.

7. Jacques Lacan, *The Seminar of Jacques Lacan, Book XVII: The Other Side of Psychoanalysis*, ed. Jacques-Alain Miller, trans. Russell Grigg (New York: Norton, 2007), 183.

8. Franco Moretti, *Distant Reading* (New York: Verso, 2013).

9. Jacques Lacan, *Écrits: The First Complete Edition in English*, trans. Bruce Fink (New York: Norton, 2006), 298–300.

10. Joel Faflak, *Romantic Psychoanalysis: The Burden of the Mystery* (Albany: State University of New York Press, 2008), 15.

11. Sigmund Freud, *The Standard Edition of the Complete Psychological Works of Sigmund Freud*, trans. James Strachey (London: Hogarth Press, 1964), 10:221–27.

12. Terry Castle, "The Spectralization of the Other in The Mysteries of Udolpho," in *The New Eighteenth Century: Theory, Politics, English Literature*, ed. Felicity Nussbaum and Laura Brown (New York: Meuthen, 1987), 231–53; Mladen Dolar, "'I Shall Be With You On Your Wedding-Night': Lacan and the Uncanny," *October* 58 (1991): 5–23; Joan Copjec, "Vampires, Breast-Feeding, and Anxiety," *October* 58 (1991): 24–43, doi:10.2307/778796; Dale Townshend, *The Orders of Gothic: Foucault, Lacan, and the Subject of Gothic Writing, 1764–1820* (New York: AMS Press, 2007); Ed Cameron, *The Psychopathology of the Gothic Romance: Perversion, Neuroses and Psychosis in Early Works of the Genre* (Jefferson, NC: McFarland, 2010).

13. Robert Young, "The Eye and Progress of His Song: A Lacanian Reading of 'The Prelude,'" *Oxford Literary Review* 3, no. 3 (1979): 78–98; Laura Claridge, *Romantic Potency: The Paradox of Desire* (Ithaca: Cornell University Press, 1992); Ghislaine McDayter, *Byromania and the Birth of Celebrity Culture, Studies in the Long Nineteenth Century* (Albany: State University of New York Press, 2009); David Collings, *Monstrous Society: Reciprocity, Discipline, and the Political Uncanny*, c. 1780–1848 (Lewisburg: Bucknell University Press, 2009); Daniela Garofalo, *Women, Love, and Commodity Culture in British Romanticism* (Farnham: Ashgate, 2012); David Sigler, *Sexual Enjoyment in British Romanticism: Gender and Psychoanalysis, 1753–1835* (Montreal: McGill-Queen's University Press, 2015).

14. Jacques Lacan, *The Seminar of Jacques Lacan, Book V: Formations of the Unconscious*, ed. Jacques-Alain Miller, trans. Russell Grigg (Cambridge: Polity, 2017), 14.

15. Jacques Lacan, *The Seminar of Jacques Lacan, Book VII: The Ethics of Psychoanalysis, 1959–1960*, ed. Jacques-Alain Miller, trans. Dennis Porter (New York: Norton, 1992), 24. See also Lacan, *Seminar XVII*, 124.

16. Lacan, *Seminar VII*, 24–25.

17. Lacan, *Écrits*, 466; Freud, SE, 12:44.

18. Lacan, *Seminar VII*, 25.

19. Faflak, *Romantic Psychoanalysis*; Alan Richardson, *The Neural Sublime: Cognitive Theories and Romantic Texts* (Baltimore: Johns Hopkins University Press, 2010); Richard C. Sha, *Perverse Romanticism: Aesthetics and Sexuality in Britain, 1750–1832* (Baltimore: Johns Hopkins University Press, 2008).

20. Wilfred R. Bion, *Attention and Interpretation* (London: Karnac Books, 1984); Richard E. Webb and Michael A. Sells, "Lacan and Bion: Psychoanalysis and the Mystical Language of 'Unsaying,'" *Theory & Psychology* 5, no. 2 (May 1, 1995):

195–215; William Betts, "Negative Capability," *Psychoanalysis Downunder*, no. 7B (2007), http://www.psychoanalysisdownunder.com.au/issues/8/papers/106.

21. Jacques Lacan, "The Seminar of Jacques Lacan, Book XII: Crucial Problems for Psychoanalysis, 1964–1965," trans. Cormac Gallagher n.d., 165 (meeting of March 3, 1965).

22. David Collings, *Wordsworthian Errancies: The Poetics of Cultural Dismemberment* (Baltimore: Johns Hopkins University Press, 1994); Lacan, *Seminar VII*; Mark Lussier, " 'Rest before Labour': The Pre-Text/s of Blake's The Four Zoas," *Romanticism on the Net*, no. 27 (2002); Jacques Lacan, *The Seminar of Jacques Lacan, Book XX: Encore: On Feminine Sexuality, the Limits of Love and Knowledge, 1972–1973*, ed. Jacques-Alain Miller, trans. Bruce Fink (New York: Norton, 1998).

23. Claridge, *Romantic Potency*, 4.

24. Jacques Lacan, *The Seminar of Jacques Lacan, Book I: Freud's Papers on Technique, 1953–1954*, ed. Jacques-Alain Miller, trans. John Forrester (New York: Norton, 1988); Lacan, *Seminar II*; Jacques Lacan, *The Seminar of Jacques Lacan, Book III: The Psychoses*, ed. Jacques-Alain Miller, trans. Russell Grigg (New York: Norton, 1993); Lacan, *Seminar VII*; Jacques Lacan, *The Seminar of Jacques Lacan, Book XI: The Four Fundamental Concepts of Psychoanalysis*, ed. Jacques-Alain Miller, trans. Alan Sheridan (New York: Norton, 1978); Lacan, *Seminar XX*; Jacques Lacan, *Écrits: A Selection*, trans. Alan Sheridan (New York: Norton, 1977).

25. Lacan, *Seminar V*; Bruce Fink, *Lacan on Love: An Exploration of Lacan's Seminar VIII, Transference* (Malden: Polity Press, 2016); Jacques Lacan, *The Seminar of Jacques Lacan, Book X: Anxiety, 1962–1963*, ed. Jacques-Alain Miller, trans. A.R. Price (Cambridge: Polity, 2015); Lacan, *Seminar XVII*; Jacques Lacan, *The Seminar of Jacques Lacan, Book XIX: . . . Ou Pire, 1971–1972*, ed. Jacques-Alain Miller, trans. A.R. Price (Cambridge: Polity, 2017); Jacques Lacan, *The Seminar of Jacques Lacan, Book XXIII: The Sinthome, 1975–1976*, ed. Jacques-Alain Miller, trans. A.R. Price (Cambridge: Polity, 2016); Jacques Lacan, *My Teaching*, trans. David Macey (New York and London: Verso, 2008); Jacques Lacan, *The Triumph of Religion*, trans. Bruce Fink (Cambridge: Polity Press, 2013); Jacques Lacan, "On a Reform in Its Hole," trans. John Holland, S: *Journal of the Circle for Lacanian Ideology Critique* 8 (2015): 14–21.

26. Forest Pyle, *Art's Undoing: In the Wake of a Radical Aestheticism* (New York: Fordham University Press, 2014), 189.

27. Daniela Garofalo, "The Uses of Lacan in Recent British Romantic Studies," *Literature Compass* 10, no. 7 (2013): 559.

28. Mark Sandy, *Romanticism, Memory, and Mourning* (New York: Ashgate, 2013); Guinn Batten, *The Orphaned Imagination: Melancholy and Commodity*

Culture in English Romanticism (Durham: Duke University Press, 1998); Evan Gottlieb, *Walter Scott and Contemporary Theory* (London: Bloomsbury, 2013), 11–31; Neil Fraistat, "The Material Shelley: Who Gets the Finger in Queen Mab?," *The Wordsworth Circle* 33, no. 1 (2002): 35–36; George E. Haggerty, *Queer Gothic* (Urbana: University of Illinois Press, 2006), 9; Brian C. Cooney, "Rev. of Maximilien Robespierre. Virtue and Terror. Intro. Slavoj Žižek. Ed. Jean Ducange," *Romanticism and Victorianism on the Net*, no. 47 (2007): para. 6, doi:10.7202/016711ar.

29. Paul A. Vatalaro, *Shelley's Music: Fantasy, Authority, and the Object Voice* (Farnham: Ashgate, 2009), 24.

30. Sam Warren Miell, "Slavoj Žižek Is Wrong about Stuff," *Different Coloured Hats*, August 3, 2016, https://differentcolouredhats.wordpress.com/2016/08/03/slavoj-zizek-is-wrong-about-stuff/.

31. Diane Long Hoeveler, *Gothic Feminism: The Professionalization of Gender from Charlotte Smith to the Brontës* (University Park: Pennsylvania State University Press, 1998), 53; Townshend, *The Orders*.

32. Joel Faflak, "Jane Austen and the Persuasion of Happiness," in *Romanticism and the Emotions*, ed. Joel Faflak and Richard C. Sha (Cambridge: Cambridge University Press, 2014), 100; Laurence W. Mazzeno, *Jane Austen: Two Centuries of Criticism* (Rochester: Camden House, 2011), 202.

Chapter One

THE GAZE OF *Frankenstein*

PAUL A. VATALARO

MARY SHELLEY foregrounds the formidable and often devastating power of vision when, in the 1831 Introduction to *Frankenstein*, she tells the story of how she conceived her first novel. Looking back on the ghost story writing contest in which she, her husband, Lord Byron and his personal physician, John Polidori, participated during the summer they spent together in Geneva in 1816, she recollects that, while Byron "began a tale, a fragment of which he printed at the end of his poem Mazeppa," and Percy Shelley, unsuited as he was "to invent the machinery of a story, commenced one founded on the experiences of his early life" (334), Polidori managed to draft something that stuck with her.[1] She remembers that

> he had some terrible idea about a skull-headed lady, who was so punished for peeping through a key-hole—what to see I forget—something very shocking and wrong of course; but when she was reduced to a worse condition than the renowned Tom of Coventry, he did not know what to do with her. (334)

The legend of Tom of Coventry, punished with blindness because he peeked while Lady Godiva rode her horse naked through village streets, and Polidori's adaptation of this story about voyeurism and retribution, provoked the nightmare that inspired *Frankenstein*, specifically what in a dream Shelley "saw—with shut eyes, but acute mental vision,—I saw the pale student of unhallowed arts kneeling beside the thing he had put together" (339). After rushing away from the scene of "his odious handywork," the student seeks refuge in sleep, but when "he opens his eyes," she writes, "behold the horrid thing stands at his bedside, opening his curtains, and looking on him with yellow, watery, but speculative eyes. I opened mine in terror" (339). The spectacle haunts Shelley as it does the protagonist of her novel and over the course of his narrative, the activities of looking, watching, and gazing (a word Frankenstein himself uses to describe conditions at his remote Scottish workshop: "I lived ungazed at and unmolested") are never far from punishment and in the creature's case they escalate to voyeurism, surveillance and aggressive scopophilia (252).

Vision determines the creature's personal history: his creator flees when waking to find the creature staring at him above his bed; the creature travels "only at night, fearful of encountering the visage of a human being" (221); he finds voyeuristic pleasure in watching the daily activities of the cottagers; a rustic, upon "seeing" him, wounds him with a rifle shot; the insults levied by William Frankenstein fill him with homicidal fury; he keeps Victor Frankenstein under constant surveillance; a shadowy specter of himself haunts him in the moonlight. Emphasis in the novel on seeing and being seen exposes the hypocrisy and shallowness Shelley witnessed in her culture; however, the traumas the creature experiences as he navigates the visual field originate at a deeper psychological stratum.

Interpretations of *Frankenstein* that have applied concepts taken from Lacan's theories about psycholinguistic development have focused on what befalls Frankenstein-the-subject once his creature opens its eyes and forces its maker to experience the disruptive capacity of the uncanny. Though Frankenstein's trials and escalating anxieties leave little reason to question this approach, the creature's disproportionately large body suggests he is more than just the specular instrument of his creator's punishment. He, too, becomes vulnerable to the liabilities that haunt those who can be seen. In order to appreciate the extent to which Shelley's novel illuminates visual expressions of the uncanny, therefore, the histories of creator and creature require equal attention. As much as the creature obsesses over his ostracism from his creator's life and society, his ghastly physical appearance and vulnerability in the visual field trouble him almost from the instant he becomes conscious. From the beginning, the creature's story emphasizes the physical and aesthetic grounds informing his creator's rejection of him, exemplified best when he places his hand in front of Frankenstein's eyes to shield him from his creature's monstrous appearance (174).

The keynote of the creature's autobiography, however, involves the unavoidable peril of being exposed prematurely to the paternal gaze and, therefore, to the uncanny awareness of loss and lack he cannot escape. This occurrence short-circuits the creature's experience during the mirror stage of his development by eliminating the emergence of his imago and propelling him toward a symbolic order that excludes him. Lacan has indicated that, very early on in its development and well before the onset of the mirror phase, the infant looks at the world from the center of a boundless circle, perceiving everything in that world as an extension of its being. Eventually, the child realizes that, as it can see, so it can be seen, and this recognition, for Lacan, constitutes an alteration in the child's perception that amounts to a loss, a symbolic castration. He refers to that castrating recognition as the "gaze." The gaze represents a lost object the subject cannot control, fuels the desire for its recapture and reintegration into the subject's perceptual field, and makes the subject vulnerable to the sudden and destabilizing irruption of the gaze into normative reality. Its capacity to function as both familiar and alien at the same time unites the gaze with the uncanny; it triggers an anxiety in the subject that he or she is not what he or she desires to be.

The uncanny emerges at the contact point at which extremes interlock, an experience Freud and Lacan believed forces the observer to confront something that is intimate and threatening at the same time. Lacan regarded the uncanny, or "*extimité*," as something "located there where the most intimate interiority coincides with the exterior and becomes threatening, provoking horror and anxiety."[2] From this perspective, the sutured and scarred creature jeopardizes convention and signals to other characters in the book that achieving subjectivity requires amputation. For Lacan, all individuals must gradually be shorn from a state of unbounded being—the "real"—in order to enter a symbolic order where boundless desire drives each subject to compensate for that lack.

Inability to escape the visual field curses the creature and, within the context of the novel's symbolic order, Frankenstein's physically imposing monster dominates every sight line he crosses. He magnifies the unavoidable liabilities attendant upon the faculty of vision with each grand appearance he stages. Whether towering above Frankenstein's bed, bounding unexpectedly toward his maker over crevices cut into the Mer de Glace, leering at his unfinished mate through a moonlit window casement, springing from his hiding place on William Frankenstein, shocking the De Lacey children at their cottage, or facing Walton from beside his creator's coffin, the creature forces every onlooker to confront the fragility of his or her own subject status. Ironically, the creature's dominance of the visual field belies his inability to escape his own image and find any compensatory fantasy that would offer him coherence and acceptance.

Mladen Dolar, Denise Gigante, and David Collings have applied Lacan's interpretation of the uncanny to *Frankenstein* as a way of elucidating the myriad ways in which Shelley exposes the flaws of Enlightenment aspirations. Dolar has asserted that Frankenstein's creature participates in the Enlightenment quest to realize a "'zero degree' of subjectivity, the missing link between nature and culture."[3] Frankenstein's rejection of the creature forces it outside the symbolic order, making it a threat to the fabric of that order, and for Dolar it comes to present itself as the gaze each time it catches its creator's eye, serving as an

> irruption of the real into "homely," commonly accepted reality. We can speak of the emergence of something that shatters well-known divisions

and which cannot be situated within them.... The status of both subject and of "objective reality" is thus put into question.[4]

In Dolar's estimation, the creature tears the fictional screen against which all subjects appear as inherently indeterminate and incomplete images. The creature performs an account of his own "subjectivation,"[5] and one of the results of that process is that the creature seeks a social contract that would install him in the symbolic order, where he would no longer represent disruption. Denied that contract, the creature's case illustrates the failure of eighteenth-century social ideals. "The paradox of the creature," says Dolar, "lies in the fact that this embodiment of the subject of the Enlightenment directly disrupts its universe and produces its limit."[6]

Recognizing that the creature's hideous appearance places it in a nonexistent aesthetic category, Denise Gigante has observed that, though the ugly generates an effect similar to the uncanny, the two phenomena differ in scope, in that the uncanny remains specific to issues repressed within the individual whereas the ugly is universal. In her view, the creature, as a manifestation of the ugly, stands outside of Enlightenment era aesthetic categories, and represents an excess of the real, which bursts through the protective covering of the symbolic. The creature is, she says, "like the blood and guts oozing from the fissures in his skin, an excess of existence, exceeding representation, and hence appearing to others as a chaotic spillage from his own representational shell."[7] According to Gigante, as an irruption of the real, the creature becomes not a lack of beauty but an excess of that which lies beneath the symbolic and threatens to consume it, an angle that inflects William's characterization of the creature as an "ogre" (224). The creature eats away at all representational structures, which include the currency of the Frankenstein family name, its civic service record, and its position on the social register. Gigante writes,

> Once we confront him, as Victor does, in the raw ugliness of his own existence, we discover that he symbolizes nothing but the unsymbolized: the repressed ugliness at the heart of an elaborate symbolic network that is threatened the moment he bursts on the scene, exposing to view his radically uninscribed existence.[8]

Her reading provides a compelling account regarding why Frankenstein's "uninscribed" issue never acquires a name.

David Collings has established that Frankenstein's creature embodies a political and philosophical form of the uncanny. Shelley, expanding her father's critique in his novel *St. Leon* of Enlightenment values, including his own former views, in *Frankenstein* takes aim at "any ideology that would reduce society to an expression of itself and by so doing deny that it is given by an unknowable and unmasterable Other, that its collective life will forever transcend its representation."[9] For Collings, Frankenstein sets out to create a being that will become the "demonstration model" of an abstract human object free of its "biological past" and therefore beyond inherited and other pathological imperfections. He succeeds, however, at constructing a being from the bodies of others that "is not human at all."[10] In seeking to achieve the abstraction Man, in other words, Frankenstein eliminates the man from the abstraction and he fails to recognize his error until the moment when the creature stares back at him, indicating to Frankenstein that his progeny embodies something—subjectivity—his maker did not put there.

What unnerves Frankenstein most, according to Collings, is that he has somehow bestowed subjectivity onto a "*dead object*, producing a creature who looks back not with a genuinely human gaze but with the hollowness of a sentient *thing*."[11] What began as a project attempting to master "natural laws" by means of a technological process ends up producing something that exceeds both: "[T]he creature," writes Collings, "assaults the integrity of human embodiment on several counts at once, desecrating the human in a visual image so powerful that it inevitably terrifies any human being who encounters him."[12]

Following Dolar and Gigante, Collings has underscored the distortions and reversals that occur during this mock-up mirror stage in which the creature serves as his creator's "monstrous double," the material realization of Frankenstein's abominable intention, but also the fiction of embodied human coherence. He reads the creature's compound uncanniness as a product of "his inexplicable subjectivity and his incoherent embodiment," an opposition that "collapses the difference between them, suggesting that the uncanny subject is already a version of the incoherent body and vice versa."[13] Ultimately, Frankenstein manages what Collings refers to as a "magnificent demystification of the human, disclosing the literal form that underlies the fiction of its sanctity," something Frankenstein remains unable to face, because the implication would be that "every person is at least potentially a monster" once "the attribution of the human is stripped away."[14] Viewed from the angles supplied by Dolar, Gigante and Collings, Shelley's *Frankenstein* succeeds at undermining by means of the uncanny Enlightenment faith in the superiority of empirical knowledge and the capacity of a social community to pressure out of existence human imperfections and indeterminacies.

The readings of *Frankenstein* performed by Dolar, Gigante and Collings have regarded Frankenstein the scientist as a representative embodiment of the

Enlightenment project and as a vehicle for Shelley's skepticism about its aspirations. Specifically their views have suggested that Shelley composes Frankenstein's story as a way of illuminating the inevitable failure of this particular intellectual agenda. Collectively, however, this approach moves to the background the creature's story, even though his account would seem to qualify as a competing case study of the psychological damage Enlightenment activity might inflict on its test subjects. The fact that Shelley gifted the creature with the power of narrative indicates that delivering this point of view mattered to her as much as extending her father's critique in *St. Leon* of himself and his contemporaries.

It would appear that for the creature the moment of stripping away "the attribution of the human" occurs as soon as he witnesses his own image in a pool of water during the De Lacey phase of his development. Dolar has implied that, because the creature belongs to the same category as other " 'zero degree' " Enlightenment representations, he never enters a "mirror phase," a misfire that makes him "a nonimaginary subject from which the imaginary support in the world has to be taken away."[15] The creature's version of his own development indicates, however, that he traverses a broken, compound mirror stage and acquires an imaginary support structure soon after his birth. He recounts:

> I had admired the perfect forms of my cottagers—their grace, beauty and delicate complexions: but how was I terrified, when I viewed myself in a transparent pool! At first I started back, unable to believe that it was indeed I who was reflected in the mirror; and when I became fully convinced that I was in reality the monster that I am, I was filled with the bitterest sensations of despondence and mortification. Alas! I did not yet entirely know the fatal effects of this miserable deformity. (190)

Certainly, experiences leading up to this watershed event have amplified the creature's despair. Among its earliest memories, the creature recalls departing Frankenstein's workshop and foraging for food in the woods outside Ingolstadt. The local shepherds and villagers fled from him and in this retrospective account the creature acknowledges the disabling consequences of the curse he bears.

Even more damaging, however, might have been the trauma he experienced once he viewed his own image transmitted by the language of his creator's journal, which the creature found "in the pocket of the dress which I had taken from [Frankenstein's] laboratory" (210). This event transpired "soon after my arrival in the hovel" (210) attached to the De Lacey cottage, possibly prior to the appearance of his image in the pool. The actual unfolding of the sequence notwithstanding, the two events mutually compound one another. Recounting this moment in his history for Frankenstein, the creature remarks:

> It was your journal of the four months that preceded my creation . . . the whole detail of that series of disgusting circumstances which produced it is set in view; the minutest description of my odious and loathsome person is given, in language which painted your horrors and rendered mine ineffaceable. I sickened as I read. (210)

The creature's comments suggest that Frankenstein's journal sets "in view" a different account of Frankenstein's labors than the one he narrates to Walton. The journal indicates that the creature's appearance disgusted Frankenstein before it first returned its maker's gaze and this crippling judgment evidently effaced any possibility of the creature seeing himself as a coherent "I" well before the moment when it opened its "yellow eye" (114).

Lacan describes the dynamic moment when the infant, somewhere between the ages of six and eighteen months, stretches away from the arms restraining it toward the image of itself it sees reflected in a mirror. An imago, the reflection provides the child with a "*gestalt*"—that is, with a superior version of its own imperfectly coordinated body.[16] At this moment, writes Lacan of the mirror stage, the "rudimentary I" is born:

> This jubilant assumption of his specular image by the child at the *infans* stage, still sunk in his motor incapacity and nursling dependence, would seem to exhibit in an exemplary situation the symbolic matrix in which the *I* is precipitated in a primordial form, before it is objectified in the dialectic of identification with the other, and before language restored to it, in the universal, its function as a subject.[17]

This developmental moment is crucial for two reasons. First, it prepares the individual for the "dispossession" of being that will characterize its existence as a subject *of* desire in the symbolic reality that will give it meaning.[18] Second, it marks the origin of an early stage in the competition between the child and the imago—now an object of the child's desire and an object desired by others—from which it has been dispossessed. According to Lacan, "it is in this erotic relation, in which the human individual fixes upon himself, an image that alienates him from himself, that are to be found the energy and the form on which this organization of the passions that he will call his ego is based."[19] Passions that accompany the emergence of the imago include tension consisting of "aggressive competitiveness," an internal state of unrest that will remain with the fully formed subject always.[20]

The creature's narrative, composed after its entry into the world of language, elides that half of the dynamic that includes the imago. The creature never reaches after its image in the pool, nor does it regard that image as the object of desire, an "ideal unity, a salutary imago" distinct from the sutured physical body in plain view.[21] One reason for this scotoma would be that the creature composes his life story from his retrospective position as a subject in the symbolic order. Traumatic rejections of his physical image have destroyed all vestiges of the imago. Depending on his formational curve, furthermore, the creature's account suggests that language came before confrontation with what might have been his imago. A fusion of parts, the creature never found himself presented with the image of wholeness.

A more compelling reason for the creature's blind spot might be that he became subjugated prematurely to the father's gaze and judgment, a developmental crisis that would have foreclosed on the possibility of the creature's "ideal-I" emerging in the first place. The father's gaze does not normatively assert itself until the Oedipus stage. In the creature's case, though, it emerges in the form of Frankenstein's journal and consequently subverts the possibility of the creature forming a normative relationship with the image of its ideal-I. Frankenstein's eight-foot infant son learns to read his father's language before completing the mirror phase. Hence, the creature resorts to substitutes—well coordinated, physically beautiful creatures that he desires at a distance without running the risk of rejection. The creature's imagination casts the members of the De Lacey family into this specular role.

During the phase in which he watches them through a peephole in the wall, the creature reveals that the admirable cottagers inhabited his dreams:

> When I slept, or was absent, the forms of the venerable blind father, the gentle Agatha, and the excellent Felix, flitted before me. I looked upon them as superior beings, who would be the arbiters of my future destiny. I formed in my imagination a thousand pictures of presenting myself to them and their reception of me. I imagined that they would be disgusted, until, by my gentle demeanor and conciliating words, I should first win their favour, and afterwards their love. (192)

The creature's imagination persuades him that he can renovate his "image" without remaking his body by mimicking the language and manners of the cottagers. He goes so far as to take ownership of the little group, referring to them as "my friends" and "my cottagers" (189–90). What's more, though the creature obviously possesses superlative motor skills even at this early stage in his compressed development, he remains in so many ways a "nursling" in need of emotional nourishment and guidance. The De Lacey family promises to provide the creature with the "imaginary support system"—that is, with the imaginary raw materials he will need to overcome the loss of the ideal-I. He recalls holding out hope that they would "overlook my personal deformity," but found himself checked by additional mirrorings, such as when he "beheld my person reflected in water, or my shadow in the moon-shine, even as that frail image and that inconstant shade" (210, 211).

For Lacan, the mirror stage marks the individual's first step toward subjectivity. "This development," Lacan observes,

> is experienced as a temporal dialectic that decisively projects the formation of the individual into history. The *mirror stage* is the drama whose internal thrust is precipitated from insufficiency to anticipation—and which manufactures for the subject, caught up in the lure of spatial identification, the succession of phantasies that extends from a fragmented body-image to a form of its totality that I shall call orthopaedic.[22]

The creature's reflection captures in exaggerated form his literally "fragmented body-image" and the visual, or "scopic"[23] models provided by the De Lacey family promise to serve as a preliminary treatment—an "orthopaedic" remedy—for the correction of his deformities. This benchmark in his development also projects him into history. At the microcosmic level, he learns about the political injustices suffered by Agatha, Felix, Safie, and their parents, creating a context for him in which to view his own treatment at the hands of the humans he had encountered in his earliest days, including the actions of his creator. At the macrocosmic level, the creature learns about Western culture from books contained within the portmanteau he finds and from the reading lessons Felix prepares for Safie: Volney's *Ruins of Empires,* Milton's "*Paradise Lost,* a volume of Plutarch's *Lives,* and the *Sorrows of Werter*" (197, 207). Once he acquires language, he takes the next step necessary in the formation of subjectivity, earning the resources necessary to function in the abstract, symbolic world.

The symbolic world is the conventional reality that envelops and defines all subjects. It is the world of language, custom, law, and contract that predates the individual subject; it is the world into which our parents deliver us, the world in which words give substance to things. The power of symbols to determine reality likewise determines each one of us. Lacan contends that symbols

> in fact envelop the life of man in a network so total that they join together, before he comes into the world, those who are going to engender him "by flesh and blood;" so total that they bring to his birth, along with the gifts of the stars, if not with the gifts of the fairies, the shape of his destiny.[24]

Yet as ominous as this all sounds, in language, with its vast capacity for nuance and interplay, there might remain some capacity for hope. In Lacan's view, "[I]t is the world of words that creates the world of things . . . by giving its concrete being to their essence, and its ubiquity to what has always been . . . Man speaks, then, but it is because the symbol has made him man."[25] Lacan's explanation resonates with the creature's aspirations, for the creature embraces the possibility that words will refine him, refiguring his "fragmented body" and thereby converting an abomination into a whole man. At this point in his development, the creature apparently intuits what, according to Lacan, "the psychoanalytic experience has rediscovered in man"—namely, "the imperative of the Word as the law that has formed him in its image."[26] Despite the decidedly bleak atmosphere that suffuses *Frankenstein* and Mary Shelley's success at exposing the ways in which culture ultimately fails us, the dramatic way in which language initially shapes the creature into something special illuminates common ground she shares with Percy.

The galvanic moment that occurs during the De Lacey period in the creature's history consists of his passage through the Oedipal crisis and into the symbolic. In his report from 1948 called "Aggressivity in psychoanalysis," Lacan comments on the relationship between the Oedipus complex and "correlative tensions of the narcissistic structure in the coming-into-being . . . of the subject."[27] According to Lacan, "in its normal state" the Oedipus complex "is one of sublimation, which designates precisely an identificatory reshaping of the subject, and . . . a *secondary identification* by introjection of the *imago* of the parent of the same sex."[28] Ultimately, this secondary identification represents another form of loss, in that, in the case of the creature, the male subject relinquishes the mother and transfers his focus toward the father and toward the world of "Law" he represents. Though the creature has no mother, the general contours of the Oedipus dynamic play out in the confrontation between himself, the blind De Lacey patriarch (on whom the creature rests all hope, since the De Lacey father is incapable of subjecting him to the gaze), and the patriarch's biological son Felix.

Flights of imagination relate him to the De Laceys. He performs oversight duties, such as gathering firewood and performing other daily chores, despite lacking the authority to behave as a familiar. And, though there is very little indication that he covets the De Lacey women, the symbolic castration he receives from the blows administered by Felix during his introduction to the family awakens the creature's sexuality at the same time that it notifies him of the conventional ground rules governing sexual expression. The moment shocks the parties on both sides:

> Agatha fainted; and Safie, unable to attend to her friend, rushed out of the cottage. Felix darted forward, and with supernatural force tore me from his father, to whose knees I clung: in a transport of fury, he dashed me to the ground, and struck me violently with a stick . . . I quitted the cottage. (216)

The cottagers' rejection of the creature smashes almost entirely the hope he placed in the refinements provided by language and speech to subordinate his physical appearance. He will, after all, use his well-cultivated tongue to sway Frankenstein to grant his wish for a wife. Some portion of the creature understands the symbolic resonance of this event, for he decides after a short delay to seek out his "birth" father. He cannot become a De Lacey. However, he can be like one—specifically father De Lacey and Felix. The creature formulates the prospect of requesting a heterosexual mate of his own kind. She will represent an object of desire cut from the same cloth as he, yet at the same time a better half to fill the very gap that forged his subjectivity:

> I demand a creature of another sex, but as hideous as myself: the gratification is small, but it is all that I can receive, and it shall content me. It is true, we shall be monsters, cut off from all the world; but on that account we shall be more attached to one another. (228)

According to Lacan, a vestige of the imago forged within the imaginary boundaries of the mirror stage remains even after language has conveyed the individual into the world of the symbolic. Having failed to maintain collectively the De Laceys in the role of surrogate imago, the creature envisions a replacement imago in the form of a wife that shares his origin.

The creature's dream of living happily ever after with a grotesque version of the biblical Eve contains the elements of its and his undoing, and as such it is difficult to ignore what appear to be key terms in the creature's proposal. The status of being "cut off from all the world" preoccupies the creature, and he and his bride must substitute one visual field for another, attaining, at best, a specular paradise. Within the dominant scopic arena, their corporeality reminds all subjects who see them of the visceral real lurking beneath the overlapping imaginary and symbolic structures that sustain them in ordinary "reality." Within the alternative, located somewhere in the "vast wilds of South America" (229), the two creatures will become subject to one another's harmful gaze, constant reminders of their permanent exclusion from the symbolic world. By default, the desperation of a joint sentence would make the couple "more attached to one another," but the marriage would only demonstrate for them that together they comprise a hole rather than a whole.

As important as the mirror stage is to the creature's development, his relationship with the gaze proves just as crucial, particularly when we consider that his figure dominates the "scopic field" of Shelley's novel and his creator's world.[29] The creature's body is preternaturally athletic and powerful. However, all who observe that body recoil at its appearance, and this inescapable materiality subjugates him to the judgment of others and renders him unable to exceed through education the sum of his physical parts. Walton's recollection of his own reaction during the final confrontation between the creature and its maker exemplifies the issue:

> Over him hung a form which I cannot find words to describe; gigantic in stature, yet uncouth and distorted in its proportions. As he hung over the coffin, his face was concealed by long locks of ragged hair; but one vast hand was extended, in colour and apparent texture like that of a mummy.... Never did I behold a vision so horrible as his face, of such loathsome, yet appalling hideousness. I shut my eyes involuntarily.... I dared not again raise my looks upon his face, there was something so scaring and unearthly in his ugliness. (319–20)

Because the creature lacks the capacity to escape his "gigantic" bodily projection, he amplifies for others the emptiness of ordinary reality. He illuminates blind spots to subjects of desire living in a world consisting, as it were, of signs interacting on a gossamer screen. The creature's power, in other words, is consummate with the power of the gaze.

When a subject looks out and experiences that uncanny feeling that the world, from an infinite number of perceptual points, gazes back, anxiety lays temporary siege to the subject's stability. The anxiety—what Lacan specifies as "the lack that constitutes castration anxiety"[30]—originates from the subject's poignant sense of inadequacy: a recognition that he or she is not one integrated whole living a "real" existence, an inviolable center point around which a world revolves, but a sign that signifies only in reference to other signs: "Let me simply say," Lacan stipulates,

> that this is what leads me to object to any reference to totality in the individual, since it is the subject who introduces division into the individual, as well as into the collectivity that is his equivalent. Psychoanalysis is properly that which reveals both the one and the other to be no more than mirages.[31]

In a separate lecture he adds,

> In so far as the gaze, *qua objet a*, may come to symbolize this central lack expressed in the phenomenon of castration, and in so far as it is an *objet a* reduced, of its nature to a punctiform, evanescent function, it leaves the subject in ignorance as to what there is beyond appearance.[32]

Lacan is saying that our status as subjects depends entirely on our relation to other objects within that field of signs—part of the mirage that fails to slake the constant thirst of desire that compels the search for fulfillment. To become uncannily aware of that possibility threatens the fantasy of our status and conveys one to the margin of "reality" beyond which lurks the "real." Once captured by it, the creature's gaze traps the onlooker and forces vision to turn inwardly. Correlatively, the gaze confines the creature to that very same margin. As the representation of the uncanny, he can never evade himself.

The uncanny nature of this experience—what the creature's gaze springs on Walton and on his creator—amounts to a feeling that is at once as familiar as it is alien and threatening. Through its agency returns the knowledge of our own lack. "In our relation to things, in so far as this relation is constituted by the way of vision, and ordered in the figures of representation," Lacan posits, "something slips, passes, is transmitted, from stage to stage, and is always to some degree eluded in it—that is what we call the gaze."[33] Shielded from the crippling gaze by the symbolic screen, we navigate our reality without anxiety. When the gaze irrupts into that reality—as the creature breaks into Walton's cabin or enters the De Lacey cottage—it reminds us of some "primal separation, from some self-mutilation induced by the very approach of the real."[34] The subject desires to possess the gaze, in part so that he or she will cease to be susceptible to its disruptions and thereby escape the "real" upon which reality is predicated. If one were to succeed, however, the price would be the loss of one's subjectivity—its sliding out of the symbolic system that bestows upon it not existence so much as meaning. The paradox of our being in the world, in other words, is that the return to the oneness of being each individual theoretically experienced in the "infans" stage would mean giving up the ego on which our subjectivity depends.

By using the language of his journal entries to (dis)figure the creature, Frankenstein asserts scopophilic sovereignty over his motherless offspring, foreclosing on the emergence of "the psychic state psychoanalysis calls narcissism, namely the fantasy of unity, which the gaze of the mother and its surrogate, the gaze of the beloved, is meant to offer to the subject."[35] In many ways the creature would seem to suffer from a traumatic past not dissimilar to that experienced by the protagonist, Mark, in Michael Powell's film *Peeping Tom* (1960). While the creature's father captures him prematurely in the language of his journal, Mark's father traps him on celluloid. The dissecting gaze of the father tortures both characters from very early on in their development.

Elizabeth Bronfen points out that

> only after this illusion of plenitude has been attained ... is a disruption of the imaginary self-image meant to occur, to be more precise, a breaking up of the mother-child dyad through the father, as representative of authority, of the laws of culture and of the consistency of the symbolic.[36]

Made indelible by his words, Frankenstein's gaze becomes the signature benchmark event in his creature's development, forcing it to confront repeatedly the unfitness of its sheer materiality for the symbolic order. In this case, the father's gaze blocks the child's accession into "the laws of culture and the consistency of the symbolic." My point here is that, though the creature's gaze expresses to Frankenstein the impossible emptiness of his own lacking as well as the intuition that the real lurks at the edge of his reality, the paternal gaze of Frankenstein exacts a time-released toll on the creature.

It should come as no surprise, then, that the creature, much like Mark in *Peeping Tom*, resorts to voyeurism, seeking not just pleasure but healing in watching others. Because of his misfit status, the creature must become a distant but intimate observer of others, a proto-cinephile "alienated from the phenomenal world, that hopes to find in the darkened theater what he or she has lost elsewhere."[37] He observes the De Laceys through "an almost imperceptible chink, through which the eye could just penetrate" (183) and keeps Frankenstein under surveillance from the shadows. Freud affirms that the sexual pleasure one finds in looking "can scarcely be counted a perversion, provided that in the long run the sexual act is carried further."[38] He adds that "the sexuality of most male human beings contains an element of aggressiveness—a desire to subjugate; the biological significance of it seems to lie in the need for overcoming the resistance of the sexual object by means other than the process of wooing."[39]

Lacan, we should recall, argues that "aggressivity" results from the autoscopia that characterizes the child's fascination with its own image during the mirror stage. Typically, however, "the subject transcends the aggressivity that is constitutive of the primary subjective individuation" by means of the "Oedipal identification."[40] Since the gaze of Frankenstein asserts itself prematurely, it warps the creature's development and the available avenues of pleasure narrow steadily throughout his growth. Viewed from a Freudian angle, it doesn't take long before the creature's "satisfaction" becomes "entirely conditional on the humiliation and maltreatment of the object."[41]

Frankenstein and the creature puncture one another's fantasies of heterosexual coupling—the former dismembering the made-to-order monster bride, the latter strangling Elizabeth—which concentrates their sadism on one another. Shocking images inform the tortures they orchestrate for one another, as each one sets out to upstage and expose the fantasies of his other. The overall pattern of the creature's behavior suggests a desire to capture the object gaze, something his creator severed from him before birth, thereby mutilating him before he is prepared to face the stare of the "real" his body signals. The creature's imagination becomes programmed early in its development to indulge in fantasies that promise to satisfy his desire. The first fantasy involves his entry into a diegetic order in which he would find unconditional acceptance, becoming a family/cast member in the De Lacey drama he has been watching from his makeshift theater. A substitute for the macrocosmic narrative order that denies him membership, admission to the latest act in the De Lacey story would make him less vulnerable to the gaze and, therefore, secure him beyond the reach of the real and of his birth father. He imagines that "his" family—a replacement for the Frankensteins—would see beyond his hideous exterior and accept him without inspection, weaving him seamlessly into their daily order.

A second fantasy in the form of the monster bride emerges once the first fantasy cancels out, and this sequel furnishes the prospect of compensating for his premature castration at the hands of Frankenstein's gaze. Two goals underpin this fantasy: first, he will subjugate Frankenstein to the object gaze by forcing him to anticipate the inaugural opening of the bride's "yellow eye" during the long process of its construction; second, he puts Frankenstein on notice that he will be watching. The gaze generates anxiety by *not* appearing. Frankenstein's choice of a remote location on a Scottish island to set up his second workshop, ostensibly because there he will remain free to operate "ungazed at" (252), a condition he attributes to the blunted "sensations" of his squalid neighbors, underscores his emotional fragility under these circumstances. No subject, however, escapes the gaze permanently. At one point Frankenstein confesses that he "grew restless and nervous. Every moment I feared to meet my persecutor. Sometimes I sat with my eyes fixed on the ground, fearing to raise them, lest they should encounter the object which I so much dreaded to behold" (253). The dual valence of the word "object" in this context suggests he fears the female (a gazing subject in progress) he is "making" (a sexual breech of contract with the creature) and he dreads witnessing again the object gaze that coexists with the first creature.

Frankenstein records that he was shocked to see "by the light of the moon, the daemon at the casement. A ghastly grin wrinkled his lips as he gazed on me" (225). From the creature's perspective at this moment, the Oedipus-contract he made with his father appears to be intact and it looks as though fulfillment of the creature's desire remains immanent. Father Frankenstein will give away the bride and the newlyweds will venture off together. However, Frankenstein shelters his subject status by dismembering the creature's intended and in the process he fuels the creature's sadistic scopophilia.

The extent to which both figures have fallen prey to aggressive looking would seem to be confirmed by the care each partner in this relationship takes in staging the murder scene of his enemy's spouse. Upon seeing the creature grinning at him through the Scottish workshop window casement, for his part Frankenstein, after pausing to reflect on the "madness" that clearly informed his decision to build a monster bride, remembers that, "trembling with passion," he "tore to pieces the thing on which he was engaged" (255). Victor's choice of the word "engaged" forms a sexual pun suggesting that he and his son's unfinished bride were intimately and contractually attached to one another. Furthermore, his action aims at dramatizing for the creature the "real" nature of the creature's constitution: a thing that will never become more than the sum total of his "pieces," an assembled object, a cobbled together fantasy from which integral parts have been sundered. With the bride's destruction the creature also loses the closest relative signifier that might have made him whole in an alternative mythic-symbolic order far outside "the neighborhood of man."

Summoning the image of Fuseli's *The Nightmare* (1781), the creature plots an equally cinematic retaliation, positioning Elizabeth's corpse in such a manner that will optimize its evocative force as a special effect. Frankenstein recalls that he burst into his wedding chamber to find the body of Elizabeth "lifeless and inanimate, thrown across the bed, her head hanging down, and her pale and distorted features half covered by her hair. Everywhere I turn I see the same figure" (289). The appearance of Elizabeth's "pale and distorted features" reprises the creature's own pale and distorted appearance when it lay before its creator. Moreover, in the form of Elizabeth's eyes the corpse embodies the gaze once severed from the creature: her eyes are vacant with the look of death; they remain visibly concealed by her hair—a taunting retribution meant to punish Frankenstein for what he took from his monster. Moreover, her "figure" will continue to ignite Frankenstein's desire wherever he turns, remaining the inaccessible lost object and the image of his own lacking.

The prospective ubiquity of this haunting underscores its capacity to undermine any compensatory fantasy to which Frankenstein's imagination might cling in the future. Just as the apparent blot appearing at the bottom of Holbein's *The Ambassadors* anamorphically turns out to be a skull staring back at the viewer who looks at the picture from an angle, so the image of Elizabeth's body will function as an intrusion of the real—a trap for the gaze—into whatever "picture" Frankenstein seeks to place himself.[42] His living nightmare will be that he has nowhere to "turn."

And this result is ensured, ostensibly by fellow guests staying at the inn, but possibly by the creature, in the repositioning (or the restaging) of Elizabeth's body:

> She had been moved from the posture in which I had first beheld her; and now, as she lay, her head upon her arm, and a handkerchief thrown across her face and neck, I might have supposed her asleep. I rushed toward her

and embraced her with ardour.... The murderous mark of the fiend's grasp was on her neck and the breath had ceased to issue from her lips. (291)

It would appear that the posture of Elizabeth's corpse has been adjusted in order to mitigate Victor's initial shock; however, this second take only amplifies the potency of the first. Specifically, the placement of a handkerchief over Elizabeth's face and neck intensifies the effect of the "blot" in the image by making it a focal point of the tableau, hiding, in plain sight, as it were, Elizabeth's expression, an a priori death agony similar to the facial expressions of Mark's female victims in *Peeping Tom*, forcing the gaze perpetually into Victor's visual field. Perhaps for Frankenstein the most horrific aspect of Elizabeth's freeze-framed status is that he will never know her during the moments immediately before or after her expiration; he can never regain access to the moment she was dying and will never know her in death. The strangulation "mark" the creature inscribed upon Elizabeth's neck represents a castration of curtain call proportions, perpetually reminding Frankenstein that his creature has outperformed and out-authored him.

An earlier generation of critics has asserted that the emotional pitch produced by *Frankenstein* might well originate from the fraught circumstances surrounding Shelley's birth, the death of her first child and subsequent pregnancies, and her misgivings about the female body's function as a procreative engine and the responsibilities incumbent on maternity.[43] Interpretations of *Frankenstein* that have applied concepts from Lacan's approach to psychoanalysis in order to direct our attention toward Shelley's inclination to challenge many aspects of Enlightenment philosophy have turned away from emotional issues that might have troubled the author. However, their success at bringing into focus the devastating emotional toll exacted by the uncanny on Frankenstein (and on the reader) suggests that the two interpretive methods might not mutually exclude one another, especially if we take stock of some of the uncanny aspects of Shelley's relationship with her own father.

Freud refers to the legend of Lady Godiva and Tom of Coventry to illustrate his point concerning psychogenic visual disturbance, a disorder related to the eye that operates as though it were caused by a voice within the subject saying: "Because you sought to misuse your organ of sight for evil sensual pleasures, it is fitting that you should not see anything at all any more."[44] Shelley might have understood all too well the burden of early exposure to the paternal gaze, especially in journal form, finding her birth referenced generically in the final chapter of Godwin's *Memoirs of the Author of A Vindication of the Rights of Woman*, as "the child was born at twenty minutes after eleven at night."[45] She also knew that during her mother's pregnancy, her parents expressed hope that their baby would be a male and intended to name the child William, after its father, a fantasy into which Mary's material appearance irrupted. Furthermore, despite mortifying Godwin by indulging in the evil sensual pleasure of "seeing" Percy, Mary dedicated her first novel to her father, but published the book anonymously, putting her own "I" out of the symbolic order and remaining unnamed. The decision permitted self-punishment for erasing the figurative "I" and physical "eye" of Godwin's beloved and her namesake, Mary Wollstonecraft Godwin, canceling herself out as her mother's haunting double.

Notes

1. Mary Shelley, *The Annotated Frankenstein*, ed. Susan Wolfson and Ronald Levao (Cambridge: The Belknap Press of Harvard University Press, 2012), 334. All subsequent references to *Frankenstein* originate from this edition. Page numbers will be supplied in text.
2. Mladen Dolar, "'I Will Be with You on Your Wedding Night': Lacan and the Uncanny," October 58 (Autumn, 1991): 6.
3. Ibid., 17.
4. Ibid., 6.
5. Ibid., 18.
6. Ibid.
7. Denise Gigante, "Facing the Ugly: The Case of *Frankenstein*," *ELH* 67, no. 2 (Summer 2000): 566, *JSTOR*, www.jstor.org/stable/30031925.
8. Gigante, "Facing the Ugly," 567.
9. David Collings, *Monstrous Society: Reciprocity, Discipline, and the Political Uncanny, c. 1780–1848* (Lewisburg: Bucknell University Press, 2009), 197–8.
10. Ibid., 200–201.
11. Ibid., 206.
12. Ibid., 206–7.
13. Ibid., 208.
14. Ibid., 211.
15. Dolar, "Lacan and the Uncanny," 17.
16. Jacques Lacan. *Écrits: A Selection*, trans. Alan Sheridan (New York: Norton, 1977), 18–19.
17. Ibid., 2.
18. Ibid., 42.
19. Ibid., 19.
20. Ibid.
21. Ibid.

22. Ibid., 4.

23. Jacques Lacan, *The Seminar of Jacques Lacan, Book XI: The Four Fundamental Concepts of Psychoanalysis*, ed. Jacques-Alain Miller, trans. Alan Sheridan (New York: Norton, 1978), 106.

24. Lacan, *Écrits*, 68.

25. Ibid., 65.

26. Ibid., 106.

27. Ibid., 22.

28. Ibid.

29. Lacan, *Seminar XI*, 72–3.

30. Ibid.

31. Lacan, *Écrits*, 80.

32. Lacan, *Seminar XI*, 76.

33. Ibid., 73.

34. Ibid., 83.

35. Elizabeth Bronfen, "Killing Gazes, Killing in the Gaze: On Michael Powell's *Peeping Tom*," in *Gaze and Voice as Love Objects*, eds. Renata Salecl and Slavoj Žižek, (Durham: Duke University Press, 1996), 74.

36. Ibid.

37. Kaja Silverman, *The Acoustic Mirror: The Female Voice in Psychoanalysis and Cinema* (Indiana: Indiana University Press, 1988), 8.

38. Sigmund Freud, *The Standard Edition of the Complete Psychological Works of Sigmund Freud*, edited and translated by James Strachey (London: The Hogarth Press, 1953), 7: 156–7.

39. Freud, *Standard Edition*, 7: 157–8.

40. Lacan, *Écrits*, 23.

41. Freud, *Standard Edition*, 7: 158.

42. Lacan, *Seminar XI*, 88–9.

43. Marc A. Rubenstein, " 'My Accursed Origin': The Search for the Mother in *Frankenstein*," *Studies in Romanticism* 15, no. 2 (Spring 1976): 165–94, *JSTOR*, http://www.jstor.org/stable/25600007; Ellen Moers, "The Female Gothic," *The Endurance of Frankenstein: Essays on Mary Shelley's Novel*, eds. George Levine and U. C. Knoepflmacher (Berkeley: University of California Press, 1979): 77-87; Anne K. Mellor, *Mary Shelley: Her Life, Her Fiction, Her Monsters* (New York: Routledge, 1988); U. C. Knoepflmacher, "Thoughts on the Aggression of Daughters," in *The Endurance of Frankenstein: Essays on Mary Shelley's Novel*, eds. George Levine and U. C. Knoepflmacher (Berkeley: University of California Press, 1979): 88–119; Barbara Johnson, "My Monster / My Self," *Diacritics* 12, no. 2 (Summer, 1982): 2–10; Paul Youngquist, "*Frankenstein*: the

Mother, the Daughter, and the Monster," *Philological Quarterly* 70, no. 3 (1991): 339–59.

44. Freud, *Standard Edition,* 11: 217.

45. William Godwin, *Memoirs of the Author of A Vindication of the Rights of Woman*, eds. Pamela Clemit and Gina Luria Walker (Peterborough, ON: Broadview Press, 2001), 113.

Chapter Two

Goya's Gaze

Seeing Non-relation in *Los Caprichos*

RITHIKA RAMAMURTHY

AN ARBITRARY DESIRE, an unforeseen whim; the *capricho*—or caprice—is the invisible contingency that makes itself known. In Francisco Goya de Luciente's *Los Caprichos* (1799), we see a collection of drives that do not cohere into a whole or stand on their own. In each of the eighty etchings and aquatints, obscurities emerge unexpectedly that threaten to devour its subjects, whose stares seem to call the very possibility of sight into question. What is unseen, what repeatedly attempts to manifest itself, and what remains a constant source of anxiety in *Los Caprichos* is the impossibility of the sexual relation. *Los Caprichos* and Lacan's foundational theory of the gaze may be helpful to think together here, not only because of their obvious theoretical connection, but also because Lacan actually mentions Goya outright in his discussion of the gaze and its relation to painting. In *Seminar XI: Four Fundamental Concepts of Psychoanalysis*, Lacan observes: "Painters, above all, have grasped the gaze as such in the mask and I have only to remind you of Goya, for example, for you to realize this."[1] In his typically casual and cryptic commentary, Lacan uses Goya's oeuvre and its repeated use of the mask as exemplary of the "gaze as such."[2] What Lacan calls the "lure," the pull of attraction between the sexes, is typically represented in Goya by "the prevalence of that which is presented as *travesty*."[3] What does he mean by this?

The "travesty" of the sexual relation: its ridicule and inversion, its disguise and debasement, its cruel caricaturization. This grotesquerie recalls David Clark's readings of Goya's work in terms of the capacious concept of "the worst." Reading Goya's dark and devastating "assemblage" *Disasters of War*, Clark explores Goya's insistent invocation of the term "worst" as an ultimately undermined category, both "sublimely unimaginable ... [and] all too available to be executed, remembered, imagined, engraved, and thus in some sense both taken in and lived with."[4] In the surreal and distorted depictions of the worsts of war, each trumping the last in caption and representation, Clark argues that Goya thinks together the catastrophic and the quotidian. These "fates worse than death" are meant to "put the aesthetic into the service of thinking the worst" as well as "ensuring that there is a place in which its iniquity and enormity can pool or eddy" without forcing them to be a forum for grieving or mourning.[5] In *Disasters of War*, Goya attempts to discover a space "in which to see war and to be seen *to see* war"; in other words, Goya's etchings formulate the violence of the gaze in relation to violence itself.[6] As Clark notes, "this negation and abstention is otherwise difficult to discern if your optic is calibrated to the legible and the social," insisting on an inoperativity that does not seek to instrumentalize the aesthetic in the service of clarification or satisfaction.[7] What would it mean to depict an array of living relations in this way? Perhaps it would seek to represent the ordinary as depraved, the erotic as empty, and the banal as brutal; this impulse is almost the utter inverse of the effect of *Disasters of War*, but occurs through an identical logic. In *Los Caprichos*, non-relations abound: masked women marry to their imminent demise (plate 2, *They say yes and give their hand to the first comer*), bogey-men haunt children and seduce mothers (plate 3, *Here comes the bogey-man*), grown men wear the gowns and frowns of infants (plate 4, *Nanny's boy*), two lovers and the twin crones that gossip behind them stare blankly in the face of depravity (plate 5, *Two of a kind*), and lovers die of boredom and obstinacy (plate 9;10, *Tantalus*; *Love and Death*). Further, the captions to these strange scenes are ill-fitting; in Clark's words, the "tone is hard to pin down and ... often read like ... words muttered at images that remain insentient and wordless."[8] There is *no relation* between word and image, between frame and framing, even though the explanations attempt to mitigate this through cryptic aphorisms. However, these distortions of the everyday are not only borne out of their ironized captions or surreal subjects, or the non-relation between the two. Instead, the "worst" of this sociality is the utter failure of the sexual relation, formalized through the failure of the look. In other words, one cannot see what is crucially wrong in these plates, for the non-relation is invisible. This ocular frustration meets a different demand, the demand of the gaze, that makes apparent the failure of relation. *Los Caprichos* forms the visibility of the sexual relation in terms of travesty, in terms of its utter distortion, through a familiar vision of the worst, the worst of vision that imbricates itself into the everyday distortion of the sexual relation that simultaneously frustrates the eye but meets the demand of the gaze.

The question of the masked mediation between the sexes in Goya is also addressed by Michel Foucault, who puts forth in *Madness and Civilization*, a vague but complex thesis about Goya's work inquiring after this representation of the unruliness of the passions in Goya's oeuvre and its relationship to the discursive historicity of madness. Foucault reads *Los Caprichos* as essentially concerned with the manifestation of madness in sociality, crystalized in moments of solitude where madness recognizes itself, or when one encounters the others whose "masks [are] truer than the truth of faces" that repeat the idea of an absolute isolation within the social.[9] In other words, Los Caprichos is concerned with the social in a way that almost necessitates the relation of subjects to each other, rather than privileging the subject in isolation as a primary mode of non-relation. Taking as exemplary Goya's famous print from the series *The sleep of reason produces monsters (El sueno de la razon produce monstrous)* and his later painting *The Idiot*, Foucault attempts to illustrate a version of madness and unruliness of passion that figures the private undoing of man, free of masquerades and the trappings of bourgeois sociality. In these brief readings of *Sleep of reason* and Goya's painting *The Idiot*, it is always a solitary man who is tortured by the physical and spiritual torsions of unreason, trapped in the throes of the unruliness of the passions. Exploring the question of the "universal idiom"—after "*Ydioma universale*," the original subtitle for *Los Caprichos*[10]—or the underlying trope of unreason that he sees as animating all of Goya's work, Foucault writes:

> Goya's forms are born out of nothing: they have no background, in the double sense that they are silhouetted against only the most monotonous darkness, and that nothing can assign them their origin, their limit, their nature... in that night, man communicates with what is deepest in himself, and with what is most solitary.[11]

This disorientation of form—a ubiquitous ungrounding of the subject(s) against a backdrop of sketched darkness—is an articulate reading of Goya's forms, but arrives at an alternative—and ultimately uncharitable—conclusion. The formal confusion of Goya's work bespeaks for Foucault the eternal solitude on the path to madness, the isolating incomprehension that characterizes unreason. However, Goya's interests in both the disorientation of sociality and the ungrounding of the individual are mutually exclusive for Foucault; he cannot accept that artistic form can bring non-relation into relief, even within the sphere of the social. In other words, non-relation is impossible to think if there are others with whom the subject may relate. In these offhanded analyses, Foucault focuses on Goya's plates and paintings that explicitly engage with the representation of modern man's solitude within or outside of the social. In this way, he privileges a version of isolation or non-relation that privileges the subject in its traditional representation, a madness that is shown in the rictus of *The Idiot* or the lonely anxiety of the *The sleep of reason*. Foucault's overview of Goya's *Los Caprichos* qualifies it almost as tame—or at least less ambiguous—in comparison to his later works, the *Disparates*, *Desastres*, and others which are not concerned with the strange faces and figures that populate *Los Caprichos*, but with "the grovel of flesh in the void... new bodies, shown in all their vigor, and whose gestures, if they invoke their dreams, celebrate especially their dark freedom."[12] This panoply of persons, reveling in and recoiling from the "nothingness that imprisons" man, seems for Foucault to elude the empty looks in *Los Caprichos* but finds itself in the representation of writhing bodies themselves.[13] Again, couched in this critique of *Los Caprichos* seems to be a wish to classify this collection of strange images as a set of *clear* or *visible* representations, one that is not troubled by "glances shot from nowhere and staring at nothing."[14] What does Foucault's gloss on Goya miss? What is lacking is a specific account of the gaze in *Los Caprichos*, one which crucially circles endlessly around its object. In Foucault's reading, Goya's forms envision solitude as the event of the subject's undoing, rather than locating this "worst" in the non-relation of the social itself. Furthermore, the absence of any discussion of femininity as it relates to the representation of madness (aside from the obvious addresses to the history and discursive production of hysteria in his work) excludes the plates that formulate an absence of sexual relation in the very arrangement of bodies and looks. The obsession with the subject *qua* subject, having to see man in his isolation instead of being refused relation in form itself, is Foucault's mistake in his reading of Goya. Instead, I maintain here that it is the constant frustration of relation itself—the torturous triangulation of visual desire within artistic form—that makes *Los Caprichos* precisely a work of the gaze inherent in the sexual relation. Goya's forms do not signify the undoing of the singular subject unraveled by madness; they envision and entrap the logic of the gaze in a formal figuring of a different type of non-relationality.

A similar wish to impose a clarity or legibility on the *Caprichos* largely animates the contemporary criticism that discusses its conditions of interpretation. The series of drawings and etchings, produced over the course of two years, were published at the turn of the nineteenth century. Often allegorically read, they continue to be interpreted as unproblematically decipherable and definitively addressing various aspects of the corruption of Spanish society at this historical moment. The bulk of this scholarship, historicist and otherwise, which attempts to confine Goya's work in terms of intentional satire or realist commentary, can interpret this problem only in terms of its moral register. There seems to be two strange affinities to the scholarship surrounding Goya's work: on the one hand, there is a tension in the attempt to relegate Goya's work purely to its realist register, insisting on historical situation as an interpretive framework even for those allegorical aspects that cannot possibly be "real" in any referential sense; on the other hand, the series is typically taken as satirical in nature, as a light-hearted "caprice," or Goya's witty and incisive musings about society's ills. This insistence on both historicism and artistic intention assumes a knowledge that precludes the possibility of acknowledging the formal aspects of Goya's work that may not be immediately available to the archive, the artist, or the eye; the unseen, unseeable, yet nonetheless existing.

It is more comforting to tarry with the visible and knowable, together. Historicist interpretations of Goya's oeuvre paradoxically link the author's historical situation without considering Goya's own words on referentiality and the realism in his body of work. In this line of argumentation, the problem for Goya is the way that society has adulterated the nature of sexuality in his cultural moment. Goya's scenes survey prostitution, the marriage economy, and the mercenary quality of courtship with an equally critical eye that seems to articulate a cogent critique of sexuality's relationship to the social order. As Alfred Boime writes, the set is largely read as a social commentary, which seeks to expose the laughable nature of the social order through anthropomorphized animals, leering figures, and men in women in various states of lust or terror.[15] These are read as indictments of the reign of the clergy, the exploitation of the underclasses, and the dreadful loom of the Inquisition. The prints that register as more realist are likened to once-existing historical figures, and the more allegorical are read as speaking to some social narrative, which Goya could only obliquely represent. However, Goya's own account of the relationship between his brand of realism and reality is vexed, or at least complex. In an advertisement published on February 6, 1799, Goya comments on his exercise of artistic imagination as attempting to bring to view "the forms and attitudes that so far have existed only in the human mind, obscured and confused by lack of illustration, or excited by the unruliness of the passions."[16] Implicit here in Goya's explanation is the desire to represent the unrepresentable, or the idea that representation can uncover an element of obscurity inherent in the expression of human drives. Here, Goya implies that the "forms and attitudes" of the human mind have been heretofore "obscured and confused" because they haven't been seen, but that they are impossible to see because of their "unruliness." In other words, the desire to represent the "passions"—encompassing sexuality, madness, physical fits, desired objects, and a sense of internal affects or external effects—has always been thwarted as they are both ubiquitous and unpredictable. Although Boime insists that the controversy surrounding Goya's creation means that "the sinister forms in *Los Caprichos* nevertheless correspond to the social and moral realities in the real world" despite their fantastical nature, it seems that the artist himself knew that his work could not be interpreted as pure social critique.[17] It is not that Goya claims to see clearly the ills of Spanish society, but that his work attempts to unseat the possibility of unproblematic perception of these ills altogether, considering the element of unpredictability built in to society itself. *Los Caprichos* thus indicates an anxiety crucially bound up in this conflict surrounding representation, both the problem of the "reality" of the unruliness lurking in the mind, and whether or not the image can make it visible.

The problem of seeing in Goya has been looked at before, but with a different view to its ultimate interpretation. In "Satirizing the Senses: The Representation of Perception in Goya's *Los Caprichos*," Andrew Schulz addresses the vicissitudinal nature of vision in the album as a whole. Like Boime, Schulz reads the problematics of visual perception—sleep, drunkenness, superstition, blindness—as animating a "mechanics of satire," which mirrors the discourse surrounding sense perception during the Spanish Enlightenment.[18] In Schulz's view, in depicting the blindness of religion, the unreason of dreams, and the follies of drunkenness, Goya implicitly makes a link between sensing and knowing. Schulz locates Goya's satirical eye in a picture of perceptions out of proportion, ones that use "cognitive imbalance" between what is visible to the viewer and what is seen by the subject to humorous effect.[19] In this account, the viewer has a sovereign sensibility to which all is available; moreover, so does the artist. Schulz insists on locating Goya's work as having "specific cultural meanings that would have led its intended audience to read it as satirical," insisting on humorous and historicized interpretation in its epistemological assumptions about perception and knowledge.[20] Interestingly, Schulz also accounts for Goya's drive to depict "humans ruled by uncontrollable somatic desires," indexed in open eyes and mouths that locate desire in humorously thwarted appetites.[21] While Schulz's readings of sensory failures correctly unseat their predictability—the moments when vision fails us can be the most telling—they continue to attribute this unpredictability to the effect of humor, a joke that the viewer is in on pointing to the epistemological assumptions of Goya's time. In other words, the unruliness is precisely there to be laughed at by the viewer. Contrary to this, what if the unruliness of Goya's works existed purely in their obscurity, rather than as an index for an imagined viewer? In other words, what if these scenes of missteps embedded the non-relation in moments of error in form, rather than content; or, what if they simply did not say anything specifically about Spanish society at all? In his own description of the album, Goya insists on himself as being an "inventor" rather than "servile copyist."[22] In insisting on invention rather than reflection, Goya invests and acknowledges an element of fantasy in representation itself. In other words, the imperfection inherent to representation is its very advantage, for it may have an unimagined relation to the unruliness of the unseen. The fantasy of a Goya who details society's follies assumes, as Georges Didi-Huberman critically puts it, an "absolute, non-human" observer:

As if the eye were "pure"—organ without drive. And as if the purity of the gaze signified the act of observing everything, capturing everything, retracing everything: in other words, detailing the visible describing and depicting it, making of it an aspectual sum without remainder.[23]

In opposition to those eager appeals to reflection and historical referentiality then, Goya's is an eye invested with drive—what Lacan called the "appetite of the eye"—with the unruliness of the passions.[24] The impulse of the artist can be found in the inexplicabilities of the work—the obscurations and enigmas—that populate Goya's prints. The mode of this unruliness is not necessarily found in his subject matter, but in the sketchy and self-effacing scenes of the non-apparent nature of the sexual.

The elusive and unsettling pressure of the gaze can affect a work of art in unseen ways. The effects of this gaze can be produced by the formal qualities of the image, including the materiality of the work of art. Georges Didi-Huberman traces the relationship between the "ever defective modality of our gaze" and the dissimulative quality of painting, which makes us face the contradiction between seeing and knowing in the fact of the detail that does not speak the whole, that occludes understanding, and that evades visibility.[25] Rather than treating this detotalizing detail as an interpretive key, Didi-Huberman suggests, we should let it pose the question of from where to look. Looking is a violent act, with the "subject cutting up the visible the better to totalize, but undergoing himself the effect of such a scission."[26] This is the splintering effect of proliferating looks within one frame, destroying any relation between eyes and the gaze, or between what is seen and what is understood.[27] Looking closely, Didi-Huberman writes, does not cut up the visible into "signifying units," but rather posits within it "a simple pretension, a desire."[28] If, for Didi-Huberman, "above all, what painting shows is its material cause, which is to say paint," then perhaps for Goya, what each frame in *Los Caprichos* shows us is perhaps not the opposite of a material referentiality—the etching as a negative of meaning rather than a surplus—but an alternative type of "sovereign accident."[29] Built into the process of etching and aquatint itself is a contingency, an uncertainty, and an impossibility of foreseeing the effect of relational proportion between etched line and acid wash which "obscures the situation" of what is represented in the frame.[30] Goya's works remind us of the impurity of the visible, that what is obscured and unseen to the eye is a material fact nonetheless. In the prints that concern us, this ubiquitous presence is the unspeakable non-relation of the sexual within the social, invisible even though the sexual itself is everywhere to be found. In *Seminar XI*,

Lacan theorizes painting in terms of the disturbing forces of desire within the field of the imaginary. In "What is a Picture?" he explains that the scopic drive is a manifestation of the desire of the unconscious at work in the visual field. Within the scopic field, the subject is "suspended in an essential vacillation" from the object of fantasy; this is the gaze, "desire established in the domain of seeing" that vanishes when we see ourselves seeing.[31] In other words, the typical painting is a sort of "taming of the gaze," an appeal to the eye, which comforts the viewer by sublimating this unconscious desire into a narcissistic relation with a look within the frame.[32] Here, the gaze is almost formulated as the impression of being recognized by an unseeable look, of being watched by a look that we cannot locate. The gaze reminds us that we are eternally lacking, unsatisfied, and frustrated in the field of the visible, looked at by something that we can never meet with our own eyes.

Rather than subdue the gaze, Lacan remarks, Goya's work formulates a "direct appeal to the gaze," to make it appear rather than disappearing behind the subject's identification.[33] By this account, satisfying or sustaining the demand of the gaze means that instead of appealing to the eye, the painting will obfuscate and obstruct its scopic drive, in order to bring into relief that unlocatable looking. Mentioning the mask, Lacan explicitly interprets Goya's unique engagement with the gaze as one that imagines the problem of sexual relation through this relationship of the eye and the gaze. "Beyond appearance, there is nothing in itself, there is the gaze" Lacan insists[34]; how can we but think of *Nobody knows himself (Nadie se conoce)*, the sixth plate of *Los Caprichos*?

"The world is a masquerade," Goya's caption reads. "Face, dress and voice, all are false. All wish to appear what they are not, all deceive and do not even know themselves."[35] There are many looks in the frame, from creatures and men alike, but none meet each other in any explicit sense. In Lacan's words, this disturbing scene formalizes an acute affinity between the masculine and feminine enabled by "the mediation of masks."[36] Even between the couple, the mask mediates any true possibility of the visualizing a relation. Here, the gaze is figured in the frustration of the group of figures, shrouded in darkness, whose looks all coalesce around the female figure but cannot meet the eye. Her mask materializes the mediation of the sexual relation; furthermore, this unknowability is juxtaposed by the clarity and illumination by which Goya's hand has rendered her, as opposed to the shadowy crowd of her monstrous, faceless pursuers, including the masked man himself. Wherever there are women, there are shadowy doubles, masks, and faceless spectators whose sketchy outlines disturb and deflect the eye.

Goya's women in *Los Caprichos* continue to have a curious relationship to visibility that betrays an anxiety about the feminine; this trope is continued in

FIGURE 2.1. Francisco Goya y Lucientes (1746–1828), *Nobody knows himself (Nadie se conoce)*, *Los Caprichos*, plate 6, 1799, etching. Los Angeles, Los Angeles County Museum of Art. https://collections.lacma.org/node/203174.

FIGURE 2.2. Francisco Goya y Lucientes (1746–1828), *Even thus he cannot make her out (Ni así la distingue)*, *Los Caprichos*, plate 7, 1799, etching. Los Angeles, Los Angeles County Museum of Art. https://collections.lacma.org/node/203226.

the bevy of witches that begin to appear in the series, the early sketches of which were the inspiration for *Los Caprichos* in a smaller series called *Sueños* (dreams).[37] In every version of earthly femininity—motherhood, madwomen, prostitutes, brides, crones—we find a lack of clarity, a distortion, or contradicting formal details. Rather than passive nudes and demure brides, there are exposed women whose cries, coquetry, and cruelty are unintelligible from their depiction.[38] In each frame critiquing or commenting upon woman, we can see an antagonism between deed and word in the conflict between what is represented and its caption; there is no clear idea here of who is to blame, who is being looked at, or who is meant to be looked at. But even so, it is not in its subject matter that the prints manifest an uncertainty about feminine legibility. In each of these prints, it is the relation between the sexes that is problematized through the obscuring process of etching itself, making figures unclear and others in relief that unsettle any relation within the frame.

Of all of the prints in *Los Caprichos*, no single plate portrays this fraught problem of looking at women as perfectly as Plate 7 (Figure 1.1), *Even thus he cannot make her out (Ni asi la distingue)*, formalizes in another strange frame the slippery space of the gaze that repeats throughout Goya's series. A history of the print will find that its working proof was probably sketched around 1796, and looked very different from what we see in the etching included in the Caprichos. Andrew Schulz notes that the inspiration, a pen and ink drawing, included a crowd of sketchy spectators and an architectural background, which grants the image perspective that it does not have in its final form. Furthermore, the original caption for the print significantly reads: *Now I see what she is (Ya la percivo)*.[39] It is almost when transferred to etching, the spectators disappear and are replaced with the illegibility of the relation as formed in aquatint shadows.

The caption in the Prado manuscript for *Even thus he cannot make her out* reads as the following: "How can he make her out? To know what she is, eyeglasses are not enough; one needs wisdom and knowledge of the world, and that is precisely what this poor gentleman lacks."[40] What we see in the image is a refined man leaning close to a woman, monocle at his eye, in order to see her more clearly. The woman looks away shyly, an unreadable expression on her face. Where a crowd of people were once seated, only the ethereally etched suggestion of a woman remains, her gaze indeterminate. This work can be said to perfectly exemplify our problem simply in its subject matter, but we must look more closely. Unlike *Nobody knows himself*, no figure in this frame is masked. All would seem apparent and available for perception. The scene seems at first self-explanatory, not only because of the caption, but further because of the naming of two subjects—"he" will make "her" out—who are thought to be the focus of the frame and are undermined by a surplus of an indistinct figure of another woman. Even *thus*: a word connoting detail in the description given, an absolute signification that is nonetheless thwarted in its invocation. Knowing what will be refused—she will not be distinguished, made out, delineated in any detail—focuses the eye on the center of the scene, throwing the woman into the relief of a contradiction; she is both seen and unseen simultaneously. Goya's details focus the energy of the etching around the central woman, framed by dark, frantic lines above and below her that throw her into relief in contrast to the darkness, but also identify her with this emergent ether.

Elsewhere, looks abound to confuse the focus of the viewer's gaze. We might expect, with such a strange scene unfolding, that the looks in the frame would converge in one place, but this is not the case. One cannot even truly say, especially if the caption is to be heeded, that anyone is seeing anything at all; and yet, in Lacan's words, we are being "looked at from all sides."[41] The static moment of the scene seems to show the crystallized form of the gaze itself; not what is invisible or visible, *but the form of the unseeable*. The eternal vision of the observer, the avoidance and performance of the observed, and the implicit but immaterial spectatorship—in this and other prints in the series—triangulate bodies, eyes, and looks into a pattern that suggests that the sexual is not only an event of non-relation, but a question of artistic form. What Goya forms as the problem in this frame—the "indistinguishability" of the sexual relation—is doubled by the spacing, arrangement, and technique in the engraving that invite the viewer to look more closely in order to distinguish what its subjects cannot. The casual way in which the subjects stand and sit insinuate that this kind of scrutinizing and observation is not an extraordinary event, but part of the everyday nature of the sexual relation. In fact, the eternal and endless quality of this look without vision formalizes the anticipatory and expectant temporality of the sexual relation itself, the constant frustration of wishing for the thing to make itself appear. The distortion of the geometry of the frame, of the foreground and background in perspective, further frustrates any viewer from distinguishing the woman from the etched darkness.

Two figures help to figure this confusion: a face and a body. First, the indistinctly etched woman seated to the side of the central figures, whose gaze ends in nothing. The progressive erasure of the spectators surrounding the scene suggests an almost ghostly quality to the unstable image of the woman, or seems like an accident that Goya meant to exclude or emphasize. The thinness of the lines, their shaky and scarce nature, insinuate an uncertainty that makes it unclear whether or not she is part of the frame at all, in the sense that the lines of her body are not even completely intact in a way that would suggest a fully formed figure. But this figure, both insistence and disappearance, suggests an enigma of looking that suggests the inconsequentiality of her very dissimulation. In other words, it does not matter whether or not she is "actually" there, for there is no way, in any case, to make her out. Second, between the man and woman, a face figures itself inside the space between their two waistlines. This face, disembodied and suspended, almost occupies the central space of vision within the frame, but only slightly off-center. Perhaps these are almost the visual instantiations of a refusal to show, desire caught in the almost-center of the scene. This appearance of absence that can be observed within the frame, something like a hole in the middle of the work, draws the eye toward it. "It reflects our own nothingness," Lacan might say, this unseeing object "which is there to be looked at in order . . . *to catch in its trap*, the observer, that is to say, us."[42] But to expand Lacan's reading further, we might say here that we are not trapped as observers in *Even thus he cannot make her out* by this misleading center, nor by the representation of the gaze that is its subject, but by dissatisfaction itself, which the caption promises. In Lacan's words, we might say that *Even thus* abandons the eye in favor of the gaze in its unsettling etching of unseeing. To put this in another way, we could say that *Even thus* abandons the drive of the eye—the pleasurable relation of the painting to the inquiring look of the viewing subject—in favor of an eternal frustration to the effect of resisting the erotics of seeing.

Liberated from the concept of the representational, these plates in Goya seem to insist that the viewer is not intrinsic to the image. If not hailed by and included in the image itself, the viewer is excluded and the image forms nothing but obscurity; it is not to be looked at, it cannot be made out. To persist in unseeing, to envision erotic dissatisfaction, to inhabit indistinguishability; this logic of non-relation is the logic of Goya's gaze. The *Caprichos* are the formulation of the event of sexual relation itself, the everlasting anticipation of the unforeseen held eternally. The unruliness of the sexual relation, its capricious nature, is the thread throughout the series that finds itself in unexpected places and allows nothing to be seen, finally. In this society—if you can call this collection of relations a society at all, and not its nightmarish inverse or end—sexuality proves itself to be the problematic disaster of the social world. Every instance of the sexual relation, both ubiquitous and unrealized, is imperfect and perverse in its iteration. And yet, despite their seeming objectivity, Goya's works do not simply reflect the corruption of the sexual within the social world, but formalize the unruliness of the sexual relation in its very persuasion and its insistence on drawing the eye, to show it nothing at all.

Notes

1. Jacques Lacan, *The Seminar of Jacques Lacan, Book XI: The Four Fundamental Concepts of Psychoanalysis*, ed. Jacques Alain-Miller, trans. Alan Sheridan (New York: Norton, 1978), 84.
2. Ibid.
3. Lacan, *Seminar XI*, 107 (emphasis in original).
4. David L. Clark, "Goya's Scarcity," in *Constellations of a Contemporary Romanticism*, eds. Jacques Khalip and Forest Pyle (New York: Fordham University Press, 2016), 88.
5. Ibid., 89-90.
6. Ibid., 93.
7. Ibid., 93.
8. Clark, "Goya's Scarcity," 94.
9. Michel Foucault, *Madness and Civilization: A History of Insanity in the Age of Reason*, trans. Richard Howard (New York: Random House, 1988), 281.
10. Albert Boime, *A Social History of Modern Art, Volume 2: Art in an Age of Bonapartism, 1800–1815* (Chicago: University of Chicago Press, 1990), 269.
11. Foucault, *Madness and Civilization*, 280.
12. Ibid., 279.
13. Ibid., 280.
14. Ibid.
15. Boime, *Art in an Age of Bonapartism, 1800–1815*, 268.
16. Ibid., 269.
17. Ibid., 270.
18. Andrew Schulz, "Satirizing the Senses: The Representation of Perception in Goya's *Los Caprichos*," *Art History*, 23:2 (2000): 155.
19. Ibid., 160.
20. Schulz, "Satirizing the Senses," 168.
21. Ibid.
22. Boime, *Art in an Age of Bonapartism, 1800–1815*, 269.
23. Georges Didi-Huberman, "Appendix: The Detail and the Pan," in *Confront Images: Questioning the Ends of a Certain History of Art* (University Park: Pennsylvania State University Press, 2005), 245.
24. Lacan, *Seminar XI*, 115.
25. Didi-Huberman, "Appendix: The Detail and the Pan," 229.
26. Ibid., 233.
27. Ibid.

28. Ibid., 261.
29. Ibid., 256
30. Ibid., 261.
31. Lacan, *Seminar XI*, 83.
32. Ibid., 109
33. Ibid., 107.
34. Ibid., 103.
35. Francisco Goya, *Los Caprichos* (New York: Dover, 1969), plate 6.
36. Lacan, *Seminar XI*, 107.
37. Janis Tomlinson, "Goya: Images of Women," 56.
38. See Tomlinson: "In the *Caprichos*, Goya offered a clear indication of these women's profession in their décolletage, confident gazes, and—above all—in the company they keep. Men petition them in transactions observed by the ever-watchful bawds, or celestina" (57). Already present in this historicized reading is the positing of subjectivities of so-called prostitutes, their confidence and dress speaking to a certain element of satire seen as Goya's intention. While we are concerned with the gazes in these prints, we do not propose to guess as to their confidence rather than to read their very formal confusion.
39. Schulz, "Satirizing the Senses," 162.
40. Goya, *Los Caprichos*, plate 7.
41. Lacan, *Seminar XI*, 72.
42. Ibid., 92 (emphasis in original).

Chapter Three

Jacques Lacan and John Keats's "Noble Animal Man"

COLIN CARMAN

What is this desire?[1]
—Jacques Lacan

LACANIANS MAY NOT BE ACCUSTOMED to thinking about the famous analyst, or the so-called French Freud,[2] in relation to the environment, nature, and the animal. Lacan's suggestion, however, that we cannot rule out the possibility of animal jouissance is surprising because his theory of desire has long been applied exclusively to the human psyche and to the mysterious source of pleasure (and displeasure) around which subjectivity is constructed. This essay applies Lacan's under-examined interest in the human/non-human relation to some of John Keats's more canonical works in order to uncover the way in which the animal is constructed in direct relation to human desire and in ways that disturb man's presumed dominion over all other living things. The poems that John Keats composed in the late 1810s in England, culminating in the reptilian romance *Lamia*—composed in 1819 (the *annus mirabilis* of Keats's career) and published in the summer of 1820—approximate Lacan's most infamous of pronouncements, uttered more than a century later in *Seminar XX*, that *il n'y a pas de rapport sexuel* (or, "there is no such thing as a sexual relationship").[3] For Lorenzo Chiesa, this declamation betokens not just "the ultimate deadlock and the origin of subjectivity and sexuation" but also what he calls the "truth of incompleteness."[4] What Keats and Lacan share is a consideration of the animal as it functions in a non-transcendent fashion; both firmly ground their conceptions of love and sexuality in the earthly domain, which, in what follows, encompasses what Keats calls the "delights" of the insect ("On the Grasshopper and Cricket," l.7) and, more complicated, the "delight and pleasure" that a man such as Lycius sees in the eyes of a snake-woman named Lamia (l.327).[5] As we shall see, the insect's capacity for enjoyment—as in the post-coital sensation of feeling "tired out with fun" and a fun that cannot be fulfilled, "ceasing never" (l.7–9)—is what earns the smallest bug its respectability. Hence the author's admiration for the so-called noble insect even if, according to his letter to Reynolds in 1818, he would rather imagine himself as a "passive and receptive" flower than a busy bee (127).

Contemporary scholars in the field of gender/sexuality studies stress the enduring value of Lacan's denaturalizing of the sexual relation insofar as it confronts the inherent gridlock that inheres in desire and relationality. In their recent *Sex, or the Unbearable*, Lauren Berlant and Lee Edelman credit Lacan for resisting what they call the "imperative to resolve the structural antagonism of the Symbolic" and for focusing on what is "negative and unknowable in sex insofar as sexual difference eludes every effort to comprehend it."[6] Negatively capable, Keats plunges into the unfamiliar and potentially unknowable delights of grasshoppers, tigers, and snakes, and in ways that deepen Lacan's passing references to ethology, from female pigeons in the mirror phase to raccoons capable of reacting to a dinner menu.[7] Animal sex, or bestial enjoyment, is especially unknowable given the fact that animals do not speak in a language we can understand.

In spite of this fact—or perhaps because of it—the English Romantic poets sought to lyricize the void of animal pleasure, which he euphemizes in his letter to George and Georgiana Keats (to which I will return) as "animal eagerness" (322). The lyric, as the first-wave Romantic ecocritic Karl Kroeber pointed out, helped to facilitate the poet's capacities to "feel natural processes as if they were humanized events" and to be "filled by a lively wealth of pleasing sensations."[8] As the Romantic period's greatest celebrant of ephemerality and the fleeting nature of pleasure, Keats pursued the pleasing but also displeasing essence of desire in both human and nonhuman forms.[9] What Keats calls "passion's passing bell" in part 2 of *Lamia* betokens this (II.39); the famous personification of "Joy" as he whose "hand is ever at his lips / Bidding adieu" in 1819's "Ode on Melancholy" is emblematic of this yet (22–23). But one must not forget the insect body that follows on the heels of a humanoid Joy, as in "and aching Pleasure nigh, / Turning to poison while the bee-mouth sips" (23–24). Whenever Keats wished to explore the nature of human feeling, he pursued his object through its opposite; thus, Keats's representations of human love directly involve animal and insectile loves as well. Often he blurred the two as part of his wider effort to erode the line where humans end and animals begin. A good example of this is his description of Lamia's eyelids opening "like new flowers at morning song of bees" (l.142) and the onomatopoeic "buzzing" she produces inside her lover's head (II.1.29).

Despite the various shortcomings that Jacques Derrida has identified in Lacan's theorization of the animal, chiefly that the human animal is sovereign by virtue of its ability to respond versus to react to external stimuli, Lacan's theories offer an instructive context for investigating the poetical works of Keats nonetheless; his *Lamia*, in particular, has been examined in relation to gothic desire and the drama of false identifications but not in ways that directly involve the role of animal desire. Lacan's demystification of the sexual relationship as fundamentally impossible is also central to the following investigation of Keats vis-à-vis the possibility of animal jouissance since it involves the idea of non-power, disempowerment, or what Berlant and Edelman term "nonsovereignty" (2). Derrida underestimates the degree to which Lacan uncouples the sexual relation from biological definitions, and in this way, I wish to build on Colette Soler's claim that Lacan helped to "mark the end of any norms based on nature."[10]

As I explore in the essay's conclusion, what's un-Lacanian about Keats is that his fictional characters that combine human and animal traits (e.g., the serpentine *femme fatale* known as Lamia) are indeed capable of recognizing humans and, in doing so, threaten the sovereignty of the (masculine) self through startling speech-acts. They hover somewhere between two oppositional states, "directly materializing"—as Žižek puts it—"our innermost fantasies which support our desire."[11] Keats foregrounds the otherness of animal delight and, in doing so, exposes those very affective states—aggression, competition, non-power—that we, as subjects, expel from our conscious minds as unpleasant. His letter to George Keats, written in the winter of 1819, bears out his belief that the "human animal" has a great deal in common with the hawks, robins, worms, and lions that inhabit "wild nature," and he singles out desire—what he calls the "same instinctiveness" and "the same animal eagerness" shared by man and animal—that drives the former's will to mate, nest, eat, and entertain himself (322).

What better remedy to the Enlightenment-era attitudes that (Derrida thinks) characterize Lacan's conception of the animal than the literature of British Romanticism and the poetry of John Keats? Romanticism, in the words of Timothy Morton, often acts as the "cure for the excessive rationality of the Enlightenment," a phase in the intellectual history of the West that witnessed what Peter Edwards calls the proliferation of "pro-animal sentiment."[12] One can see the emergence of this sentiment in the first-generation Romantic lyric, such as Blake's "The Fly" (1789) in which the human speaker collapses man and insect through the rhetorical tool known as erotesis ("Am not I / A fly like thee? / Or art not thou / A man like me?"), and Coleridge's "To A Young Ass" where the speaker hails a "poor little foal of an oppressed Race" as his "brother," even if, as Tobias Menely has recently pointed out in *The Animal Claim: Sensibility and the Creaturely Voice*, that Coleridge rescinded on the liberal understanding of rights he displayed in his youth.[13] Guided by his belief in negative capability, Keats goes further than these important predecessors by plunging into the inner life and feelings of the animal other—either the "alertness of a Stoat," as he writes to George, "or the anxiety of a Deer" (322).

Derrida on Lacan

This is true of the whole animal kingdom, from which men have no business to exclude themselves.

—Freud, "Why War?"[14]

Derrida's critique of Lacan's anthropocentricism turns on the question of sovereignty and who, in effect, possesses the power to wield the phallus not as an anatomical organ, of course, but as a culturally hegemonic sign. The defining characteristic of the animal's non-power is that it does not, and constitutionally *cannot*, traffic in vocal and legible signs. "Man speaks, then," Lacan stated in 1953, "but it is because the symbol has made him man."[15] The core of man's identity, in the structuralist paradigm, depends upon his ability to make and interpret signs and, within the Lacanian rubric, operate under the aegis of what Spivak once termed the "transcendental signifier."[16] What sets our species, *Homo sapiens*, apart is that it alone can recognize signs and, what's more, use symbols in the dialectic of recognition; unlike the animal, he proceeds teleologically toward symbolization. On this, Madan Sarup writes: "Desire is the desire for recognition. If a person says 'You are my master' the implication is 'I am your slave.' If one says 'You are my wife' the implication is 'I am your husband.'"[17] Where does of all this leave the animal, asks Derrida, since the animal presumably does not look to, much less speak to, other species in order to gain such a complex and reflexive sense of self. What rights can we guarantee a species that, lacking what Coleridge's Ancient Mariner calls "strange power of speech," is nothing more than raw reflex and basic instinct (188)? Man, or the species Charles Taylor has recently called "the language animal," transcends a simple responsiveness to signs, like "rats responding to triangles, and birds responding with cries to the presence of predators," to operate in a more sophisticated linguistic field, to articulate emotional states and to communicate with his fellow man.[18]

Two years prior to his death in 2004, Derrida situated Lacan in a Cartesian tradition that refused to grant the animal any kind of agency beyond the ability to react to external stimuli.[19] In contemporary animal studies (a recent offshoot of environmental philosophy, also known as "eco-studies"), René Descartes has long functioned as the *nom-du-père* since he codified, in his *Discourse on Method* of 1637, a binary of human-animal that privileged the *cogito* of thinking-man over the unthinking and clocklike animal.[20] To this day, Descartes remains, in the parlance of Keats, like "stout Cortez" with "eagle eyes," the single most influential theorist in terms of drawing a strict border between man and beast, a border that helped to justify such practices as hunting, meat eating, and vivisection (l.11–14).[21] Believing the animal to be a soulless, insensate creature, Descartes's followers argued that the cruelty toward animals was morally justifiable since they could not feel pain. Englishmen, for example, could follow a recipe such as the one found in the cookery manual, *Secrets of Nature* (1660) by John Wecker, which instructed gourmands to first de-feather, then burn a goose or duck alive, for maximal taste.[22] In Early Modern England, people could easily finish such a meal with a clean plate *and* a clean conscience, while today, people are more squeamish and conflicted about the issue of animal welfare and the so-called face on your plate. We are slowly recognizing the ideological investment man has in maintaining a strict separation between human and animal since it serves his narcissism and satisfies his dietary habits; in order for a carnivore economy to function, the animal must be abjected as all body, all instinct, all nature. It wasn't until the early nineteenth century, and the rise of a rights-based political paradigm inspired by the French Revolution, that England saw the founding of the Society for the Prevention of Cruelty to Animals (led, in part, by the tireless abolitionist William Wilberforce) in 1824.[23] The Romantic period in England cultivated sentimental thoughts about the flora and fauna that shared the environment, and its greatest literary artists, Keats included, crawled inside and inhabited the mind of the animal in order give it a voice, however much that voice sometimes sounded—by way of the pathetic fallacy—like his own.

This belief in man's intrinsic superiority over all of the natural world was based in the biblical as well as Aristotelian faith in man's unique possession of a soul and the rationality to make decisions in accordance with a free will, two crucial faculties thought to be radically lacking in the animal. In effect, Descartes authorized man's ability to shrug off the reality of animal suffering as not an important concern, and he has attracted critics ever since, including Voltaire who, in his popular *Dictionnaire philosophique portatif* of 1764, addressed Descartes indirectly, asking, "So tell me, mechanist, has Nature arranged all the springs of feeling in this animal so that it will not feel anything?" before warning, "Do not suppose Nature capable of such an impertinent contradiction."[24] In the age of Voltaire, animals existed only as objects to be caged, killed, and consumed. Parisian society got into a swivet, in the spring of 1798, when a pair of Indian elephants was showcased at the *Jardin des Plantes*. The arrival of these pachyderms prompted naturalist Bernardin de Saint-Pierre to remark that the elephants would help scientists and animals lovers recognize all of the emotions that man and animals had in common.[25] London, meanwhile, was home to St. Bartholomew's Fair, which enthralled William and Dorothy Wordsworth during an 1802 visit after which time the former recalled, in *The Prelude*, the sound of "chattering monkeys dangling from their poles" and "the horse of knowledge, and the learned pig" (a reference to "Toby the Sapient Pig," exhibited in 1817, and believed to be capable of prognostication and card playing).[26] No less fascinated with beastly spectacles was Keats who, in "The Cap and Bells," marvels at Tipoo Sultan's toy tiger, the "Man-Tiger-Organ"—sexual pun intended—which Keats probably saw in the reading room of the East India Company in 1819 (333). What he saw was a wooden automaton devouring a European officer. He wrote *Lamia* in the same year and did so, harnessing the reading public's fascination with beastly spectacles, in the hope of capitalizing on its erotically charged mythological themes of metamorphosis and seduction.

In the final phase of his career, Derrida sternly rebuked what he saw as Descartes's *and* Lacan's faulty concept of the animal as a mechanical beast that reacts rather than responds.[27] On several fronts, Derrida struggled to level the playing field between man and animals, which, in fact, was never a horizontal plane but a hierarchical chain of being with humanity on top. Compared to man, with his power to recognize himself and others, the animal "does not respond," writes Derrida, "it only *reacts*" and insofar as the animal communicates, reacting to signs and stimuli, such reactions fall short of more sophisticated "responses."[28] Certainly the role that bees play in Lacan's "The Function and Field of Speech and Language in Psychoanalysis" (1953) confirms Derrida's view, for, as Lacan points out, bees communicate with other bees, via a dance directed toward the sun (upon which their honey-gathering lives depend). "But is it necessarily a language?" Lacan asks, to which he decidedly says no, for the big Other plays no role, nor does the unconscious, repressed desire, which leaves nothing but a Saussurean economy of signifiers and signified.[29] By contrast, only the human subject orients the other (his listener/reader) through what Lacan terms the "highest function of speech," which, again, interpellates man into the meta-relational roles of master/slave, husband/wife, teacher/student, etc. (85). Furthermore, only man is able to recognize himself in others.

Derrida parts ways with this anthropocentric tradition that (including Heidegger and Levinas) denies the animal an essential place in Western philosophy and, consequently, facilitates man's abdication of his ethical responsibility to preserve and protect anything that shares his environment but lacks the ability to think and speak in ways that deems recognizable and, therefore, worthy of his consideration. This is the "logocentric metaphysics" that, through its construction of a coherent human subject that speaks and writes on the back of a mute and merely mechanistic animal other, has perpetuated man's destructive dominion over the earth as "natural" and just.[30] Derrida's later comments, which emerged in a dialogue with his friend Jean-Luc Nancy, were essentially a continuation of the remarks he made in "L'animal que donc je suis (à suivre)" [or "The Animal That Therefore I Am (More to Follow)] in a 2002 issue of *Critical Inquiry* where, for the first time, he singled out Lacan for advancing the dangerous thesis that it is man's right, given his exceptionality among all species and his divinely ordained access to *logos*, to speak for animals (*bêtes*) lacking in the powers of speech and recognition. Even conceding to the animal "some aptitude for signs and for communication," Lacan uncritically inherited a tradition that subordinates the bestiary to the human on the specious premise that animals possess only the simplest ability to react versus what Derrida calls "the power to respond—to *pretend*, to *lie*, to *cover its tracks* or *erase* its own traces."[31] Even the seemingly incidental addition of the definite article "the," as in the "the animal," relegates what Derrida calls the vast multifariousness of nonhuman life to a "catch-all concept"—as in "a virgin forest, a zoo, a hunting or fishing ground, a paddock or an abattoir, a space of domestication"—that negates man's continuity with the nonhuman world and the inclusiveness inherent in more communal formulations such as "his fellows, his neighbors" and "*all the living things*" (402). While eco-feminists such as Susan Fraiman have recently questioned the ascendance of Derrida (based upon this influential essay from 2002) as the "founding father" and framer of animal studies, the text remains an indispensable one, not only for its post-humanist deconstruction of the rhetoric deployed by Lacan but for its liberating effect on key ontological questions concerning man's relation to himself and to the world outside those subjective delimitations (e.g., What is the animal? What is it in relation to the human? Does the animal recognize man and, if so, does man operate in the animal's imaginary? If an animal can dream, does it have an unconscious?).[32]

Derrida's characterization of Lacan as the poster boy for an anthropocentric logocentrism is not an entirely fair one since Lacan's acknowledgment of bestial, even insectile, enjoyment does open new lines of animal-positive inquiry. In 1963's seminar on anxiety, he reasoned that if the phallus is the *sine qua non* of masculine jouissance, then there is no reason to suppose that the "black-beetle" is "deprived of "amorous jouissance."[33] The same can be said of any "mammals who most resemble us" and, no doubt, it was the bilateral mirror symmetry of the beetle's carapace (akin to the human body) that caught Lacan's eye (167). The fact that Lacan sexualizes the continuum that fuses man and the natural world puts him more squarely in line with Aristotle and his "principle of continuity" rather than in dualizing school of Descartes and Locke who, according to Kate Rigby, sought "mastery over a de-animated Nature devoid of ethical considerability."[34]

In his recent *Lacan on Love,* Bruce Fink stresses that the role of the animal in Lacanian theory is interwoven with the fundamental role of images in identity formation and sexuation. Influenced by Chavin's 1941 research into grasshoppers, Matthews' 1939 work on pigeons, and Lorenz's study of aggression in the animal kingdom, Lacan singled out the chimpanzee as capable of self-recognition in a proto-mirror stage, thereby broadening the self-reflexive capabilities of the psyche to animals. But only barely: animals in Lacanian theory only rarely transcend the reactionary modes of mimicry and aggression.

In this way, Lacan follows Freud in terms of the hostility he associated with animality. Susan McHugh, in *Animal Stories,* points out that animals play a vital function in Freud's case studies not simply as surrogate humans or as abstract figures with totemic qualities but, instead, as "reminders of how animals can function as 'demonic' or menacing figures of multiplicity."[35] The animal in classical psychoanalysis is typified mainly by its aggression: leering wolves perched in trees, snakes coiled on the skull of Medusa, vultures perched beside baby cribs—as in the case of Leonardo da Vinci's "phantasy of a vulture" that forcibly inserts its tale in the infant's mouth as an obvious substitute for the breast/phallus.[36] The Wolf Man is the paradigmatic case study because the neurotic subject is besieged by what Freud twins as "anxiety-hysteria (animal phobia)" the most shocking of which involves the image of a wolf (which is, contra McHugh, his father in wolf's clothing) and, worse, the image of two canines copulating which Freud unlocks as the boy's repressed memory of his parents copulating doggy-style in view of his sickbed.[37] Regardless, Derrida favors Freud over Lacan for better absorbing the scientific discovery known as Darwinism. David Krell notes that, for Derrida, Freud not only learned from but overcame the great Darwinian humiliation and was "not so keen" as Lacan was in distinguishing humankind from the animal kingdom.[38]

With Darwin in the air, it bears mentioning that the rise of animal rights throughout the nineteenth century in England is easy to trace to the works of Erasmus Darwin (1731–1802), the polymath and grandfather to Charles, the evolutionary biologist and author of *The Origin of Species* (1859). Erasmus Darwin wore many hats: he was an outspoken critic of Christianity in the 1770s, a translator of Linnaeus's works in the 1780s, and a nature poet and author of *The Loves of the Plants* (published in 1789 by Joseph Johnson, the infamous printer of works by Wollstonecraft, Godwin, and Paine), *The Botanic Garden* (1791–1792), and *The Temple of Nature* (released posthumously). Even if *The Botanic Garden* is now regarded as minor poetry, Desmond King-Hele's observation that its pre-evolutionary ideas "knocked the literary world sideways" is instructive because Darwin's lifelong effort was to flatten the artificial distinctions between human beings and all the other life-forms that were, according to Judeo-Christian moralism, believed to be lesser and baser than humanity.[39]

Again, my contrarian objective here is to perform a rescue effort of sorts since Lacan is unfairly positioned as anti-Darwinian and anti-Romantic in terms of subordinating any species that does not speak to logocentric man. Instead, Lacan's musings on nature and animal sex contain some illuminating contradictions. Again, my contrarian objective here is to perform a rescue effort of sorts. Lacan follows Freud in this respect, but his musings on nature and animal sex contain some illuminating contradictions. On the one hand, he states in "Function and Field" that desire does not exist outside of the Symbolic; thus, "the moment in which desire becomes human is also that in which the child is born into language."[40] On the other, Lacan would state the biologically obvious ("A penis is not limited to the field of mammals") but go onto locate the phallus (in the form of the cockroach's dart, or hook-like instrument) as the "locus of jouissance" and as the "function of the object" (167). Clearly the non-human penis, then, functions in the same way and facilitates a state of pleasure totally alien to human phenomena.

Just because animals lack the libidinal investment in an image discovered externally (in accordance with Lacan's foundational 1936 paper, "The Mirror Stage") does not mean they do not experience jouissance, which lies outside of the signifying mode as a site of pleasure but also as a site *beyond* pleasure (thus, the ineffable *Unlust, deplaisir*, or in the words of Paul Verhaeghe, "that which escapes symbolization").[41] While I concur with Fink, who claims that "unlike Freud, Lacan does not think that we cathect our*selves* automatically, like animals do," given their indifference to the self-image generated by a mirror image, a new angle needs to be developed.[42]

Cat Got Your Tongue?

The hawk wants a Mate—so does the Man.
         —Keats, *Letters*, February 19, 1819

Though he predates Lacan, Keats can help in that development since his lyric poetry grants agency, in the forms of dreams and voices, to animals and shares Lacan's interest in the delights of nonhuman biota. Paul Vatalaro notes that hearing one's own voice and the voice of the (m)other, traditionally "regarded in Western tradition as the initial and superior signature of self-presence," likely precedes the ability to "recognize oneself in the mirror."[43] The human voice, therefore, plays a vital role in the Symbolic and man's ability to communicate sounds aurally. It should not be hard to see how the animal also functions to construct, through a negative contrary, man's exceptional status as the so-called paragon of animals, equipped, as he is, with the tools of elocution and voice-recognition. Yet observe, in the following sonnet, how Keats extends these tools (customarily reserved for humans) to insects and how he grounds the ability to sing in the animal. Susan McHugh has credited the author with producing the "most famous animal representation of the Romantic artist's transcendence of human society" in his 1819 "Ode to a Nightingale."[44] This earlier poem, which Keats wrote under an hour as part of a sonnet-writing contest with Leigh Hunt, is a playful kind of trial run for his great avian *Ode* except that it is resolutely non-transcendent; the artist, instead, drops out of the scene and if he remains behind at all, he is, at most, "half lost" in the process of translating the sounds of insects. That loss originates in the fact that the animal is the origin of song while the human swoops in to reorganize insectile sounds into something poetic: the Petrarchan sonnet. Keats's "On the Grasshopper and Cricket" aestheticizes the mating call while stressing the lack of fulfillment inherent in creaturely jouissance, thereby naturalizing the continuity between human and animal vocalization:

> The poetry of earth is never dead:
> When all the birds are faint with the hot sun,
> And hide in cooling trees, a voice will run
> From hedge to hedge about the new-mown mead;
> That is the Grasshopper's—he takes the lead
> In summer luxury,—he has never done
> With his delights for when tired out with fun
> He rests at ease beneath some pleasant weed...
> And seems to one in drowsiness half lost,
> The Grasshopper's among some grassy hills. (ll. 1–14)

Significantly, the fairly facile projections on the poet's part—surely grasshoppers do not have "fun" nor experience "ease" in the way humans do—are balanced by the sheer otherness of animal enjoyment, for it "seems to one," which signals considerable indeterminacy on the speaker's part. The degree to which this trio of poets—grasshopper, cricket, and the sonneteer—forms a harmonious whole is undercut by the adjectival "half lost," which inscribes the *objet petit a* (or, the missing object) in what seems, only from the outside, a self-regulating ecosystem. In this way, Keats undercuts the fantasy of a fully unified Nature to expose instead a cacophony at the core of desire. It also undercuts human supremacism since, on an evolutionary level, vocalization regresses to its animal origins. To this end, he accords something epistemologically inaccessible to the insect's capacity for "delight," which is paradoxically limited *and* limitless, as in "never done / With his delight" (reinforced by the enjambment of lines six through seven) and "ceasing never:" (line nine, with its open-ended use of the colon to introduce the grasshopper's surrogate in the wintertime: the cricket). Together, the grasshopper and cricket are capable of two distinct but related functions: first, symbolization, or sign making ("a voice") in ways only they can decipher, which, then, parallels the poet's own power of representation and equates the writer and the bug as choristers singing the "same" song.

Another poem in which Keats turns back the clock, from an evolutionary perspective, is a short and playful fragment that begins "Where's the Poet?" (1). Usually dated from 1819 because of its similarities with the "camelion poet" letter to Woodhouse in the fall of that same year, this fifteen-line lyric—quoted *in toto* below—parallels the close conceptual connection that Keats makes between human and animal forms of sexual expression in his earlier sonnet. Jouissance is not limited to the field of humans alone, and this poem's interest in the full range of a bird's "instincts" will be crucial to my reading of *Lamia* as this poem puts "animal eagerness" and human desire on an even footing:

> Where's the Poet? Show him! show him!
> Muses nine, that I may know him!
> 'Tis the man who with a man
> Is an equal, be he King,
> Or poorest of the beggar-clan,
> Or any other wondrous thing
> A man may be 'twixt ape and Plato;
> 'Tis the man who with a bird,
> Wren or eagle, finds his way to
> All its instincts;—he hath heard
> The Lion's roarings, and can tell
> What his horny throat expresseth;
> And to him the Tiger's yell
> Comes articulate and presseth
> On his ear like a mother-tongue. (1–15)

It should be easy to see how the anti-monarchical ideology at work here, putting princes and paupers on the same plane, stretches beyond the human to the vaster animal kingdom. While the fragment cannot exactly be categorized as Darwinian, its purpose is to erode man's supposed superiority over all other species and to stress that one power in particular—vocalization—is foundationally animal and intelligible only to the poet. Elizabeth Grosz considers this a Darwinian explanation of language. In *Becoming Undone: Darwinian Reflections on Life, Politics, and Art*, she writes that by insisting on the "primarily erotic and attractive nature of vocalization," Darwin proved that language is a tool not simply for securing a species' survival (according to the logic of natural selection) but for attracting a mate through "rhythmic and melodic" means that only gradually, over time, develop and coalesce as language."[45] Symbolization originates in the prelinguistic animal even if, as we see in Keats's sonnet, poetic male genius alone has the power to aestheticize these sounds in the role of nature's spokesman. Indeed the unspoken commandment to round out the lyric might be *Hear him! hear him!*

What other "slips of the tongue"—as Freud describes the accidental articulation of the unconscious in *The Interpretation of Dreams*—lie in the tongue of Keats's tiger/mom?[46] Closer to home, the "mother-tongue" may allude to Frances Jennings, the author's mother, whose death in 1810, when Keats was fourteen and a half, caused him to hide under his master's desk at Clarke's School in Enfield.[47] The most foreign tongue of all, for which there is no translator, belongs to the animal whereas the mother is she who gives the boy his desire. Displacing, then, his oedipal fantasy of returning to his "mother-tongue" (a site foreclosed forever due to death) is a predator's "yell" and "roarings" inexplicably transformed into something comprehensible, even caressing. The tongue is connected to the mouth, after all, and, as Žižek has recently noted, Lacan's figuration of the mother as a crocodile with its mouth open symbolizes that "subject with the open mouth" who remains fiercely unresponsive to the desiring child.[48]

Beyond the simian and avian allusions, however, the function of the tiger's throat, which recalls the feline sexuality found in the "Man-Tiger-Organ" of "The Cap and Bells," is the most surprising. Its horny throat has at least two connotations, dental and sexual, respectively. "Horny" may signify his fangs, or the brassy sound of his roar, but, by the 1810s in England, "horny" had already become a slangy synonym for sexual arousal. Five of the six definitions beginning with "horn" in Francis Grose's 1811 *Dictionary in the Vulgar Tongue* refer either to cuckoldry or priapism (as in, "horn colic" and "hornified").[49] The poet, meanwhile, is in the unique position to receive those sounds as man and tiger share that "same animal eagerness" Keats identifies in his letter to George and Georgiana as the very thing that bridges man and beast (322). "The greater part of Men make their way with the same instinctiveness, the same unwandering eye from their purposes, the same animal eagerness as the Hawk" who "wants a Mate" as intensely as Man" (322). What may have triggered this epistolary outpouring, as rambling as it is obsessed with "pure desire" versus the self-interestedness of animal instinct, was a cricket of a different sort—that is, the cricket bat which struck the poet and left him with a black eye. As a remedy, his friend Charles Brown attached a leech to Keats's eyelid, bringing him face-to-face with the bloodsucker known as *Hirudo medicinalis*. Bloodletting was a standard medical practice and, as Roy Porter points out, big business: from Wordsworth's 1807 poem on leech-gatherers in England, which indicates an economic incentive among rural laborers, to France, which was importing thirty-three million leeches by 1837, the leech signified the therapeutic linkage between human bodies and the absolute other: a blood-sucking slug with ten stomachs that could expand six times its size upon feeding.[50]

Together with Keats's sonnet on the "delights" of insects, the fragment and letter from 1819 serve as important precursors to *Lamia* because they illustrate how animal jouissance sits on a continuum with the poet's own delight in giving voice to the natural objects that, in turn, make his own sensual instincts intelligible. Playing close attention to the role of the animal and vocalization in *Lamia*, the final section of my argument considers a snake-woman whose "throat was serpent" (l.63), rather than feline, but whose horniness and overt desire for a human animal propel Keats's fable to its irresolvable end. *Lamia* lays bare Lacan's logic of the sexual relation, or what Žižek has called the acknowledgment that the "relation between sexes is by definition 'impossible,' antagonistic," and that "there is no final solution."[51] Yet the animal's function in that preordained impossibility has heretofore not been uncovered.

Recognizing Keats's *Lamia*

We know nothing of the amorous *jouissance* of the cockroach or the black-beetle.

—Lacan, *Seminar X*[52]

Of the poems considered here, *Lamia* is the one that has been the most exhaustively psychoanalyzed.[53] Most persuasive is Orrin N. C. Wang's masterful essay, "Coming Attractions: *Lamia* and Cinematic Sensation" wherein Wang historicizes the poem's fascination with the feminine *and* the animal body by stressing the popularity of public shows, exhibitions, and phantasmagoria in Romantic-era London, such as the aforementioned toy tiger that would savage a man to the shrieks of its pipe organ built into its side. Wang provides a prehistory to cinema's unique power to facilitate the kind of visual pleasure that Lacan associates with the impossibility of desire, and by focusing on the visually unrestful and shifting image of Lamia's body, he connects her status as a *femme fatale* to the specular world of consumerism that Keats himself inhabited. Therefore, the poet's highly sensual descriptions of Lamia's eyes, mouth, and throat yield an equivocal shape that metonymizes heterosexual desire itself. "Mouth and throat together also make *voice*," he notes, "which along with the gaze is another prominent member of Lacan's list of partial objects that externalize for the subject the *objet petit a*, the object cause of desire."[54] Accordingly, all eyes are on Lamia throughout the poem, but especially at the poem's start where the fact that there is something missing (namely Hermes's wood nymph) helps to set the narrative (driven by the rhythm of neoclassical couplets) in motion. As part of a *quid pro quo* arrangement with Hermes, Lamia shrewdly agrees to assist the god in locating his lost nymph but only if he agrees to transform her into a human woman, so that she may, once again, "move in a sweet body fit for life, / And love and pleasure" (39–40). Yet pleasure, according to Keats, can never be fulfilled, which makes erotic love doomed from the start yet never done. Here his sonnet written for Fanny Brawne is in evidence, for the speaker of "Bright Star" wishes to touch her breast "*for ever*, its warm sink and swell, / Awake, *for ever*, in a sweet unrest" (my emphasis, 11–12). Here, too, delight can never rest—the caesura, from the Latin for *cutting*, contravenes a breast that rises and wakens—while, at the same time, incompleteness is what puts noble man and noble animal on the same plane.

Due to the fact that Keats never resolves the question of whether Lamia's body is animal or human, special attention must be paid to her ability to recognize versus merely react to external stimuli, which will by now be familiar as Lacan's qualification for humanness. The god Hermes is the first of two male lovers beguiled by the sight of the eponymous female figure who appears to him as a "Gordian shape of dazzling hue, / Vermilion-spotted, golden, green, and blue; / Striped like a zebra, freckled like a pard, / Eyed like a peacock, and all crimson pard" (I.47–50). The knottiness of Lamia's identity, or the "knotty problem" (as it's described in the poem's second part), speaks to the ontological ambiguities underlying the entire romance, for Keats provides no definite answer to the question of what Lamia is exactly: immortal? mortal? human? animal? All of the above? (l.160).[55] Speaking to this central question, she asks of Lycius, the young Corinthian and second male enchanted by the mysterious sight and sound of her, "My essence?" (l.283). Lamia's impact on this youth of Corinth rings Lacanian bells for myriad reasons, not least of which is the fact that his gaze (as the visual medium of desire) is as dazzled as it is distorted by her appearance. Following Wang, who reads Lamia's body as a "hybrid zoo whose exotic exhibition fails to secure Lamia's image in any mentally synthetic manner," I read the bestial body of Lamia as that which cannot be assimilated into normative cross-sex desire and as the missing object/hole at the poem's center (486). She is analogous to Lacan's account of the sardine can shimmering in the sun.[56] Note the description of Lycius's desire for Lamia as unquenchable in the lines: "And soon his eyes had drunk her beauty up, / Leaving no drop in the bewildering cup, / And still the cup was full" (251–3). On desire, Keats and Lacan are decidedly half-cup-empty thinkers. The fact that Lamia will never satisfy Lycius's desire, despite his ceaseless striving, is due to the fact that she can melt down and reshape to fit the fantasy of any onlooker—not "as she is," in the words of Victorian poet Christina Rossetti, "but as she fills his dream."[57] What matters most for our purposes here is that Lamia straddles the human-animal divide, all the while, "shut up in mysteries" (I.241). Keats's description of her reptilian body as "rainbow-sided" is especially fitting since it evokes Žižek's formulation of the *objet petit a* as "curved space," for "the nearer you get to it, the more it eludes your grasp (or the more you possess it, the greater the lack)."[58] Keats's fairytale opening to the poem ("Upon a time, before the faery broods") soon unravels into death and lack on all sides (1).

The ironic reversals at the end of *Lamia* are not limited to the fact that what the Corinthians have gathered to see, like any guests at a wedding banquet, is the fulfillment of two person's desire though they depart in total disappointment. They come together as celebrants but leave as eyewitnesses to a murder. One matter of critical concern has been what drives Lycius to display his fiancée, whom he is convinced is "real woman," for all of Corinth to see (I.332)? For Jack Stillinger, it's his "arrogance and vanity" in "showing off his bride at a wedding feast."[59] Stillinger is only partly right about Lycius's motivation, however, since he is also driven by the desire for others to recognize the identity he has bestowed upon this "knotty problem" through the patriarchal solution of matrimony. Yet Lacan instructs us that recognition is always *mis*-recognition, and that the mirror plays a defining and distorting role in the formation of human desire and selfhood. That crucial stage of misperception is spatial in nature since the self sees itself in the eye of someone else, or, in Wordsworth's formulation, "drinks in the feelings of his Mother's eye!"[60] As Teresa Brennan puts it, there are "three factors at work" in Lacan's theory of *méconnaissance*: "one's self, one's image, and the other who validates the image."[61] In the scene that concludes *Lamia*, there is zero validation, only renunciation, leaving Lamia no other option but to vanish once the sage Apollonius succeeds at exposing her animal nature.

The poem is driven by multiple desires—Hermes's, Lycius's, and of course Lamia's—but it is her regression into her erstwhile beastliness that short-circuits the poem. The most unsympathetic character in *Lamia* is the old wise man Apollonius who struggles to put the animal-woman in her place and to reinstate the Cartesian divide discussed earlier. Lamia's animality precludes what Daniela Garofalo has termed "full jouissance" in another romance of Keats's, *The Eve of St. Agnes*, that also ends in lack and loss, or the "insufficiency of the beloved and the failure of courtly love fantasies."[62] Keats's fable, in which the animal's role cannot be minimized, ponders and plays with the eroticism involved in its antiheroine being both snakelike woman *and* a womanly serpent with the aim of disturbing the difference between human and animal forms of jouissance and rendering both, ultimately, incomplete. The two are incompatible since Lamia's existence depends on Lycius's blindness while inhabiting the same plane in full view of each other results in death; thus "[h]e look'd and look'd again a level— No!" (304). Whatever Lamia is in the end, she exposes the animal's elusive and only partially knowable place in the field of desire, which is attributable to the fact that Lamia never really existed in the first place. Lacan teaches in Seminar XXIII that the "mark of the real is that it is tied to nothing."[63] In the eye of Hermes at the start, she exists only as a mirage at the end of what he calls his "serpent rod" (89) while under the Medusan eye of Apollonius at the wedding feast, she blurs with the sage's conception of her in a complete role reversal, for it is his gaze that is suddenly serpentine: "lashless eyelids" (l.288) and "stinging" (like a snake's) (301). Lycius is no different since, as he screams in fear and collapses fatally in shock and revulsion, Keats describes his arms as "empty of delight, / As were his limbs of life" (307). Wedding guests traditionally gather to view *and* validate the love-is-blind fantasy that drives heterosexual union in the first place but what Keats stages, perversely so, in *Lamia* is the ultimate emptiness of the groom's arms and bride's evacuation from the scene, which explains the poem's last word, which reinforces the knottiness of Lamia's real identity: "wound," as in the groom's corpse wrapped in his robe ("the heavy body wound") (311). Gilbert D. Chaitin, in *Rhetoric and Culture in Lacan*, comments that in accordance with Lacan's dictum that the unconscious is structured like a language, metonymy is essential to the unconscious since, as an elusive substructure, the "unconscious is precisely that which escapes expression in language" yet remains behind, traceable only in "slips, dreams, and symptoms."[64] Lycius's heavy body, wound up tight and emptied of life, metonymizes the deeper, irresolvable conflicts below the poem's surface: the cancellation of total pleasure, and the chaos and confusion that arise when humans and animals come into close erotic contact with one another.

In addition to the fact that Keats depicts the men's desire for Lamia as fundamentally unfulfillable, the confusion over whether Lamia has the ability to recognize others—the hallmark, for Lacan, of one's humanness—is reflected in the scholarly divide over this very issue. Bate described Lamia like so: "[S]he is dependent on human recognition and response" in light of her shape-shifting ability to melt down and reform in order to "fulfill different—even conflicting—desire and demands, and do so with innocence and clairvoyance, with beauty and unparalleled knowledge."[65] Meanwhile Levinson writes that the "death-dealing horror, for Lycius, [is] Lamia's inability to *recognize* him," for "she can only blankly reflect his own image."⁶⁶ *Lamia* stages a drama of desire and disavowal and ends abruptly as man realizes that Lamia's jouissance is not his own and that the unrecognizability of her eyes jolts him into a deathly state of panic. Simply put, he cannot recognize himself in Lamia's "orbs," which, like her mouth, are shut tight. The crucial lines are as follows:

> He gaz'd into her eyes, and not a jot
> Own'd they the lovelorn piteous appeal:
> More, more he gaz'd: his human senses reel:
> Some hungry spell that loveliness absorbs;
> There was no recognition in those orbs.
> "Lamia!" he cried—and no soft-toned reply. (256–61)

A gap has suddenly opened at the poem's ending as Lamia is exposed as the animal she really is; she stands outside of the human self and sociability ("no recognition," "no . . . reply"). But it is through this gap, this place of lack, that constitutes Lycius's humanness, Lamia's animalness, and the dissolution of both these constructed selves. She has the eye of a peacock and the tongue of a snake, both of which are completely inscrutable to Lycius. Following Richard Sha (who deploys a queer explanation of jouissance, handed down to him by the likes of Lee Edelman and Leo Bersani) as disruptive and self-annihilating), I see the poem as connecting jouissance with what Sha calls "anti-relationality, the death of the heteronormative social" through its undoing of the marriage plot.⁶⁷ The eroticized animal has ruined the marriage-feast, killed off the fiancé, any chance of reproduction, and disrupted the optics of love and marriage.

There are a great number of new avenues opened by Lacan's conceptualization of the animal, and Keats's animal poems in particular lend themselves to a Lacanian analytic since they grant the "noble animal man" special status as nature's interpreter while blurring the boundaries between his pleasures and the pleasures of the animal other. What might be considered Lacanian is Keats's definition of the human animal in relation to language since he upholds man's superiority over other species as the master sign-maker and -interpreter but this does not mean that the essential sameness between man and animal is unimportant. What's un-Lacanian is that he ascribes an erotic interiority to the animal and ponders, less in passing than Lacan and more in concerted ways that peaked in the poetical works written in 1819, the inner feelings and desires of nonhuman biota. As I show, sexual difference and human-animal difference are overlapping constructs that, together, drive an ideology of anthropocentricism, or what Rigby calls the "human supremacism" that preserves man's unshakable position atop the "evolutionary pyramid."⁶⁸ Biopower as we know it depends on abjecting the animal, a strategy which Lacan and Keats appear to undermine through the curiosity these two thinkers shared about animal jouissance and its mysterious circuits of feeling and erotic desire. In Keats, the animal cooperates in the formation of the human subject and in the symbolic by assuming a name and a language that presses on the poet's ears and shapes the substructure of his imagination.

Notes

(The author would like to thank Beth Lau for her generous input on this essay.)

1. Jacques Lacan, *The Seminar of Jacques Lacan, Book XI: Four Fundamental Concepts of Psychoanalysis*, trans. Alan Sheridan (New York: Norton, 1978), 156.

2. See the introduction to Lacan in *The Norton Anthology of Theory and Criticism*, ed. Vincent B. Leitch (New York: Norton, 2010), 1157.

3. For extensive debate over what Bruce Fink calls Lacan's "bombshell expression," see *The Lacanian Subject: Between Language and Jouissance* (Princeton: Princeton University Press, 1995), 104–5 and 193; see the discussion of "Sexuation" in *Reading Seminar XX: Lacan's Major Work on Love, Knowledge, and Feminine Sexuality* (Syracuse: SUNY Press 2002), 6–7. For the concept of *jouissance*, as David Sigler writes, as a "notorious sticking point" for translators, see his *Sexual Enjoyment in British Romanticism: Gender and Psychoanalysis, 1753–1835* (Montreal: McGill-Queen's University Press, 2015), 10 and Leo Bersani and Ulysse Dutoit's *Forms of Being: Cinema, Aesthetics, Subjectivity* (BFI Publishing, 2004), 126–7. Lacan concedes that his negation of the sexual relation is an "embellishment" in "On *Sens*, Sex, and The Real" in *The Seminar of Jacques Lacan, Book XXIII: The Sinthome*, trans. A. R. Price (Malden: Polity Press, 2016), 104.

4. Lorenzo Chiesa, *The Not-Two: Logic and God in Lacan* (Cambridge, MA: The MIT Press, 2016), 1.

5. Unless otherwise noted, all references to Keats's works are cited by line number (for poetry) and page number (for prose) and found in *Keats's Poetry and Prose*, ed. Jeffrey N. Cox (New York: Norton, 2009).

6. Lauren Berlant and Lee Edelman, *Sex, or the Unbearable* (Durham: Duke University Press, 2014), 1–2.

7. Lacan, *Écrits*, trans. Alan Sheridan (New York: Norton, 1977), 62.

8. Karl Kroeber, *Ecological Literary Criticism: Romantic Imagining and the Biology of Mind* (New York: Columbia University Press, 1994), 69.

9. The source of pleasure in Keats's schema—Beauty, Joy, Fame—are always subject to erasure; thus, according to the melancholic logic of his "Ode on

Melancholy," beauty is doomed from the start ("She dwells with Beauty—Beauty that must die") (l.21). The parallel to the "aching pleasure" in "Ode" is the coexistence of pain and pleasure in *The Eve of St. Agnes* wherein the birdlike Madeline feels, in her nest, "blissfully haven'd both from joy and pain" (xxvii.240).

10. Colette Soler, "The Curse of Sex," *Sexuation,* ed. Renata Salecl (Durham: Duke University Press, 2000), 39–53, 39.

11. Slavoj Žižek, "The Thing from Inner Space," *Sexuation* (2000), 216–59, 231.

12. Timothy Morton, *The Poetics of Spice: Romantic Consumerism and the Exotic* (Cambridge: Cambridge University Press, 2000), 211. For Edwards, see his "Nature Bridled: The Treatment and Training of Horses in Early Modern England," in *Beastly Natures; Animals, Humans, and the Study of History,* ed. Dorothee Brantz (Charlottesville: University of Virginia Press, 2010), 155–75, 156. For further discussion of how men displaced onto animals their own anxieties about bodily functions, specifically "ferocity, gluttony, sexuality," see Keith Thomas, *Man and the Natural World: Changing Attitudes in England, 1500–1800* (Oxford: Oxford University Press, 1983), 36–50, 41.

13. William Blake, *The Complete Poetry and Prose of William Blake,* ed. David V. Erdman (New York: Anchor Books, 1988), 23. Samuel Taylor Coleridge, *Poems* (London: Everyman's Library, 1991), 50–1. For Menely's reading of Coleridge's "To a Young Ass" and the author's volte-face in terms of the humanitarian verse of his early days, see *The Animal Claim: Sensibility and the Creaturely Voice* (Chicago: University of Chicago Press, 2016), 200–1.

14. Sigmund Freud and Albert Einstein, "Why War?" (1932), *Character and Culture,* introduction by Philip Rieff (New York: Collier Books), 134–47, 135.

15. Lacan, *Écrits,* 65.

16. Spivak, *Of Grammatology,* trans. Gayatri Chakravorty Spivak (Baltimore: Johns Hopkins University Press, 1976), lxv.

17. Madan Sarup, *Modern Critical Theorists: Jacques Lacan* (Toronto: University of Toronto Press, 1992), 104.

18. Charles Taylor, *The Language Animal: The Full Shape of the Human Linguistic Capacity* (Cambridge: The Belknap Press of Harvard University Press, 2016), 25.

19. Late in his career, Derrida distanced himself from any anthropocentric line of thought, even playfully likening his existence (on camera, in a 2002 documentary about his life) to a "fish's experience" as it is "exposed to the endless scrutiny of aquarium visitors" (541); see Max Cavitch, "Criticism in Translation: Contrejour," *PMLA* 131, no. 2 (2016): 540–2. For more on Derrida's conceptualization of the animal in relation to queer ecology, see my "Grizzly Love: The Queer Ecology of Timothy Treadwell," *GLQ: A Journal of Lesbian and Gay Studies* 18, no. 4 (Fall 2012): 507–28.

20. For Descartes's role in the rhetoric of Western anthropocentricism, see "Rhetorics of Dehumanization" in Élisabeth de Fontenay's *Without Offending Humans: A Critique of Animals Rights* (Minneapolis: University of Minnesota Press, 2012), 72–95.

21. Unless otherwise noted, all references to Keats's works are from *Keats's Poetry and Prose*, ed. Jeffrey N. Cox (New York: Norton, 2009).

22. Patricia Fumerton connects the grotesque details of Wecker's goose recipe to the importance of spice as a crucial commodity in Renaissance culture; see (if you can stomach it) her "Introduction: A New New Historicism" in *Renaissance Culture and the Everyday*, ed. P. Fumerton and Simon Hunt, (Philadelphia: University of Pennsylvania Press, 1999), 1–10.

23. For more on the history of animal rights and organizations in the Romantic period, see "The Animal Question and Women" in Barbara Seeber, *Jane Austen and Animals* (Burlington: Ashgate, 2013), 15–31.

24. Voltaire, *Pocket Philosophical Dictionary* (*Dictionnaire philosophique portative*), trans. J. Fletcher (Oxford: Oxford University Press, 2011), 41.

25. For elephants in 1790s French culture, see Michael E. McClellan's "'If We Could Talk with the Animals': Elephants and Musical Performance during the French Revolution" in *Cruising the Performative*, ed. Sue-Ellen Case (Bloomington: Indiana University Press, 1995), 237–45.

26. William Wordsworth, *The Prelude*, ed. J. Wordsworth et al. (New York: Norton, 1979), Book 7, ll. 694–708.

27. A concise review of Judeo-Christian and fourth-century attitudes (articulated by Aristotle) toward the animal can be found in Edwards (2010), 155–8, Rigby (2014), 63–4.

28. Jacques Derrida, *For Strasbourg: Conversations of Friendship and Philosophy*, trans. Pascale-Anne Brault and Michael Naas (New York: Fordham UP, 2014), 82.

29. Lacan, *Écrits*, 85.

30. Derrida, *Of Grammatology*, 46.

31. Derrida, "The Animal That Therefore I Am (More to Follow)," *Critical Inquiry* 28 (Winter 2002): 369–418, 401. For more on the question of *Homo sapiens* and its "exceptional" status, see Alenka Zupančič, *What Is Sex?* (Cambridge, MA: The MIT Press, 2017), 84–93.

32. Susan Fraiman, "Pussy Panic versus Liking Animals: Tracking Gender in Animal Studies," *Critical Inquiry* 39 (Autumn 2012): 89–115, 93.

33. Lacan, *Anxiety: The Seminar of Jacques Lacan, Book X*, ed. Jacques-Alain Miller, trans. A. R. Price (Malden: Polity, 2016), 167.

34. Kate Rigby, "Romanticism and Ecocriticism," *The Oxford Handbook of Ecocriticism,* ed. Greg Garrard (Oxford: Oxford University Press, 2014), 60–79,

63. See Arthur O. Lovejoy's canonical *The Great Chain of Being: A Study of the History of an Idea* (1966) for Aristotle's intervention into the man-versus-animal debate with his "introduction of the principle of continuity into natural history" (Cambridge: Harvard University Press, 1966), 56.

35. Susan McHugh, *Animal Stories* (Minneapolis: University of Minnesota Press, 2011), 13.

36. Unsurprising in its reductionism, Freud's interpretation unveils the bird's "tail" as a phallic symbol. See *Leonardo da Vinci and a Memory of His Childhood*, trans. Alan Tyson (New York: Norton, 1961), 36.

37. Freud, *Three Case Histories* (New York: Touchstone Books, 1996), 163.

38. David Krell, *Derrida and Our Animal Others* (Bloomington: Indiana University Press, 2013), 87.

39. Desmond King-Hele, "Shelley and Erasmus Darwin," *Shelley Revalued: Essays from the Gregynog Conference* (Totowa, NJ: Barnes & Noble Books, 1983), 129–46. Also see my forthcoming book, *Eros and Environment: The Radical Ecology of the Shelleys*, for both the Shelleys' indebtedness to Erasmus Darwin's biocentric outlook.

40. Lacan, *Écrits,* 103.

41. Paul Verhaeghe, "Enjoyment and Impossibility: Lacan's Revision of the Oedipus Complex," in *Jacques Lacan and the Other Side of Psychoanalysis: Reflections on Seminar XVII*, eds. Justin Clemens and Russell Grigg (Durham: Duke University Press, 2006), 29–49, 30.

42. Bruce Fink, *Lacan on Love: An Exploration of Lacan's Seminar VIII, Transference* (Malden: Polity, 2016), 72.

43. Paul A. Vatalaro, *Shelley's Music: Fantasy, Authority, and the Object Voice* (Burlington: Ashgate, 2009), 22.

44. Susan McHugh, "Literary Animal Agents," *PMLA* 124, no. 2 (2009): 487–95, 488.

45. Elizabeth Grosz, *Becoming Undone: Darwinian Reflections on Life, Politic, and Art* (Durham: Duke University Press, 2011), 18.

46. Freud, *The Interpretation of Dreams*, trans. A. A. Brill (New York: Barnes & Noble, 1994), 472.

47. For the history of Frances Keats, her back-to-back marriages, and death, see Denise Gigante, *The Keats Brothers: The Life of John and George* (Cambridge: The Belknap Press of Harvard University Press, 2011), 48–51.

48. See Slavoj Žižek, *Trouble in Paradise: From the End of History to the End of Capitalism* (Brooklyn: Melville House, 2014), 17.

49. Francis Grose, *Dictionary in the Vulgar Tongue*, last modified Jan. 10, 2011, last accessed Dec. 29, 2016, http://www.gutenberg.org/cache/epub/5402/pg5402.htm.

50. For more on the medicinal usages of the slug, see the "Paris Medicine" section in Roy Porter, *The Greatest Benefit to Mankind: A Medical History of Humanity* (New York: Norton, 1997), 314–6.

51. Žižek, *The Sublime Object of Ideology* (London: Verso, 1989), xxviii.

52. Lacan, *Anxiety*, 167.

53. In addition to Wang, there is Marjorie Levinson (1988) who combines Freud and Marx in reading the possessive love for Lamia on Lycius's part as a sign of his narcissism but also a means of marketing Lamia as his property in a system of commodity capitalism; see 280–95. See also Bruce Clarke's "Fabulous Monsters of Conscience" in which he draws the parallel between Lamia's status as a "penised lady" and the "phallic mother," the "most monstrous of all the fabulous monsters in the Freudian bestiary"; see Clarke, "Fabulous Monsters of Conscience: Anthropomorphosis in Keats's *Lamia*," *Studies in Romanticism*, 23, no. 4 (Winter 1984): 555–79, 576.

54. Orrin N. C. Wang, "Coming Attractions: *Lamia* and Cinematic Sensations," *Studies in Romanticism* 42 (Winter 2003): 461–500, 489.

55. William Godwin's *Mandeville* of 1817 reminds us that the monstrous "Lamiae" are also identified as shark-like—"the sea-monsters of Africa, the Lamiae, that with a thousand inticements and flatteries lure their victims to their ruin"—so the exact species in the Lamiae myth is unknowable; see *Mandeville: A Tale of the Seventeenth Century in England*, ed. Tilottama Rajan (Peterborough: Broadview, 2016), 215.

56. For a Romanticist application of Lacan's sardine can to Wordsworth's *Salisbury Plain*, see David Collings, *Wordsworthian Errancies: The Poetics of Cultural Dismemberment* (Baltimore: Johns Hopkins University Press, 1994), 72–74.

57. Christina Rossetti, "In an Artist's Studio," *The Norton Anthology of English Literature*, ed. S. Greenblatt and M. H. Abrams (New York: Norton, 2006), 1463.

58. Slavoj Žižek, *The Fragile Absolute* (London: Verso, 2000), 24.

59. Jack Stillinger, "Reading Keats's Plots," in *Critical Essays on John Keats*, ed. Hermione de Almeida (New York: G. K. Hall & Co., 1990), 88–102, 94.

60. Wordsworth, *The Prelude*, Book 2, l.236.

61. Teresa Brennan, *The Transmission of Affect* (Ithaca: Cornell University Press, 2004), 108.

62. Daniela Garofalo, "'Give me that voice... Those looks immortal': Gaze and Voice in Keats's 'The Eve of St. Agnes,'" *Studies in Romanticism* 49, no. 3 (Fall 2010): 353–73, 354.

63. Lacan, *The Sinthome*, 104.

64. Gilbert D. Chaitin, *Rhetoric and Culture in Lacan* (Cambridge: Cambridge University Press, 1996), 50.

65. W. Jackson Bate, *John Keats* (Cambridge: Harvard University Press, 1963), 556.

66. Levinson, *Keats's Life of Allegory: The Origins of Style* (New York: Basil Blackwell), 1988, 280. Andrew Bennett comes to similar conclusion in *Keats, Narrative, and Audience: The Posthumous Life of Writing* (Cambridge: Cambridge University Press, 1994) when he asserts that the "congruence of Lamia's name with the poem itself" highlights the instability of both the snake-woman's ontological status *and* the signifier itself; see 173–77, 173.

67. Richard C. Sha, "Blake and the Queering of Jouissance," in *Queer Blake*, ed. Helen P. Bruder and Tristanne Connolly (New York: Palgrave, 2010), 40–49, 41.

68. Rigby, "Romanticism," 67.

Chapter Four

Abandoned by Providence
Loss in Jane Austen's *Persuasion*

DANIELA GAROFALO

JANE AUSTEN has rarely been read in conjunction with Lacanian theory. Since the groundbreaking work of Claudia L. Johnson and other feminist minded critics, scholars have understood Austen's work as engaged with some of the major philosophical and political concerns of her time. However, I argue in this chapter that the complexity of Austen's response to capitalism in her last novel has often been overlooked by historicist and feminist readings which see *Persuasion* as championing new professional possibilities for men and even women. A Lacanian reading, instead, allows us to probe *Persuasion*'s concern with capitalism's relation to loss. Lacan understands human subjectivity as founded on loss, and, by examining Austen's treatment of the theme in Lacanian terms, my reading reveals a novel much more ambivalent and even critical of a nascent capitalist culture than has often been recognized.

While Austen might appear to be the least likely Romantic writer to lend herself to a Lacanian approach, her interest in social competition and the fantasies that inform our sense of reality, as well as her focus on sexual difference and the loss sustained in particular by women, connects her powerfully to some central Lacanian concerns. This chapter examines Austen's representation of capitalism in relation to Lacan's theories of sexuation and phallic jouissance.

Jane Austen's *Persuasion* is famously considered her autumnal novel, concerned with missed opportunities, waning hopes, and broken love affairs. Pervaded with a sense of loss, the novel, nonetheless, abounds with characters who deny it or distance themselves from it, embracing, instead, an ethic of success and achievement. Thinking of loss in connection with gain or profit, the characters in the novel tend to see loss as merely a potential risk in the pursuit of wealth and success. Those who experience loss without gain are forgotten. Presumably, they are those who, lacking merit, have been justly abandoned by providence.

According to this ethic, loss functions as a sign of personal failure, a merited punishment for lacking the abilities, the drive, or the moral fortitude possessed by those who make their own fortunes. This view of loss evokes Lacan's characterization of what he called the masculine side of sexuation, a subjective position which promises enjoyment from the attainment of phallic objects, such as wealth and prestige. Phallic enjoyment offers the illusion that one may escape loss and the incompleteness and vulnerability brought on by castration.

However, a different emphasis on loss persists in the novel, which refuses to relegate the "losers" of history to the background. This emphasis, represented particularly by the protagonists Anne Elliot and, later in the novel, Captain Wentworth, brings into question the novel's commitment to narratives of economic and social success. This other, less recognized commitment to loss, aligns Anne and Wentworth with an acceptance of loss, connecting them to Lacan's feminine side of sexuation, and distancing them from phallic enjoyment.

Critics have often understood *Persuasion* as centrally concerned with economic and social change. Jessica Richard has pointed to *Persuasion*'s interest in a changing economy from that of "the landed estate owner" to that of the "the risk-taking professional."[1] For her, the romance elements of the novel suit the emphasis on gambling, on taking chances: "Romances are filled with improbable events and heroes; by learning romance, Anne learns not to calculate probabilities prudentially but to surrender herself to the improbable operations of chance" (47). Richard refers to the navy heroes of the novel as "overseas speculators" (148). While Austen is most often read as a realist novelist, Richard emphasizes the romance elements in the realist narrative that speak to this interest in chance, risk, and gambling. The changing economy put an emphasis on the unexpected event, on a willingness to risk all, on the need to "navigate an unpredictable world" (150). For Richard, Wentworth functions as "a sublime gambler" (158), one who believes that chance will serve him well. His sublime gambling "leaves him open to chance's operations, to sink to the bottom or to rise to riches as luck determines" (160–61). The course of the novel, Richard claims, sees Anne develop from a character averse to risk to one who is "willing to take risks and to engage in the romance of risk" (164). Embracing Wentworth's sense of fortune, Anne chooses a certain kind of risk that "has roots in the belief in special providence that characterized British mariners' culture" (167). This doctrine holds that "providence intervenes in the ordinary progress of affairs, improbably altering outcomes to favor good or to punish evil" (166). Essentially, this view of providence and the positive view of gambling speak to the opportunities that the "gambling-based capitalizing economy appeared to promise" (14). The interest in chance, then, is a manifestation of "the eighteenth century's cultural and economic shift to capitalism" (3). Loss becomes a necessary part of the system for anyone who wishes to participate in a capitalist economy, one in which speculation in multiple forms was becoming pervasive (5). Enlisted in a capitalist teleological narrative, loss can be understood as losses, as setbacks in the struggle for economic success.

This view of loss is a far cry from Lacan's theory of constitutive loss, a loss that occurs when the subject enters language and becomes impressed with the belief that it has lost some authentic self-presence or immediate being in the world. The notion of losses that can be reversed or made up for, participates in the phallic fantasy that the social world offers compensation for constitutive loss.

I want to expand on Richard's emphasis on a new economic model that made risk-taking an important part of participating in a venture capitalist and speculative economy, but I also want to underscore the novel's concern with the dark side of such a change. Furthermore, I qualify Richard's claims about the heroine by seeing her as only partially embracing this new view of risk. I begin by exploring the novel's interest in a new economic dispensation and how it creates intolerance toward those who cannot fulfill the success narrative. I then go on to consider alternatives to this modern ethos as manifested by Anne and Wentworth's acceptance of loss, a loss associated with the failure of what Lacan calls "fantasy." When Wentworth finds himself falling out of the narrative trajectory of Providence, of success, he is seduced by Anne's embrace of loss. By championing loss, Anne allows us to glimpse an ethic that distances us from phallic enjoyment, the struggle for the goods, and to accept, instead, "not having," what Lacan defines as the feminine position of sexuation.

Providence, Profit, and Risk

A system that celebrates risk takers, Austen's narrator suggests, cannot waste much sympathy on losers. In this moral climate, callousness towards those who fail seems so natural as to go without much notice. One moment in the novel particularly exemplifies this attitude towards loss. Mrs. Musgrove, on hearing that Captain Wentworth is in the neighborhood, recalls that her dead son was in Wentworth's service. Louisa Musgrove explains that "her head is quite full of it, and of poor Richard! So we must all be as merry as we can, that she may not be dwelling upon such gloomy things" (86).

The narrator here intervenes to describe the "real circumstances of this pathetic piece of family history" (86). These circumstances turn out to be that

> the Musgroves had had the ill fortune of a very troublesome, hopeless son; and the good fortune to lose him before he reached his twentieth year; that he had been to sea, because he was stupid and unmanageable on shore; that he had been very little cared for at any time by his family, though quite as much as he deserved; seldom heard of, and scarcely at all regretted, when the intelligence of his death abroad had worked its way to Uppercross, two years before. (86)

This begins the narrator's efforts to undermine Mrs. Musgrove's expression of feeling for her dead son. In a novel very much concerned with profit making, the Musgroves appear to have gotten little of it from their younger son, Richard. Fortune is throughout the novel associated with money getting, not only in the sense of gaining a fortune but also in the sense of having the luck which allows one to acquire it. Here it also suggests that fortune weeds out those who are unprofitable. We are told that, "though his sisters were now doing all they could for him, by calling him 'poor Richard,'" he had, in fact, "been nothing better than a thick-headed, unfeeling, unprofitable Dick Musgrove, who had never done any thing to entitle himself to more than the abbreviation of his name, living or dead" (86). While the sisters refer to him as Richard, the narrator prefers "Dick," a term that both replaces the proper name with a familiar diminutive and suggests Dick, as a word for a man, any man, as in "Tom, Dick, and Harry." The diminutive suggests Richard's indistinguishability from any other representative of average, unsuccessful man. Not having distinguished himself, Dick is only worthy of an abbreviation of his name. Undistinguished men can do no better than to die, losing their name and their individuality.[2]

Yet, when at the dinner party at the Musgroves' home, Wentworth discusses her son with Mrs. Musgrove he does so "with so much sympathy and natural grace, as shewed the kindest consideration for all that was real and unabsurd in the parent's feelings" (101). He expresses himself "naturally" even though, as the narrator informs us, he has responded to Dick's name with a "curl of his handsome mouth, which convinced Anne that instead of sharing in Mrs. Musgrove's kind wishes, as to her son, he had probably been at some pains to get rid of him" (100). Wentworth's kindness is, then, rather forced but apparently responsive to what is "not absurd" in the mother's feelings. The idea that a grieving parent's feelings contain something absurd might certainly seem surprising. But in the ledger of profit and loss, the loss of an "unprofitable Dick" hardly counts as a loss at all. If loss is connected to profit and Dick Musgrove never aimed at profit (the narrator makes clear that he only wrote to ask his parents for money), then his loss doesn't register in this world. Unproductive, he must simply be written off. The narrator's harshness only increases as the scene develops. We are told that Mrs. Musgrove appears ridiculous in her character as mourner and the narrator gives Wentworth "some credit for the self-command with which he attended to her large fat sighings over the destiny of a son, whom alive nobody had cared for" (101). The fat of the body is displaced onto the sighs of sorrow, creating a scene of broad humor. It is as though her bodily presence negates the possibility that loss can be registered at all.

Wentworth also seems to address the possibility of loss but he does so again only to negate it. Beginning by assessing the fitness of his first ship, the Asp, Captain Wentworth tells his rapt auditors at the Musgrove dinner:

> The admiralty [ ] entertain themselves now and then, with sending a few hundred men to sea, in a ship not fit to be employed. But they have a great many to provide for; and among the thousands that may just as well go to the bottom as not, it is impossible for them to distinguish the very set who may be least missed (98).

The admiralty, according to Wentworth is as careless of loss as the narrator. They face such a multitude of contenders for a good ship, that they accept losses among a thousand "that may just as well go to the bottom as not." The very fact of competition makes it impossible to miss the dead. Wentworth makes clear that the navy and the public only notice a lost man if he is a man who has profited. Wentworth explains that if he had encountered bad weather "I should only have been a gallant Captain Wentworth, in a small paragraph at one corner of the newspapers; and being lost in only a sloop, nobody would have thought about me" (99). Loss can only be registered in connection with worth—that is, when loss is associated with someone who has fortune on his side, someone who has commanded something better than a sloop.

Touching on the possibility of his death when he was only an untested captain of a sloop, Wentworth emphasizes that he would have earned only a forgotten entry in a newspaper article. Despite Anne's shuddering, her brief reaction to the possibility of Wentworth's loss, such a possibility is quickly glossed over because, as Wentworth makes clear, he never experienced loss at all. His first ship, he remarks, was hardly "fit for service then.—Reported fit for home service for a year of two,—and so I was sent off to the West Indies" (98). Although this account would seem to set us up for a narrative of disaster, Wentworth, in fact, tells a success story:

> Ah! she was a dear old Asp to me. She did all that I wanted. I knew she would. I knew that we should either go to the bottom together, or that she

would be the making of me; and I never had two days of foul weather all the time I was at sea in her; and after taking privateers enough to be very entertaining, I had the good luck in my passage home the next autumn, to fall in with the very French frigate I wanted. (98)

Luck is with him, and he never experiences bad weather, which would have undone his old ship. His good luck also allows him "to fall in with the very French frigate I wanted." Leaving out the details of battle, violence, death, and pillage, the Captain's language recalls a pleasure jaunt (at other points he refers to setting out for war at sea as a lovely cruise). Wentworth's "luck" turns a potential tragedy into a great success. Despite the Asp's condition, Wentworth "knew" she would do "all he wanted." He recognizes that he is inured to loss. What matters is knowing how to turn what might appear to be a loss, or a disadvantage, into a profit. In this way, Wentworth seems to conceive of himself as uncastrated, immune to loss. Yet, his skill is not enough. Wentworth's ventures in the Asp are successful because he avoids bad weather. He has luck on his side. It is not enough to be fit for a task: one must have providence on one's side. Wentworth is fit for his calling and for reacting to adverse circumstances successfully but even he requires higher aid. His luck with the Asp suggests the approbation of Providence or, what psychoanalytic theory would call, the big Other. Incapable of imagining real lack in himself, Wentworth also sees the big Other as consistent and whole.

Part of Wentworth's resentment towards Anne is that she did not understand his ability or trust in his good luck. Wentworth attempts to convince Anne, in the early part of their courtship, that she need not fear for the future because he "had always been lucky; he knew he should be so still" (66). Wentworth stands for "confidence" (66) and has "sanguine expectations" (67). In fact, "[h]is genius and ardour had seemed to foresee and to command his prosperous path" (67) so that "all that he had told her would follow, had taken place" (67) and he has now made a "handsome fortune" (69). What Anne has lacked, then, is a "cheerful confidence in futurity." She has shown instead "an over-anxious caution which seems to insult exertion and distrust Providence!" (69). The narrator tells us that Anne had "been forced into prudence in her youth" but that with age "she learned romance" (69). This order of things is the "natural sequel of an unnatural beginning" (69). As Richard points out, romance is aligned with exertion and providence and Anne has discovered this later in life. Because she failed to understand he was singled out for success, that the big Other had chosen him, he now finds her unworthy of his attention. Like the Dick Musgroves of the world, Anne has shown herself unable to rise to the challenge of a brave new risk-taking world. Unable to forgive, he sees her only as "wretchedly altered" (95). As critics have noted, Anne, for much of the novel, functions as a kind of non-entity, as a "nothing" whom the other characters use as a sounding board, whose voice is usually silent or unheard, and who is almost invisible to others. After all, like the unprofitable Dick, Anne has "disappointed" the Captain and has shown "a feebleness of character in doing so, which his own decided, confident temper could not endure" (95). As a character who has been bowed down by loss, Anne functions in her world for the first part of the novel as a ghostly figure, present and yet hardly visible. Her loss is all the more palpable in comparison with Wentworth who seems incapable of sustaining loss, who phallically rises to every occasion despite the odds.

This is the reason in the comical "nut" scene the reader instantly understands that the nut Wentworth holds in his hands is meant to exemplify the opposite of Anne. He tells Louisa that "*yours* is the character of decision and firmness" (117). He then goes on "to exemplify" by comparing Louisa to "a beautiful glossy nut" (117) which is "blessed with original strength" and has neither "a puncture" nor a "weak spot" (117). It is a nut "possessed of all the happiness that a hazel-nut can be supposed to be capable of" because, unlike the wretched Anne, it has held "firm" (117). The weak nuts end up trodden underfoot. The weak, the undecided, and timid, those who do not exert themselves and remain firm in the face of danger deserve, Wentworth implies, and much of the narrator's commentary agrees, to die or be forgotten. They do not matter in this brave new world of firm, decided characters who must make their own fortune in the face of serious disadvantages. The firm characters take a risky situation, rife with the potential for loss, and, by relying on providence and their own skill, emerge unscathed. Thus, Anne can be deservedly forgotten, used, insulted, and ignored. She, like Dick, is a casualty of a system in which those who cannot be strong must be discarded. From this perspective the possibility of loss and death, which might seem so reasonable, appears a cowardly failure to believe in the fantasy of phallic fulfillment.

Mrs. Smith is another, if somewhat different, example of this logic. Unlike Wentworth who risks loss but ultimately succeeds, Mrs. Smith sustains only loss until Wentworth intervenes for her at the end of the novel. However, despite her losses, she is still one of the modern characters in that her constitution makes her unable to actually register loss. A poor invalid, suffering financial and physical losses with little assistance, she, nonetheless, maintains an unexpected cheerfulness of temper under adversity. Unlike Anne who is bowed down by loss, Mrs. Smith seems impossibly untouched by pain. Furthermore, like Wentworth, she ventures forth to risk in an effort to gain. She risks by unscrupulously using her friendship with Anne to earn interest with Mr. Elliot who is legally responsible for her property. As William Galperin writes, "she is in the end a manipulative and mendacious person whose main goal is to regain her West Indian property, and the slaves that presumably go with it, even if it means encouraging Anne to marry someone—specifically Mr. Elliot—whom Mrs. Smith knows to be thoroughly ruthless."[3] Yet, this failure of friendship and loyalty goes largely without mention from the narrator or Anne. Mrs. Smith is, after all, doing what one does in a risk society: risking one's own and other's well-being in order to attain an ultimate prize. In fact she and her friend, Nurse Rook, are represented, in their small way, as enterprising women. Going to war to earn prize money and selling small goods or trading in profitable gossip are similar in the way each of these ventures entails some risk on the way to potential success. Each also depends on trusting one's fortune and one's skill. Thus, when faced with potential or actual loss, the lucky gambler takes advantage of unfavorable circumstances (Nurse Rook and Mrs. Smith profit from gossip heard in the sick room) to attain success. Galperin points out that Mrs. Smith's "principle object" has the "additional effect of deconstructing any difference that might exist between the old order and the newer democratic order under whose auspices both slavery and the continued subjugation of women are also countenanced" (233).

The narrator's callousness, Wentworth's blasé account of war, and Mrs. Smith's cheerfulness suggest how the new order cannot account for real loss. Todd McGowan points out that the "role of fantasy is to convert the subject's traumatic experience of lack into a more acceptable experience of loss in order to produce the illusion that there is somewhere a satisfying object of desire, that there is a world of things that language obscures and hints at."[4] If, for Lacan, every subject experiences a constitutive loss by entering language and giving up an imagined sense of self-presence and immediacy, and if every subsequent form of loss recalls the originary loss, fantasy is a narrative that reassures the subject that loss can be made up for, that lack is not fundamental as Lacan claims. Instead, the symbolic order holds forth the promise of phallic objects that will satisfy the subject, objects such as wealth and power. Several of the characters in Austen's novel are so caught in fantasy that loss of any kind becomes difficult to register in any significant way.

The Fantasy of Merit: All Are Welcome

The novel makes clear how seductively the fantasy of merit and risk operate. The culture of risk associated with nascent capitalism is appealing because it can potentially call on anyone to feel included and capable of overcoming lack. In the climactic scene at Lyme, in fact, the novel reverses the order of things by having Anne replace Louisa as the heroine with merit and pluck. At Lyme, Louisa famously jumps off the Cobb and cracks that hard, firm nut of hers showing that she mistook the nature of the call and did not have true merit. Lacking true merit, she proves herself only to be hard headed.

In this climactic scene, concerned that the height is too great, Wentworth attempts to persuade Louisa not to jump from the Cobb. But infatuated with the encouragement he has given her never to yield and to remain firm, "she must be jumped down by" Captain Wentworth because "the sensation was too delightful to her" (137). Yet, in doing so, she evinces a mindless determination that cannot take the circumstances into account. Peter Knox-Shaw claims that Louisa's "Tinkerbell-like dependence on" Wentworth reveals her inability to judge for herself.[5] Proving she is unfit to handle the world of risk, Louisa soon becomes an object of ridicule, rather than pity. The narrator's characteristic callousness recurs when Louisa becomes the object of spectacle for the prurient interest of the working men collected "to enjoy the sight of a dead young lady" and when, her sister Henrietta faints, to enjoy the sight of "two young ladies, for it proved twice as fine as the first report" (139). Here we see another instance of the narrative voice turning the experience of loss into a source of broad humor, recalling an affect similar to that inspired by Mrs. Musgrove's "fat" sighs. The digs at Louisa continue but this time from Anne herself who rather spitefully wonders "whether it ever occurred" to Wentworth

> now, to question the justness of his own previous opinion as to the universal felicity and advantage of firmness of character; and whether it might not strike him, that like all other qualities of the mind, it should have its proportions and limits. She thought it could scarcely escape him to feel that a persuadable temper might sometimes be as much in favor of happiness, as a very resolute character (143).

Turning the tables, Anne now wonders if being more risk averse or at least more capable of judging the probable dangers of a situation might not make one as likely to experience happiness as the most resolute character. Like all qualities of mind, even firmness should have its "proportions and limits." Anne here speaks for an awareness of particular circumstances that might require an ability to carefully calibrate the risks. If Louisa is found wanting, though, Anne proves herself able to handle adverse circumstances when she takes control of the emergency on the Cobb. She directs everyone and is recognized by others as capable. It is in this part of the novel that Anne's place in her social world changes. No longer the forgotten drab, even her looks change and she is noticed by rival men.

Attractive, capable of managing risk, Anne is allowed in at this point as one of the favored ones.[6] Like Wentworth, she now begins to feel that she too has powers and abilities, that she can manage adverse circumstances. Her inclusion shows the novel's awareness of the capitalist fantasy's power to interpellate us all, rich and poor, male and female, socially privileged or socially marginalized. The call can come for anyone. Peter Knox-Shaw points to Austen's Enlightenment feminism. Writing during the Napoleonic War, Austen was well aware of the "premium placed upon male heroism" (222). The novel provides "a corrective to the values" of wartime Britain by celebrating the "strength of women" (222). By emphasizing the skill and power of women, the novel brings them in for their share of recognition. However, I would add that while the democratic nature of such a call to include women in the narrative of heroism and merit might seem appealing, it also means that now everyone is caught in an ideological illusion that ties us firmly to the big Other. Perhaps the fantasy of merit even ties us to the big Other better than older, traditional fantasies of power and success.[7] Anne finds that her father and sister's more traditional fantasies of social advancement fail to compel her and seem entirely bankrupt of value because they do not take merit into consideration. Several of the characters find themselves alienated by the fantasies that compel Sir Walter; but they find compensation in the new idea of merit.[8] This is why it is entirely fitting that Admiral Croft should replace Sir Walter at Kellynch hall as a sign of the success of the new emphasis on merit. In its depiction of the navy, the novel suggests that the modern fantasy of merit can include everyone, regardless of status.[9] The new fantasy seems seductively democratic, offering a kind of siren call to those who wish to imagine they could fit in if only providence would smile on them. The novel engages this teleological fantasy in particularly powerful ways, which remain appealing to this day; however, Austen does not leave our fantasies untouched. Instead, she develops her narratives in such a way as to expose, to a degree, at least, the limits and problems with the romance of risk.

The first casualty of the romance of risk is Wentworth himself. If the fall physically affects Louisa, it undoes Wentworth's sense of himself. Wentworth falls apart "as if all his own strength were gone" (138). Unable to act, he cries out, "Is there no one to help me?" (138). While Anne steps in to direct everyone, Wentworth can only stagger "against the wall for his support" (138). Wentworth, in his naval ventures has not really faced loss. While loss is a possibility, it remains potential in his career. Suddenly at the Cobb he faces an unexpected loss and becomes unable to function. Lorri G. Nandrea points out that Wentworth ends up sharing Anne's position when he recognizes his own culpability in Louisa's accident. Wentworth "is forced into the pattern Austen has associated with Anne, specifically with Anne's powerlessness as a woman, and this experience seems to heighten Wentworth's sensitivity."[10] He becomes "open, expressive, porous, penetrable" (54); in other words, he is feminized "in relation to the masculine figure of the firm nut" (54). Developing this line of argument further by specifying Wentworth's position in terms of Lacan's notion of fantasy, I would argue that Wentworth comes to a point at which he fails to see himself in the big Other as he has always imagined himself to be: decided, strong, capable and favored by fortune. He finds now that there may be no one to catch him when he falls. Fantasy, for Lacan, is not a daydream, but a way to organize our reality, to cover over lack, and persuade ourselves that the object we desire exists and is attainable if we follow the proper course. The belief in Providence in the novel speaks precisely to this notion of fantasy, offering the characters a way to deny lack and to attach themselves to a symbolic order which promises phallic achievement. But if, up to this point in the novel, Wentworth has expected Providence to mark him out and protect him, here, he discovers, luck is shockingly absent. He who imagines himself so capable, lucky, and likely to always be so, finds that his own arms fail. More metaphorically, providence fails to catch him, to allow him one more instance of success. If Anne and the narrator's callous reactions here might suggest a continued inability to affectively register loss, in the novel, Wentworth leaves no doubt that he has been staggered by loss out of his usual confidence both in his abilities and in his luck.

His symbolic identity is imperiled by Louisa's fall because the accident shows him in a petty, vindictive light, and as a man who does not know his own desires or real motives. It puts him in contact with a sense of loss, the loss of the story of the fortunate son he has been telling himself; he is now in a position to doubt who he is for the Other. While throughout the novel Anne has mostly lacked any significant place in the socio-symbolic network, Wentworth has never doubted his before. Anne is marked by her out-of-placeness: she does not quite belong to anyone or anyplace. Her father and sister do not acknowledge her place and the Musgroves use her without valuing her. As Elizabeth says, Anne is no one. She begins to find a potential place for herself in the narrative of merit and risk to which the navy men ascribe. Proving herself capable, level headed, and a leader of others in times of crisis, she gains some assurance of what she might be for the Other just as Wentworth begins to lose his. The novel enacts the seductive fantasy that the Other wants, protects, and patronizes the worthy and talented who, willing to take risks, will ultimately profit. What is particularly seductive about this fantasy is that *anyone* may be favored by the Other, poor men, and even women. As I argue above, the novel offers a very compelling vision of the modern capitalist and democratic fantasy of merit in which we are all called on to "feel the call," to imagine ourselves favored of providence or the big Other. But Austen does not leave well enough alone.

Loss without Return

While Anne is, herself, enthralled by the new ethic of middle-class merit, work, and profit, she, nonetheless, ends up speaking in a crucial scene to a different ethic that aligns her neither with Sir Walter nor the navy and that allows her to sympathize with Wentworth's loss. The other characters in the novel are constantly associated with an ethic of return, of return on investment. But in the famous scene at the White Hart Inn, Anne speaks to a very different ethic.

Anne and Captain Harville converse about constancy in love while Wentworth writes a letter, overhearing their conversation. Harville draws Anne's notice to "a parcel in his hand" that contains "a small miniature painting" (241) of Captain Benwick. Harville informs Anne that he is having the miniature set for Louisa Musgrove although "it was not done for her." It was intended for Fanny Harville but now Harville has the "charge of getting it properly set for another!" (241). Harville mourns, "Poor Fanny! she would not have forgotten him so soon!" Anne replies that "it would not be the nature of any woman who truly loved" to forget her dead lover (241). But Harville insists that men are more devoted than women, that as their bodies are stronger so are their attachments. Anne offers a series of arguments against this claim: first, men are distracted from any loss by "a profession, pursuits;" men have "business of some sort or other, to take you back into the world immediately, and continual occupation and change soon weaken impressions" (242). Second, she suggests that if the difference lies not in their modes of life, then it must lie in the different natures of men and women. Women, she claims, are "the most tender." Because men must exert themselves in their professions, it would be impossible for them to have tender feelings: "You have difficulties, and privations, and dangers enough to struggle with" (242).

In response to Harville's claims that literature has always represented women as fickle, Anne replies that "if you please, no reference to examples in books. Men have had every advantage of us in telling their own story. Education has been theirs in so much higher a degree; the pen has been in their hands. I will not allow books to prove anything" (243). The pen has just fallen from Wentworth's hand as she speaks. Taking the pen away from Wentworth, Anne appears poised to seize the phallus Wentworth has ceded. However, she does no such thing. Instead, she claims that

> [W]e never can expect to prove any thing upon such a point. It is a difference of opinion which does not admit of proof. We each begin, probably, with a little bias towards our own sex; and upon that bias build

every circumstance in favour of it which has occurred within our own circle (243).

The conversation between Anne and Harville begins as an argument about who will have the power to determine meaning, who, in other words, will successfully seize the phallus. But in the above statements Anne renounces the position of having the phallus. Lacan writes that what "the phallus denotes is the power of signification" (*Seminar XIX*, January 19, 1972 quoted in Fink).[11] Whereas Harville and Anne begin by trying to assert the truth of their own position, Anne abandons this effort by claiming "we never can prove anything." Instead, she gives up that aspect of the phallus associated with seizing power through meaning and claims that she and Harville can speak only for a contingent point of view that cannot be backed by proof. If she does not claim the power of setting down the meaning of things but insists instead on a subjective point of view, she does claim something (which no one need covet); rather than seizing meaning and power, she exposes an attachment to lack: "I believe you equal to every important exertion, and to every domestic forbearance, so long as—if I may be allowed the expression—so long as you have an object. I mean while the woman you love lives, and lives for you" (244). As long as men have a return on their love, a woman who "lives" for them, then they are capable of perpetual attachment. But, all "the privilege I claim for my own sex (it is not a very enviable one; you need not covet it), is that of loving longest, when existence or when hope is gone" (244). Anne refuses to take up the phallus as a signifier of power and embraces, instead, a perpetually lost object. She holds on to this object even though she can now imagine herself participating in phallic jouissance, striving for recognition by the Other. She has been invited to participate in the social world as someone who can seize the phallus, who can enter into a teleological fantasy that allows one to strive for an object. As Bruce Fink points out, the "symbolic phallus is what is socially valued,"[12] offering the possibility of a "jouissance that might possibly be attained through the pursuit of what the Other values" (137). Having the phallus is what most of the characters in the novel seek: whether they seek it in their pursuit of wealth, marriage or social authority.

The curious thing about this passage, though, is that Anne knows very well that Wentworth is not lost to her; in fact, she knows he loves her but holds back because he fears Anne will marry Mr. Eliot who will inherit Kellynch Hall. Wentworth is neither lost to her nor dead. He is more available than ever having come to value Anne as he has never done before. I want to propose a reading of this scene that takes into account Anne's position of enunciation. While she speaks like the Anne of the beginning of the novel, who mourns her lost love, she is no longer the "nothing" with no place and no hope. She can now see herself in the fantasy of merit that animates the Navy officers and their families. She is so interpellated by this fantasy that she can even believe in the likelihood that Wentworth loves her and would ask for her if he could believe in *himself.* Her real concern is not that she doubts his love but that he does not believe in his own luck and the likelihood of his success. The trauma of the fall at the Cobb has shaken him out of his fantasy of being favored by Providence. While Anne's words most directly describe the loss of the love object through death, they might also be read as pointing to another kind of loss.

There is another loss experienced in the novel beside the loss of wealth, of love or life, and that is the loss of Wentworth's fantasy about what he is for the Other. Wentworth has lost his certainty about his place in relation to Providence. What he overhears convinces him to declare his love and this decision has usually been read as the simple result of Anne persuasively assuring him that she remains faithful to her original lover. Perhaps, though, we can also see fidelity here to loss itself. One way to read the loss of "existence and hope" that Anne describes might be to consider the loss of Wentworth's fantasy. The lost object might be understood as the Captain Wentworth of the first part of the novel, the favored son who expects everything to turn out his way.

Wentworth and Anne's first engagement ends when Anne fails to believe in Wentworth's fantasy of success. In the first part of the novel, Wentworth speaks of himself as a man who thinks he is uncastrated, who can go to war without any real fear of death or loss, who can refer to patrolling the seas at war as a pleasure cruise. He seems to believe he has a special dispensation that inures him to loss and guarantees success. The trouble is Anne does not appear to share his fantasy. She imagines him as subject to loss, castrated like any other man.

However, in the Cobb scene, Wentworth himself is forced to assume his castration. What he experiences in that moment is a traumatic encounter with the big Other. Providence does not respond, does not step in to save the favored son, leaving him helpless and destitute of his place for the Other. At the Cobb, in other words, he experiences for the first time, what it means to be the victim of circumstances without any support from fantasy.

Earlier, Wentworth has reacted to Anne's inability to buy into his fantasy by assuming her unworthiness and her lack of love. Seeing him as a castrated being, she cannot value him for what he values in himself. However, in the climactic scene in which he overhears her, she declares her allegiance to loss, to castration. If he were dead, he would be erased from the fantasy of Providential support; his luck would have run out or never have existed, and he would be nothing more than the gallant Captain Wentworth in a newspaper article, which he describes at the Musgrove dinner party. In saying she would be loyal to him even if he were dead, Anne can be understood to love Wentworth even without his exalted place in the Other; she claims to love him even if he were nothing for the Other, a mere mention in a newspaper. She can love him without the fantasy of profit and success.

This speech, in sum, reveals her allegiance to the new, fallen Wentworth, the one he refused to imagine he could be at the end of their first courtship. Anne declares in this climactic scene that her love does not depend on the Providential fantasy, that it is not about having, but about circling around an absence, a lack. Perhaps the lack is both about not having Wentworth and about his not having "it" either. That he doesn't have "it," he has come to recognize after the incident on the Cobb. Anne maintains an attachment to the lost object suggesting that, where Wentworth is concerned, she does not ally herself to the fantasy of having, of success and profit. Although she gave him up, Anne indicates here that her love was not connected to his success or to hers. In other words, she indicates to Wentworth that he is not the object of her fantasy, a reward for meritorious conduct, the object that indicates her success in the eyes of the big Other. He is beloved even though the favored son of Providence is lost to both her and himself. If Anne knows she has not lost Wentworth's love at this point and if he is very much alive and available to her, the one loss they have between them now is that of his own self-image, of his fantasy. He need not be jealous of Mr. Eliot, she communicates, because having is not what interests her. As Todd McGowan points out, while male enjoyment is "always futural, and it depends on the act of obtaining or having its object, female subjectivity "provides enjoyment through what it doesn't have" (158). This is a difficult position to sustain because it "places subjects in a position where their lack is completely exposed" (158).

Nandrea argues that the novel connects an ability to detach oneself from teleological narratives and phallic rewards with women who are less driven by the goal oriented work of the career. Unlike professional men, women wait on the sidelines. This condition of hopelessness and powerlessness can heighten "sensitivity" (54) and increase openness to "change and differentiation" (54). Nandrea proposes that it "is as if derailment of one's narrative trajectory redirects desire, permitting a greater sensitivity to the nuances of the present" (54). If a more masculine focused narrative has a goal, an end in sight, a more feminine one, the novel suggests for Nandrea, offers "a different logic of desire" (55) that allows women to live "a difference between the sequence of events that shapes a story, and the presence of a desire that persists, in time, outside of any narrative sequence or trajectory" (56). Desire's aim having "been cancelled, without being replaced" (56), allows for a state in which one can be open to the possibility that "radical change is not only possible but perpetually proximate" (59). I want to take up

Nandrea's claims about the unique position for which Anne's experience allows, but to go beyond by focusing specifically on loss and desire in more specifically Lacanian terms.

What Anne's experience allows for is an, at least, partial separation from the injunctions of the big Other. That Anne has rejected a very suitable offer of marriage from Charles Musgrove is the first hint perhaps that Anne does not simply follow the trajectory laid out for her as the daughter of a penniless baronet who must marry well. In fact, she twice refuses this option, the second time with her cousin Mr. Elliot, marriage to whom would ensure not only wealth but possession of Kellynch hall, the ancestral home. Like the navy men, then, she too could ascribe to a teleological narrative of success. The marriage market itself might be seen, like a career in the navy, a space of risk, rife with potential loss and profit. If, for Richard, gambling is the metaphor for Wentworth's career, it could be used as well for ventures in the arena of marriage. Competition and the struggle for the prize can inform both men and women's lives ("Everyone knows there are phallic women").[13] Lacan's theory of sexuation helps us see how the masculine position need not only be associated with biological males. Women, too, can attempt to seize the phallus. Lacan's more nuanced view of sexual position helps to explain why none of the women in the novel function like Anne who interrupts the teleological fantasy and circulates instead around the lost object.

Austen places her heroine in a condition in which she occupies two positions at once: she has taken on the teleological function of fantasy (i.e., the masculine position), but has also remained connected to loss. From this position it is conceivable to imagine that she can attain a certain distance from the masculine position of having. The novel also makes clear that if women can take on the masculine position, men can take on the feminine one. Wentworth approximates this condition, when still caught in the fantasy of profit, he suddenly experiences an unexpected loss, the failure of the story he has been telling himself about himself.

Tellingly, Wentworth declares himself to Anne not when she is flush with success and admired by others but when she aligns herself with loss. When Wentworth hears Anne's declaration of her commitment to loss without hope, he takes action to gain the woman who, at least in part, maintains a distance from the narrative trajectory of ambition held out by the Other. The decisive erotic moment in *Persuasion* involves a moment when two losses overlap: Anne's declaration of her commitment to loss and Wentworth literally and symbolically dropping the pen, an action prepared for by the loss of his secure place with respect to the Other. Here Wentworth gives up the prerogative of men to write about women as faithless as they have historically done and as he himself has done in regards to Anne. Instead, in this moment he simply forgoes the capacity to write at all, allowing Anne to have the word. When he does pick up the pen again he does so not to assume phallic power but to express his lack: he writes that "You pierce my soul," that he hopes she has "penetrated" his feelings, that her words "overpower[ ]" him (245). As Nandrea points out, this is the language of feminization; far from identifying with the image of the impenetrable nut, here, Wentworth emphasizes his vulnerability.

However, the ending of the novel has often been read as a celebration of the new culture of merit and as showing how Anne becomes fully embraced by it. After all, the last pages focus on Mrs. Smith recovering her West Indies property and on her imperviousness to a sense of loss. The narrator offers an ironic commentary emphasizing how she "might have been absolutely rich and perfectly healthy, and yet be happy" (258). The joke, however, is suggestive of the possibility that achieving one's goals, one's success, may not lead to happiness; it may lead to the recognition that one cannot make up for loss, that the Other cannot give us what we desire. That Mrs. Smith is impervious to such a recognition makes her an improbable and mindless representative of the ethic of profit and risk. Anne and Wentworth, even though they are connected to the profession that is if possible even "more distinguished in its domestic virtues that in in its national importance" (258) (suggesting the seemingly totalizing hegemony of the new ethic as it permeates both private and public, domestic and national spheres), maintain a connection to loss. It is because of this very profession that loss permeates their lives in the "dread of a future war" (258). If war has throughout the novel been understood as good fun, a pleasure cruise, a means to a profitable end, on the last page, it appears as something to be dreaded. One might recuperate such a dread as merely the potential loss or risk to be faced in pursuit of profit. However, considering the moments when both Anne and Wentworth embrace loss, this dread might suggest the possibility of registering the horrific loss associated with war, a loss that might sever one's alliance with fantasies of success and profit that promise to make loss disappear.

Notes

1. *The Romance of Gambling in the Eighteenth-Century British Novel* (Houndmills, Basingstoke, Hampshire: Palgrave 2011), 146.
2. Elizabeth Kosmetatou attempts to dismiss this scene as a family joke about the name Richard, revealing how the novel was still in the draft stage. She finds no other significance in the narrator's cruelty. "What's in a Name? Jane Austen's Persuasion and the Puzzle of Poor Richard," *Persuasions: The Jane Austen Journal*

23 (2001): 215–18. Other critics have attempted to connect this callousness to Regency attitudes. See, for example, Jill Heydt-Stevenson, "Unbecoming Conjunctions: Mourning the Loss of Landscape and Love in Persuasion," in *Eighteenth-Century Fiction* 8 (1995).

3. William Galperin, *The Historical Austen* (Philadelphia: University of Pennsylvania Press, 2003), 232.

4. McGowan, *Enjoying What We Don't Have: The Political Project of Psychoanalysis* (Lincoln: University of Nebraska Press, 2013), 199.

5. Peter Knox-Shaw, *Jane Austen and the Enlightenment* (Cambridge: Cambridge University Press, 2004), 236.

6. Laura Vorachek points to how Anne and Wentworth occupy similar positions that connect them to the ethos of merit:

> Because Anne loses all but her name at the start of the novel she is, in effect, in the same position as Wentworth who had only his name when she ended their engagement eight years previously. She has no land or fortune and is considered 'nobody' by her family (5), much as Wentworth was when he proposed to Anne the first time. However, she has the opportunity to prove herself worthy of Wentworth's affections, as he has proven himself worthy of hers.

"Crossing Boundaries: Land and Sea in Jane Austen's Persuasion," *Persuasions* 19 (1997): 37 (36–40).

7. Several critics have celebrated this ethos of merit and success, perhaps none more enthusiastically than Nina Auerbach. See "O Brave New World: Evolution and Revolution in Persuasion," *ELH* 39 (1972): 112–28.

8. Claudia Johnson writes, "[I]f in Persuasion the landed classes have not lost their power, they have lost their prestige and their moral authority for the heroine." *Jane Austen: Women, Politics and the Novel* (Chicago: University of Chicago Press, 1988), 145.

9. For Charles Rzepka, the novel attempts to imagine how women might participate in this ethos of merit by being useful to the nation. "Austen points up the natural affinities between Anne's desire to 'be of use' through the exercise of her nurturing and healing skills, her personal 'domestic virtues,' and the 'national importance' (254), or 'utility,' of the profession she is destined to join." "Making It in a Brave New World: Marriage, Profession, and Anti-Romantic Ekstasis in Austen's Persuasion," *Studies in the Novel*, 26, no. 2 (1994): 109 (99–120).

10. "Difference and Repetition in Austen's Persuasion," *Studies in the Novel*, 39.1 (Spring 2007): 54 (48–64).

11. Bruce Fink points out further that the "phallus denotes the power of the signifier to bring the signified into being, that is, the signifier's creative power." *Lacan to the Letter: Reading Écrits Closely* (Minneapolis: University of Minnesota Press, 2004), 139.

12. Fink 137.

13. Lacan, *The Seminar of Jacques Lacan, Book XX: Encore*, trans. Bruce Fink (New York: Norton 1999), 71.

Chapter Five

LOGICAL TIME AND THE ROMANTIC SUBLIME

ZAK WATSON

MARK AKENSIDE writes in his *The Pleasures of Imagination: A Poem* (1744): "From heav'n my strains begin; from heaven descends / The flame of genius to the human breast, And love and beauty, and poetic joy / And inspiration."[1] This speaker is sure of his source of inspiration; his words are evidence of his ontological vocation, proof that genius has descended to his breast. He has turned the gap between himself and the "heav'n" into a profitable resource. The proto-Romantic poets of the 1740s are bursting with similarly inspired passages. The rhetorical move of invoking heavenly inspiration is so common as to meet most readers without impact or meaning. In William Collins's "Ode on the Poetical Character" (1747), the speaker returns to no less than three different literary fathers, trying to find a place for himself in the pantheon of makers. Through strong misreadings of their texts, the speaker returns to Spenser, God, and Milton to seek inspiration. Three times, Collins's speaker tries to close the loop of inspiration, and three times the loop remains open. Collins distinguishes himself from other triumphantly sublime poets of the day by his failure to achieve decisive divine inspiration. Where Akenside and so many others turn the sublime gap between creator and creature to profit, Collins seems to come up short. I want to return to that failure because it interrupts the sublime narrative, particularly its powerful sense of closure, which becomes an important strand in the romantic sublime. Before the romantic sublime, and even after it is named as such, there is a gap of loss that can't be turned wholly to profit. A psychoanalytic reading of the sublime reveals persistent loss.

In *An Essay on the Sublime* (1747), John Baillie explains the relation between vast ideas and the human mind: "Vast objects occasion vast sensations, and vast sensations give the mind a higher idea of her own powers."[2] The elevation of the mind or expansion of the soul is the feeling of the sublime. That mirroring between vast sensations and the mind's estimation of its own powers informs Collins's poetic sublimity. His "Ode to Fear," also included in his 1747 collection, dramatizes encounters between the speaker and Fear, who flees before terrifying monsters. "Ah Fear! Ah Frantic Fear! / I see, I see thee near. / I know thy hurried step, thy haggard eye! / Like thee I start, like thee disordered fly."[3] The speaker assumes the physical responses of Fear herself as vast sensations are reflected in his mind. The epode and antistrophe narrate the history of Fear, proposing to connect the speaker to the vast objects of literary history from Sophocles to Shakespeare. By the close of the poem, the speaker is still imploring Fear: "Hither again they fury deal, / Teach me but once like him [Shakespeare] to feel: / His cypress wreath my meed decree, and I, O Fear, will dwell with thee!"[4] The speaker's continued request suggests that the reflection of poetic greatness in the speaker is incomplete. While Collins works in the realm of the sublime, his poems do not enact achievements of the sublime. The narrative that should lead from vast objects to the mind's own power is interrupted.

Psychoanalysis lives in the disruption of narratives. Their smooth connection from beginning to end, from heaven to the human breast, and their resolution of crises are overdetermined. The subject of psychoanalysis disappears from narratives and appears in parapraxes whose meanings are assigned only partially and retroactively. Lacan's take on psychoanalysis began with a return: something had been missed in Freud. Suffused throughout his work was a meeting with the real that the discourse of psychoanalysis was, predictably, missing. In that spirit, I want to return to the romantic sublime. Like psychoanalysis, the sublime began by setting our teeth on edge, tearing everything up like a whirlwind and exhibiting the power of an orator at a single blow, but it was domesticated by the discourse on the sublime. I return to the narrative of the sublime to refind the encounter with the real that its writers and analysts have hidden under successive layers of criticism, speculation, and reasoning. Uncovering the impossibility of taming the loss of the sublime with the tools of the symbolic points to the ideologically motivated nature of all adjectival sublimes. The phrase structure "the [adjective] sublime" is itself another symbolic attempt to squeeze profit from the real.

As Freud's work did for Lacan, the sublime still holds onto truth that needs to be mobilized by analysis. The sublime is an experience and a discourse of limits: the experience of travelers and poets is recorded in travel writing, poetry, and philosophical treatises, which form the discourse on it. Both the experiences and the discursive attempts to explain it are caught in structures, which lock subjects and readers in circuits of repetition circling around the unrepresentable, the hole in the symbolic and the real that ex-sists to it. Lacan's logic of sexuation provides alternative ways to think about limits. Slavoj Žižek examines the deadlock of sublime representation from Kant to Hegel, distinguishing between Kant's solution, external reflection that places the Thing-in-itself beyond phenomenal representation, and Hegel's solution, the determinate reflection that says beyond representation is the "Nothing of absolute negativity."[5] Both of those alternatives present a finished picture of the sublime inscribed on the masculine side of sexuation. Kant's external reflection relies on the existing exception to castration (the first line of the masculine side of the sexuation graph) while Hegel's determinate reflection reads the all of castration in phenomenal representation (the second line of the masculine side).

Instead of turning the sublime into a conclusion defined by a masculine logic of limits, we need to understand the sublime and the discourse on it through the pull of the automaton and the (missed) encounter with the real, the tuché, because this approach lets us ask not where the limit of representation is, but when it is. Tracing the logical time of the sublime reveals the inexpressible difference, the difference that Jean-François Lyotard says "is to be found at the heart of sublime feeling" by refusing the synthesis typically achieved in the discourse on the sublime by giving the last word to the understanding.[6] Returning time to the sublime also moves us beyond what Joan Copjec calls the masculine "superegoic logic of exception or limit" and into the feminine logical space of the not-all in which "the status of the world is not infinite but indeterminate."[7] Insisting on the necessity of experiencing the sublime moment by moment makes possible an "ethics of inclusion or of the unlimited" that keeps open the circuit of signification, refusing even the seemingly benign "position of respect in response to an incalculable otherness" offered by Barbara Claire Freeman as a component of the feminine sublime.[8] Furthermore, thinking of the sublime as a form of repetition that is always novel, an intersection of the necessary and the impossible, provides a way to understand the romantic dialectic between Promethean defiance of the father and abject confrontation of belated human limitation. In short, I propose that we read key moments in the discourse on the sublime as narrative attempts to solve the impossible dialectic between the subject and signifier. The sublime impasse is the moment in which the subject confronts the possibility of his own annihilation not at the hands of a powerful Other, but by its indifference or non-existence. If the subject is a gap, it appears in the symbolic only through the defiles of the signifier, which offers only partial representation. The difference between the subject and the signifier is the force that propels the action of signification forward and supports the necessary/impossible illusion that a consistent Other exists. The sublime begins with the recognition that there is a gap between the subject and signifier, and it typically ends with a suturing of that gap. That suturing is the work of the discourse on the sublime. At the end of my argument, I return to Collins's "Ode on the Poetical Character" as a refusal of the sublime conclusion and consider the fate of adjectival sublimes.

This narrative solution is apparent in Kant's description of the dynamic sublime, which I offer here as a paradigmatic example. This selection does not reduce the sublime to Kant's third critique. The narrative in which terror follows with relief and edification is present in work on the sublime by Longinus, Addison, Burke, and most recently Skorin-Kapov.[9] I choose to use Kant only because his model is particularly detailed and familiar. The subject is confronted with the absolute power of nature over him. That is the first moment of recognition of the mismatch between the subject and the Other. The effect of this recognition is terror. After reflection, the Kantian narrative says the subject realizes that even if his body were absolutely destroyed, his connection to the supersensible would be unharmed. The conclusion to the narrative is the end of terror and the restoration of the calm that comes from being re-harmonized with this Other that transcends nature as a might. The dynamic sublime initially looks like a description and explanation of a dangerous experience (a vacillation between the pain and pleasure of danger and release), but it finally is an already-decided drama of the discovery of the supersensible substrate.

I claim no novelty in thinking of the sublime as an experience with successive stages. Such an approach is the centerpiece of Theodore Weiskel's *The Romantic Sublime*. Taking a Freudian approach and applying Kantian and structuralist terminology, Weiskel splits the sublime confrontation of subject and object into three phases as follows. The first phase is "the state of normal perception or comprehension, the syntagmatic linearity of reading or taking a walk or remembering or whatnot."[10] This is the state we should find ourselves in most of the time, signifiers and signifieds cooperating nicely to keep us on track. Its lack of novelty (Weiskel even mentions a certain boredom associated with this phase) suggests there is nothing sublime about the first phase; it is a mere prelude, though necessary in Weiskel's scheme. "In the second phase, the habitual relation of mind and object suddenly breaks down. Surprise or astonishment is the affective correlative, and there is an immediate intuition of a disconcerting disproportion between inner and outer."[11] We might think of Collins's "As once, if not with light regard, / I read aright that gifted bard."[12] Here is where the real interest in the sublime lies, in its potential to upset boundaries and realign consciousness. Something in experience or memory creates an imbalance, which must be addressed. Weiskel says the second phase is marked by a failure or an excess of signification: "[W]e are reading along and suddenly occurs a text which exceeds comprehension, which seems to contain a residue of signifier which finds no reflected signified in our minds."[13]

> In the third, or reactive, phase of the sublime moment, the mind recovers the balance of outer and inner by constituting a fresh relation between itself

and the object such that the very indeterminacy which erupted in phase two is taken as symbolizing the mind's relation to a transcendent order.[14]

For Kant, this transcendent order is human vocation, our participation in the supersensible. For Longinus, this is the moment that fills us with pride, and it makes us feel as if we are responsible for the greatness of the discourse we have just heard. For Addison, it is the moment of the delightful expansion of the imagination. The canonical writers on the sublime all agree that the sublime benefits people, in a more or less calculated way, depending on which writer is in question. Weiskel recognizes that the conclusion is ideological: "What happens to you standing at the edge of the infinite spaces can be made, theoretically, to 'mean' just about anything."[15] After this point, the sublime subsides, and the experience is over.

Weiskel's take "renders the sublime moment as an *economic* event," one which serves to dispel "mystical" explanations for the sublime.[16] The schema works well with his Freudian reading (in which the second and third moments are the fear of and subsequent love for the father as superego) and fits in smoothly with received accounts of the sublime. In fact, it fits too well. Of the "Ode to Fear," Weiskel writes that Collins was "stuck in Romance, the literary mode appropriate to phallic ambivalence.... Ahead was a symbolic, Longinian identification with Shakespeare, Spenser, and Milton which he could not quite perform."[17] The attempt to reflect in one's mind the greatness of vast objects is an Oedipal struggle whose conclusion is successful identification with the father. Collins's failure to get there in his poetry signals an unresolved Oedipal complex.

To write about the sublime poses an obvious problem: how is one to write coherently about a category that deranges the subject who experiences it? How to avoid the *mise en abyme* of sublime writing that, itself, becomes sublime? We can conceptualize this problem as one of exerting control, keeping the discourse from getting off course by imposing certain bounds, defining key terms (such as Burke's separation of the sublime and the beautiful) or creating a complex apparatus to explain the workings of the mind (such as Kant's account of the faculties). In each case, including Weiskel's, we see an author acting out the sublime drama of confronting excess, and in each case we see excess turned toward a purpose without concern for the residue of that excess, which cannot be accounted for by the newfound purpose.

For Weiskel, objects are signifiers, and the mind is the container of signifieds.[18] The sublime is a rupture in discourse, which can come from an excess either on the side of the signifier (in which case it leads to what he calls the metonymical or negative sublime) or on the side of the signified (the metaphorical or positive sublime). It is an elaborate scheme that finds either the poet or reader as the one experiencing the sublime, and asserts the differences in terms of metaphor and metonymy, similarity and contiguity. It provides the kind of model for which structuralism is so deservedly famous. Weiskel recognizes the potential of building too nice a system, and he questions the division between positive and negative sublimes: "[W]e ought to be wary of the tendency in structuralist thinking to turn a preliminary heuristic into a deduction."[19] However, to state that objects are signifiers is an oversimplification that obscures a fundamental part of the sublime.

Rather than locating the signified on the side of the subject, or Weiskel's "mind," and putting the signifier on the side of things in the world, Lacan holds that the subject is made only of signifiers. A phrase found repeated across Lacan's work is "the signifier represents the subject for another signifier." This phrase makes at least two important points that concern us here. First, it highlights the importance Lacan puts on the signifier over the signified. Questioning the Saussurean writing of the sign (the capital S of the signifier separated by a horizontal bar from the lower case *s* of the signified) that would seem to provide meaning through the conjunction of the two terms, Lacan reminds us that the signifier can hope to find meaning only in reference to another signifier. Signifiers are reduced to "ultimate differential elements," which means they exist only insofar as they are different from one another.[20] The relation of signifier to signified cannot be solidly established, but there are chains of signifiers which can be followed. For Lacan, this chain-like structure of signifiers is what matters in language, and it accounts for the anticipatory nature of meaning making in speech. " 'I'll never . . . ,' 'The fact remains . . . ,' 'Still perhaps . . .' Such sentences nevertheless make sense [despite the fact the meaning is interrupted], and that sense is all the more oppressive in that it is content to make us wait for it."[21] Lacan's examples highlight the anticipation of meaning which the structure of signifiers, each depending on the next for its meaning, gives to language. Instead of reading a poem as a signifying mediation between subject and world, in which the terms of the dialectic contain its conclusion, this structure asks us to read a poem as a signifying chain in which meaning occurs through metaphor and metonymy, the latter drawing us from line to line looking for satisfaction. The relation between signifier and signified is a process, not a given. The power that draws us along the chain arises from the lack that makes the symbolic. Collins's failure, in the "Ode to Fear," to identify with Shakespeare is a shortcoming not of the subject, but of the symbolic order. Fear is the one "to whom the world unknown / with all its shadowy shapes is shown," not the speaker.[22] What she sees is beyond representation, the primary repressed whose inaccessibility drives the sliding of signification.

Second, Lacan's dictum shows that the subject is caught up in this anticipatory (and retroactive) play of the signifier. Unlike Weiskel's subject/object scheme, the Lacanian subject is not a mind that perceives, providing meaning to the objects of the world it contacts. Rather, it is a lack-in-being affected by signification. The essential problem of the subject is that it can be represented only by signifiers (which Lacan writes as the S of the signifier over the barred $ of the subject, which can be read as a revision of the Saussurean schema mentioned in the previous paragraph), for this is the cost of the intervention of the Name of the Father, but these signifiers cannot completely represent the subject. Because of the failure of representation, the subject is left to the famous Freudian parapraxes (dreams, slips of the tongue, and so on) that express themselves in spite of the subject. Far from being a simple matter of connecting signifiers "out there" to signifieds "in here," this conception of the network of signification and the subject's problematic place in it (it functions as a gap) gives us a richer system within which to consider the sublime than Weiskel's. In the context of the "Ode to Fear," it lets us read the speaker not as a late-arriving poet exercising his capacity to reflect greatness, but as the empty space waiting for the Other to answer him back. The status of the subject as a null point requires the speaker to continue asking for inspiration.

For Weiskel, the sublime cannot happen without its resolution through identification with the superego, or what he calls the participation of "god terms."[23] He writes: "It is inconceivable that Wordsworth should have given us the Mount Snowdon vision without the subsequent editorializing in which he turns experience into emblem and takes possession."[24] Wordsworth liquidates experience and produces poetry. As an alternative, I seek a discourse that does not turn experience to profit through closure. Instead, this discourse needs to account for experience at precisely the moments it is shut out of accounts such as Weiskel's. Lacan's idea of logical time explains how such a discourse might work, and Collins's poetry, which frequently recounts the speaker choking on the missing signifier, shows it in action. The essential point that Lacan makes by introducing the concept is that classical logic presents its solutions in the eternal space of reason, and there are logical problems which the spatial mode cannot answer. To translate this logical point into poetic terms, logical time reminds us to read poems as events rather than statements. Their unfolding matters as much as their conclusions. At the root of this alternative approach to the sublime is the value of the concluding moment.

Lacan first discusses logical time in "Logical Time and the Assertion of Anticipated Certainty," first published in 1945 in *Les Cahiers d'Art*, then updated for his 1966 *Écrits*. Lacan's argument would hold that "logical time" is already a strange idea, if approached from the classical perspective. Consider the truth tables created by classical logic. If one wants to know if the sentence "A or B is true" when A is false, one need look no further than the proper table to find out.

The truth value of the statement has already been decided, and there is no temporal element to its decision. According to Lacan, his

> sophism... presents itself as an aporia for the forms of classical logic, whose 'eternal' prestige reflects an infirmity which is nonetheless recognized as their own—namely, that these forms never give us anything which cannot already *be seen all at once*.[25]

Lacan argues that classical logic excludes time as a deciding factor in determinations of truth, preferring a method in which a single instant of sight is the guarantor of truth. Lacan elevates the place of the unseen over the seen in the assertion of certainty, as he presents a case in which time is an ineluctable modality.

The second half of the title, "the Assertion of Anticipated Certainty," indicates that there will be something of a recursive structure in place here. I argue that it is just this recursive step, the forward and backward movement of the subject in determining a certainty that is anticipated (and which could not be reached without this anticipation), that Lacan refuses to spatialize. In other words, this approach provides a way out of the problems of closure, of reconceiving the whole affair of the sublime from the perspective of final certainty. Rather, central to his "sophistry" and to my rereading of the moments of the sublime, is the value of their unfolding. The conclusion cannot be understood outside of the logical moments understood to reach it, and the logical moments cannot happen without the anticipation of the conclusion.[26]

Lacan's article professes to contribute to "the logical notion of collectivity" and to provide a model for "*collective logic* with which one could complete classical logic."[27] Knowing that Lacan takes Hegel as a starting point for the foundation of the subject's identity in the mirror stage, this so-called collective logic takes on a different character than it would if Lacan were a thinker interested in "genuine intersubjectivity" or "I/Thou" relations. Logical time is actually much closer to the functioning of the subject than it may seem here. A final footnote, added in 1966, concludes "the collective is nothing but the subject of the individual."[28] The drama of the three-prisoner game is not to be read literally, as making a point about subjects working together (recall that the only relation between the subjects consists of false imputations of cogitation, a forerunner of Lacan's concept of *méconnaissance*, which characterizes the false mirror stage assumption of corporal wholeness engendered by the reflected image). Rather, it explains the logical function of time in identification (note that each prisoner tries to answer at least a version of the question "what am I?"), and the unconscious (the prisoners have to find their identities within a given limited symbolic matrix: the last four words could work as a definition of the unconscious from a Lacanian perspective).

Lacan makes this connection between logical time and the unconscious more explicit in his *Seminar XI: The Four Fundamental Concepts of Psychoanalysis*. Building on Freud, Lacan says the unconscious is pre-ontological: "[N]either being nor non-being, but the unrealized."[29] Lacan likens the unconscious to a slit which opens and closes in rhythmic fashion, which gives the unrealized a temporal dimension: it appears at one moment, and it disappears at another. In everyday experience, a slip of the tongue is an opening of this slit, most often quickly closed. The illicit meaning which comes through in speech is taken back up into the licit meaning of every day discourse.

> The appearance/disappearance takes place between two points ... between the instant of seeing, when something of the intuition itself is always elided, not to say lost, and that elusive moment when the apprehension of the unconscious is not, in fact, concluded, when it is always a question of "absorption" fraught with false trails.[30]

Thus Lacan connects logical time to the unconscious. The opening and closing of the unconscious is structured by three moments: a moment of seeing, a time for understanding, and a moment to conclude. In the passage above, the important point for my purpose is that "the unconscious is not, in fact, concluded." The third logical moment, based as it is on an error (in the 1945 article, recall that the anticipated certainty is based only on the false premise made by A: "[M]y disc is black"), does not conclude anything. The assertion that the unconscious is not closed by the conclusion reached about it applies as much to the denied or forgotten slip of the tongue in everyday speech as to speech given under the conditions of free association in analysis. Regardless of our intentions in coming to a conclusion about the unconscious, the Freudian category of the primary repressed (*Urverdrängt*) stands as a limit to interpretation. In structuralist terms, there is a point beyond which there may be signifying material, but it has no context which can provide it meaning. "Non-communativity," Lacan says, "is a category that belongs only to the register of the signifier."[31] The third moment conclusion, then, must always be good enough to ensure the subject's purposes (or to satisfy the jailer's demand for logical explanation), but can never be the final word. The weakness of the third moment is critical in my reappraisal of the sublime.

Consider "a signifier represents a subject for another signifier" in terms of logical time. The first moment is marked by the appearance of a signifier, a mark of difference. Something appears to the subject, and it is enigmatic because this signifier has not found a place in the signifying order. I choose the word "enigmatic" because the signifier may present several alternative, even contradictory meanings, or no meaning at all. The second logical moment is the time of suspension.

The subject considers ways in which this newly arisen signifier may fit into the Other, understood here as the limited symbolic matrix that preexists the subject. The third logical moment, the time of the closing of the unconscious, is the time when the subject reaches a decision about the meaning of the signifier by putting it in relation to at least one other signifier. The subject is neither more nor less than the lack found between the signifiers, the part of the world that cannot be covered by signification. This is the fundamental problem of the subject: it is at once barred from the field of signification (because signification always leaves something over) and required to represent itself there (because there is no other way to be represented). The cost for the subject is the loss of jouissance, but the reward is dialectically constructed meaning, and desire that can be satisfied, at least momentarily, in the symbolic. These third-moment conclusions are always in some part false because the circuit of repetition (which is nothing but the insistence of signifiers and the representation of the subject) will bring them around again.

These three moments map onto Weiskel's three moments uneasily. Between the "immediate intuition of a disconcerting disproportion between inner and outer" and the recovery of "the balance of outer and inner," Weiskel leaves out the moment of suspension.[32] In that syncope, Weiskel follows the sublime tradition that moves immediately from disproportion to restoration. That exclusion is symptomatic of a discourse that closes out the possibility of the failure of signification. Logical time lets us restore that moment and see that the possibility of symbolic failure is present between the second and third moments. Again, the key to this system of signification and time is that it always misses something; the difference introduced by the signifier cannot completely cover the real.

Neil Hertz recognizes the place of symbolic failure in the sublime. According to Hertz, the sublime exceeds the Oedipal organization precisely where it touches on the unspeakable. In his reading of Longinus's stricture on the collapse of the sublime into the merely disgusting, Hertz says, "What is literally 'unspeakable' is not the shame of sexuality or of Oedipal desire but the figurativeness of that shame; that is, the figurativeness of every instance of the figurative, including those figures that inform our sexual meanings."[33] The unspeakable emerges from the failure of language to represent. The sublime orator must conceal that failure, Longinus advises his student. Merging the sublime with logical time demonstrates that this concealment opens precisely on the failure of representation.

I turn now to William Collins's proto-romantic "Ode on the Poetical Character" as an early attempt to apply the structure of the sublime to the problem of claiming a poetic identity from powerful literary fathers. Collins fails to reach a conclusion that would allow him to claim the gap in the symbolic as a space for his own identity, and in that failure lies the interest of this poem. His subjective lack, rather than being blissfully represented as in a Wordsworthian egotistical sublime, overlaps with the lack in the Other, resulting in a poem whose syntactical and tropic uncertainty fails to claim the poetical character for its author. Whether Collins got a glimpse of paradise before the curtain was closed is a question which, perforce, cannot be answered by his poem. By placing the conclusion outside the scope of the poem, Collins reveals a sublime impasse without an end, a break in the signifying chain where a signifier does not represent the subject for another signifier. This poem exploits the suspension of the second sublime moment and the impossibility of adequate closure in the third moment.

The well-established reading of Collins's finest ode as an admission that the persona or poetic self has no chance at greatness is at odds with the speculative and open nature of the work. From Samuel Johnson's "Poor Collins" to Harold Bloom's perverse celebrant of loss, the author of the "Ode on the Poetical Character" has been judged a failure of one kind or another repeatedly.[34] Indeed, Bloom has initiated an entire school confident of Collins's status as a late-coming failure at the feet of Milton.[35] Martha Collins, expanding William Collins's failure to the poetic enterprise in general, writes that Collins's "self-conscious awareness of his poetic role and limitations" make the "Ode on the Poetical Character" "ultimately a poem about the difficulty, if not the impossibility, of writing poems."[36] She also cites Alan D. McKillop, who finds in Collins "an idea of inspiration which is conceived and intensely desired, but never fully realized."[37]

This ode, which winds its quest for recognition across the varied three-part structure expected of the form attributed by the English to Pindar, but which reflects a mannered wildness more English than Greek, has been called "arguably the most difficult English lyric poem written before the 1790s and one of the most difficult of any era."[38] It is a sign of the author's times that the poem is deeply concerned with establishing what poetry is; in the wake of Pope's death, Collins nearly issued his collection of odes together with those of Joseph Warton, who explicitly stated his intention to bring poetry back into its "right channel," away from "didactic poetry" and "moral essays."[39] Modern and contemporary critics risk taking Collins too much at Warton's words by missing the public, rhetorical functions of the former's poetry. I read this poem not as a private paean to Collins's poetic masters, but as a public bid to himself be numbered among them, even though his rhetoric is quite different from the putatively more public Augustan poets who preceded him.

The structure of the false third moment elevates William Collins's proto-romantic "Ode on the Poetical Character" from a mere hymn to indeterminism to an existential question about identity and influence that may not be answerable. Like Akenside, Collins seeks inspiration: he wants his strains to descend from heaven, too. His attempt to be inspired by the Other is a bid for recognition, as much a question of signification as of inspiration. Looking to answer the question of his poetic identity, he turns to his literary fathers, Spenser, God, and Milton. Collins's recreations of Spenser's "solemn tourney," the Creator's heaven and Milton's Eden provide the respective scenes of these paternal returns. In each case, Collins attempts to capture inspiration in language: first through extended simile, then through allegory, and finally through syntax. Each attempt to make meaning and identity coalesce under a chain of signification slips his grasp.

The subject of the strophe is the contest for Florimel's girdle that takes place in book 4 of *The Faerie Queene*. Spenser's contest, recast in an extended simile as one for poetic greatness, does not name a clear winner in Collins's revision. The uncertainty of "if not with light Regard, / I read aright that gifted Bard," raises the possibility that the speaker has missed Spenser by reading incorrectly or with the wrong kind of attention.[40] The question of who the poet is as subject overlaps with language's inability to accurately and unquestionably transmit its message, the message that would give the subject his identity. Like one of the prisoners in Lacan's logic game, the speaker is forced to wait for a sign that would reveal his identity. So Collins's sentence spins across sixteen lines, still settling in the uncertainty of the moment between the call to the Other and its response. That time of anticipation of meaning is the extension of the second logical moment. Even as the sentence reaches a grammatical conclusion, part of its meaning still escapes, unbound by signification. As the strophe concludes, the extended simile is completed: just as only one woman in *The Faerie Queene* "[m]ight hope the magic Girdle wear," only one subject might hope to gain Fancy's "God-like Gift" of poet-hood.[41]

Collins's reading of Spenser is, inevitably, a rewriting. In spite of the completion of the simile, there are important differences between Spenser's competition for Florimel's belt and Collins's competition for fancy's prize. Where Spenser's competition is a zero-sum game, fancy "[t]o few the godlike gift assigns."[42] Spenser's Other bestows (or withholds) her prize with certainty; Collins's muse offers no such certainty in her prize. Far more problematic is the element of certainty about the victor present in the contest of Spenser's ladies. In their competition, there is immediate and undeniable evidence of success or failure: if the wrong "Nymph" tried the band, "[i]t left unblest her loath'd dishonour'd Side."[43] The competition of poets for fancy's prize is not so certain. The identity of the poetical character cannot be indicated by a magic belt that would burst from the side of the unworthy poet. As a signifier of identity, fancy's prize is unable to cover the real of what ex-sists to the symbolic. It is also telling that Collins's reading of Spenser in the strophe stops short of showing the winner of the contest. In leaving the winner out, Collins opens the space of uncertainty which characterizes the second logical moment. Spenser's nymphs and Collins's speaker live in the space of the question of their identity in the eyes of the Other, but by stopping short of the contest's conclusion, Collins's revision leaves the poetical character hanging, waiting for another kind of closure than Spenser provides in his narrative, risking annihilation in twisted syntax. In the strophe, signification misses the subject.

The most celebrated and frustrating figure in the poem is its personification of the "rich-hair'd Youth of Morn," who appears at the poem's climax.[44] His birth is the poem's central event, and its meaning has long been disputed. This line's resistance to easy interpretation reveals the way in which the ode relates to the Other. Like the connection between the subject and the Other, the referent of the "rich-hair'd Youth of Morn" is not settled. Some hold that it refers to the sun, some to Apollo, some to the poet, and some to a combination of these.[45] That many critics have approached this personification as requiring a specific and singular referent is not surprising; according to Thomas Maresca, this is how personification works. In his essay "Personification vs. Allegory," he argues that personification is a univocal trope, in which a concrete element stands precisely for the abstract thing it embodies, with no room for slippage.[46]

Those critics who are satisfied with multiple referents for the "rich-hair'd Youth of Morn," the critics with whom I am compelled to agree, are clearly violating the rules of personification. The lack of a single referent for the personification indicates that Collins is not really engaging here in personification as we usually apply the term. Rather, he is creating an allegory, in the sense that Maresca opposes the term to personification. He compares allegory to a pun, arguing that "[j]ust as a pun cannot be paraphrased and still exist as a pun, so too allegory."[47] There is something irreducible in the multiplicity of the referent of allegory. This multiplicity does not destroy meaning, but delays it. As Marshall Brown notes in the "Ode to Evening," "[p]ersonification is here liberated from the constraints of visualization."[48] The purpose of Collins's personifications is not to create a single image to comprehend an idea. Janice Haney-Peritz writes that Collins's allegorical mode is "neither purely constative nor purely performative" and that "the odes constantly turn on themselves, thereby denying the reader any determinate understanding."[49] In this poem, allegory works to disrupt the univocal, determinate relationship between inspiring source and poet that usually obtains in pre-Romantic poetry. In this allegory, Collins confronts the possibility of inspiration, not its conclusion. In Haney-Peritz's words, "neither the 'I' nor the 'thou' remains an uncontested basis for the production of meaning."[50] The "rich-hair'd Youth of Morn" presents the irruption of the possibility of subjective contact with the Other rather than its uncontested certainty. In the poem's mesode, this disputed signifier reaches for meaning, but it still has not found it unequivocally.

In the antistrophe, the speaker scales the heights of Milton's Eden, returning us to his mythic past. However, Collins's revision lets him rewrite time and pose the possibility of having received the inspiring vision without concluding that it has been seen. What exactly is meant by "now" in the second to last line is not entirely clear; John Sitter suggests that "[p]erhaps the Edenic 'scene' is closed to any *future* view, but Collins and his readers have just had a good look."[51] If there is a positive sense granted by this "now," its modesty is in keeping with the rest of the poem, which has questioned throughout how the poet and the divine come together. Likewise, the final line offers another possibility, that the "kindred Pow'rs ... curtain'd close such Scene from ev'ry future View. If by "such" Collins means every scene which could inspire a future poet, then we have something like the closing of the canon of prophecy. However, "such" could also refer to this specific Miltonic scene, and "Such bliss to one alone . . . / was known" seems to support this reading. The speaker's veneration of Spenser in the strophe seems to indicate that he has felt fancy's flame, though it would be absurd to make Spenser's scene of inspiration look like Milton's Eden, so there may be more scenes of inspiration to come. The provocation of the first moment of the sublime is made, and readers are left to labor in the second moment, searching for closure. If we can imagine Collins responding to Freud's injunction, "*Wo Es war, soll Ich werden*," we would have to conclude that he is always trying to get there, but every time he arrives, words cannot tell him he is there. The third moment that Weiskel describes, in which the "mind's relation to a transcendent order" is symbolized, never arrives.[52]

Collins gives us the romantic sublime before the discourse on it had boiled off its possibilities into easier certainties. His sublime dwells in the suspension between terror and certainty just as his poetry dwells uneasily among its contemporaries. As his tropes fail to make the closure that would grant the speaker an identity, critics continue to struggle to place his work. He is logically pre-romantic because his sublime doesn't reach the kind of conclusion that later poets and critics reach.

Reading Collins and the sublime tradition through the lens of logical time lets us see that before the egotistical sublime or the national sublime or any-other-adjective sublime, there is an experience of the suspension of signification. Beyond that, third-moment conclusions and adjectival sublimes are only ever ideological solutions to the impossibility of closure in the symbolic order. They proliferate as the symbolic order always does, by producing marks of pure difference bound at once by the necessity and impossibility of their connection to the real.

Notes

1. Mark Akenside, *The Pleasures of Imagination* (Printed for R. Dodsley, 1744), ll. 56–9.
2. Andrew Ashfield and Peter De Bolla, *The Sublime: A Reader in British Eighteenth-Century Aesthetic Theory* (Cambridge: Cambridge University Press, 1996), 89.
3. William Collins, "Ode to Fear," in *The Poems of Thomas Gray, William Collins, Oliver Goldsmith*, ed. Roger Lonsdale (New York: Longman, 1969), ll. 5–8.
4. Ibid., 68–71.
5. Slavoj Žižek, *The Sublime Object of Ideology* (New York: Verso, 1989), 206.
6. Jean-François Lyotard, *Lessons on the Analytic of the Sublime: Kant's Critique of Judgment* (Stanford: Stanford University Press, 1994), [Sections] 23–29, 123–24.
7. Joan Copjec, *Read My Desire: Lacan against the Historicists* (Cambridge, MA: The MIT Press, 1994), 236, 221.
8. Copjec, 236; Barbara Claire Freeman, *The Feminine Sublime: Gender and Excess in Women's Fiction* (Berkeley: University of California Press, 1997), 10–11.
9. For Longinus, see D. A. Russell and Michael Winterbottom, eds., *Classical Literary Criticism* (Oxford: Oxford University Press, 2008). See Addison's papers on "The Pleasures of the Imagination" in *The Spectator*, vol. 5, ed. Donald F. Bond (Oxford: Clarendon Press, 1965); Edmund Burke, *A Philosophical Enquiry into the Origin of Our Ideas of the Sublime and Beautiful* (Notre Dame, IN: University of Notre Dame Press, 1986); Jadranka Skorin-Kapov, *The Aesthetics of Desire and Surprise: Phenomenology and Speculation* (Lexington Books, 2015).
10. Thomas Weiskel, *The Romantic Sublime: Studies in the Structure and Psychology of Transcendence* (Baltimore: Johns Hopkins University Press, 1986), 23.
11. Ibid., 24.
12. William Collins, "Ode on the Poetical Character," in *The Poems of Thomas Gray, William Collins, Oliver Goldsmith*, ed. Roger Lonsdale (New York: Longman, 1969), ll. 1–2.
13. Weiskel, *The Romantic Sublime*, 24.
14. Ibid.
15. Ibid., 28.
16. Ibid., 25.
17. Ibid., 121.
18. Ibid., 26.

19. Ibid., 31.
20. Jacques Lacan, *Écrits: The First Complete Edition in English*, trans. Bruce Fink (New York: Norton, 2006), 418.
21. Ibid., 419.
22. Collins, "Ode to Fear," ll. 1–2.
23. Weiskel, *The Romantic Sublime*, 37.
24. Ibid., 53.
25. Lacan, *Écrits*, 166.
26. For a full exploration of the details of the logical puzzled treated in "Logical Time" and its implications for the subject and the symbolic order, see Dieter De Grave, "Time to Separate the Men from the Beasts: Symbolic Anticipation as the Typically Human Subjective Dimension," vol. 718 (AIP Conference Proceedings, AIP, 2004), 435–44, and Bruce Fink, "Logical Time and the Precipitation of Subjectivity," in *Reading Seminar I and II: Lacan's Return to Freud*, ed. Bruce Fink and Maire Jaanus, vol. 1 (New York: SUNY Press, 1996).
27. Lacan, *Écrits*, 174.
28. Ibid., 175.
29. Jacques Lacan, *The Seminar of Jacques Lacan, Book XI: The Four Fundamental Concepts of Psychoanalysis*, trans. Alan Sheridan (New York: Norton, 1978), 30.
30. Ibid., 32.
31. Ibid., 40.
32. Weiskel, *The Romantic Sublime*, 24.
33. Neil Hertz, *The End of the Line*, Critical Studies in the Humanities (Colorado: Davies Group, 2008), 18.
34. Harold Bloom, *The Anxiety of Influence: A Theory of Poetry* (Oxford: Oxford University Press, 1997), 111.
35. Paul H. Fry, *The Poet's Calling in the English Ode* (New Haven: Yale University Press, 1980); Paul S. Sherwin, *Precious Bane: Collins and the Miltonic Legacy* (Austin: University of Texas Press, 1977).
36. Martha Collins, "The Self-Conscious Poet: The Case of William Collins," *ELH* 42, no. 3 (Autumn 1975): 375.
37. qtd. Collins, "The Self-Conscious Poet."
38. Christine Gerrard, ed., *A Companion to Eighteenth-Century Poetry* (New York: Wiley Blackwell 2006), 265–39.
39. Joseph Warton, *Odes on Various Subjects: By Joseph Warton* (printed for R. Dodsley; and sold by M. Cooper, 1747), A2.
40. Collins, "Ode on the Poetical Character," ll. 1–2.
41. Ibid., 6, 20.
42. Ibid., l. 20.

43. Ibid., l. 13.
44. Ibid., l. 39.
45. Those reading the Youth of Morn as the sun include Roger Lonsdale, Earl Wasserman, and A. S. P. Woodhouse. See Roger Lonsdale, ed., *The Poems of Gray, Collins, and Goldsmith* (New York: Longman 1969), 432; Earl R. Wasserman, "Collins' 'Ode on the Poetical Character,' " *ELH* 34, 98; A. S. P. Woodhouse, "The Poetry of Collins Reconsidered," in Frederick W. Hilles (ed.) *From Sensibility to Romanticism: Essays Presented to Frederick A. Pottle* (Oxford: Oxford University Press, 1965), 129. Partisans of Apollo include Harold Bloom, Edmund Blunden, P. L. Carver, and Northrop Frye. See Harold Bloom, *The Visionary Company: A Reading of English Romantic Poetry* (Ithaca: Cornell University Press, 1971), 3–10; Edmund Blunden, ed., *The Poems of William Collins* (London: Frederick Etchells and Hugh, 1929), 168; P. L. Carver, *The Life of a Poet: A Biography of William Collins* (New York: Horizon Press, 1967), 128; Northrop Frye, *Fearful Symmetry: A Study of William Blake* (Cambridge: Harvard University Press, 1969), 169–70. Paul S. Sherwin reads here the archetypal poet. See Sherwin, *Precious Bane*, 24. Paul H. Fry and John Sitter both see a combination of the sun and the poet. See Fry, *The Poet's Calling in the English Ode*, 108; John E. Sitter, *Literary Loneliness in Mid-Eighteenth-Century England* (Ithaca: Cornell University Press, 1982), 139.
46. Kevin L. Cope, ed., *Enlightening Allegory: Theory, Practice, and Contexts of Allegory in the Late Seventeenth and Eighteenth Centuries* (New York: AMS Press, 1993), 25. To illustrate this, consider Maresca's example, *The Pilgrim's Progress*, of which he notes, "Christian flees the City of Destruction to seek the Celestial City. That is not a metaphor but a literal narrative statement, and it does not figure anything significantly other than what it says" (Ibid., 24). He further notes that the one-to-one correspondence created by personification is perfectly suited to Bunyan's didactic purposes.
47. Ibid., 36.
48. Marshall Brown, *Preromanticism* (Stanford: Stanford University Press, 1994), 54.
49. Janice Haney-Peritz, " 'In Quest of Mistaken Beauties': Allegorical Indeterminacy in Collins' Poetry," *ELH* 48, no. 4 (Winter 1981): 738.
50. Ibid.
51. Gerrard, *A Companion to Eighteenth-Century Poetry*, 274.
52. Weiskel, *The Romantic Sublime*, 24.

Chapter Six

The Eros of Thanatos

Eighteenth-Century Graveyard Poetry and Melancholic Sublimation

ED CAMERON

Romanticism has from its inception been lit by two lights: the star of revolt and the black sun of melancholy.

—Michaël Löwy and Robert Sayre

If happiness is a seamless assent of the subject to his life..., it is clear that this is refused to anyone who does not abandon the path of desire.

—Jacques Lacan

THE PLANET SATURN has long been recognized for its metonymic affiliation with melancholia because, in the words of Michael John Kooy, it not only "governed the lower earthly regions and drew men downward" but also, "as the highest planet, pulled them furthest upward."[1] Saturn, in other words, pulls humans in two opposing directions; it *elevates* toward higher regions of thought as it also forces a *condescension* to the lower depressive depths at the margins of sociality.[2] As melancholia has been strongly tied to creativity since Aristotle, it is not a stretch to see how this Saturnine pull in two different directions—elevation and condescension—anticipates Jacques Lacan's two differing notions of sublimation that he developed throughout his career. In *Seminar VII*, he articulates his commonly understood notion of sublimation as an *elevation* of the object to the level of the Thing.[3] However, in *Seminar X*, he recognizes a form of sublimation pulling in the other direction when he claims that sublimation can also allow *jouissance* to *condescend* to the lower level of desire.[4] These two differing modes of sublimation can help demarcate the two modes of sublimation utilized by mid-eighteenth century English graveyard poets in their sublimatory attempt to ward off the influence of Pope and his generation by introducing a search for the sublime and a new romantic poetics.

The inability to mourn, which results from the withdrawal of desire and attachment to the dead that characterizes melancholia in graveyard poetry, can be seen as a means to sublimate the lost object of enjoyment, which was viewed as missing from Augustan poetics. Following this logic, the early graveyard poets (Elizabeth Carter, Robert Blair, Edward Young, James Hervey) attempt an elevating religious mode of idealization where the fantasy of full *jouissance* can be maintained and regained in the transcendental future, while the later graveyard poets (Thomas Gray, William Collins, and the Warton Brothers) develop, in response, an artistic sublimation that condescends to the level of desire because it posits jouissance as always only partial, making us aesthetically cognizant of the illusion of full jouissance. In this narrative, while the early graveyard poets manage to alienate their poetic voice from the Augustans, the later graveyard poets create the more radical separation necessary for the birth of Romanticism.

While all eighteenth-century graveyard poetry exhibits the melancholic withdrawal of the libido into the tomb of the ego that eventually characterizes the inward turn indicative of Romanticism, these post-Augustan poets of Sensibility perform this introspective turn through the appropriate theme of melancholia, traditionally associated with an artistic activity rooted in the type of withdrawal from reality necessary for the unreal to become real.[5] Replacing the restrained, unemotional, and controlled Augustan poetics with an emotionally self-indulgent, sentimentally introspective aesthetics,[6] much poetry of the midcentury used melancholia for its elegiac purposes. According to John Sena, "probably more of the leading poets were melancholic" during this era "than in any other comparable span of English history."[7] Among these melancholic poets, Thomas Parnell, James Thomson, Elizabeth Carter, Edward Young, Robert Blair, Thomas Warton, William Shenstone, William Collins, William Cowper, Christopher Smart, and Thomas Gray are all considered, to one extent or another, graveyard poets. These poets exchanged Horatian moderation for a mood, theme, and setting generally influenced by Miltonic sublimity along with a dose of the graveyard scene from *Hamlet*, a play itself about a young prince who is plagued by an insufficient mourning.[8]

The extremely subjective expression that emerges in mid-century poetics reflects the anxiety about Pope and his poetics that characterizes the origin of the Romantic movement. Robert Griffin and Marlon B. Ross have each argued that Romanticism should be viewed less as a style or as a poetic interest in specific content and more as a discourse. That discourse is a revolt against the comforting notion, typical of the neo-classical poetics and ethics of Pope and his generation, that "whatever is, is right." Defining Romanticism thus, Griffin argues, is to define Romanticism "negatively as a phenomenon that is intimately bound up in what it dislikes. The unity of Romanticism, that is to say, is discovered in the agreement over what it rejects. From this perspective, the Wartons and Young are key figures, for they, in conscious but ambivalent rebellion against Pope, helped create the new paradigm out of old materials."[9] Romanticism as a discourse, therefore, begins in the mid-eighteenth century with the poetic turn that is often associated with the graveyard poets whose desire for the pathetic and the sublime functions as a response to what they felt were the limitations on enthusiasm and the lack of experimentation in Augustan poetics. Characteristically, for instance, in his treatise on poetics *An Essay on the Writings and Genius of Pope,* Joseph Warton privileges Pope's early pathetically inclined poems "Elegy to the Memory of an Unfortunate Lady" and "Eloisa to Abelard" over any of the author's more mature poetry composed after 1717. In Warton's estimation, the early Spenserian Pope reaches a height and possesses a value never reached in the later Francophile Pope. Warton praises the early poetry of Pope because he feels that it stems from Pope's own poetic infancy prior to the repression created by his poetically restrictive "petticoats"; it is a poetry more in line with Warton's own theory of pure poetry.[10] These early poems of Pope's can, given Warton's enthusiasm, expectedly be considered Pope's own proto-graveyard poems. From this perspective, the graveyard poets of mid-century can be seen as exchanging a "sunny classicism" for a "melancholy Gothicism that offers deeper pleasures."[11] In psychoanalytical terms, these mid-century graveyard poets attempted to move poetry beyond the comforting confines of the reality and pleasure principles, uncomfortable as they were functioning within the established poetic coordinates.

Exchanging the probable for the marvelous accounts for the main alteration in mid eighteenth-century poetics. Joseph Warton argued for the distinction between what he referred to as a mere "Man of Wit" and a "True Poet," notably linking Donne, Swift, and Pope with the former and Spenser, Shakespeare, and Milton with the latter.[12] His famous rhetorical question "What is there very sublime or pathetic about Pope?"[13] attempts to create a distinction between the early century Augustan poetics of the everyday and the ruminative vein that characterizes the mid-century poetry of the graveyard school. According to Joan Pittock, Joseph Warton—and, by association, any poet in his vein—not only composed from his own subjective feelings but also sought out from poetic tradition "whatever enabled him to escape from the everyday and mundane." This was the primary method, Pittock continues, "to bring back true poetry into the English tradition and to defeat the pervasive irony and denial of straightforward emotion in verse of Pope and his school."[14] Turning toward the pathetic and the sublime became, for the mid-century poets of sensibility, a poetic means of turning away from the everyday and a method of indicating alienation from the prevailing reality principle: "Possessed as many of them were by sensibilities which isolated them from the complexities of social life, they established as the hallmark of their work [. . .] a melancholy nostalgia."[15] Of course, "cessation of interest in the outside world" is one of the "distinguishing mental features" of melancholia, according to Freud.[16] Due to a grave loss, the melancholic displaces his or her libidinal attachment from external reality into what Charles Shepardson characterizes as "the withdrawal of libido into the tomb of an ego that is no longer even his own, but rather the sacrificial tomb in which the object remains alive."[17] Rather than displacing the libido onto a new external object after mourning a loss, the melancholic, according to Freud, internalizes the lost object as part of the ego itself. The object that is lost in reality becomes identified with the ego, leading to Freud's famous observation "[t]he shadow of the object fell upon the ego."[18] By turning away from reality in this highly subjective displacement, not only does the lost object never become lost, but a space opens up in excess of the prevailing reality principle.

This anti-classicist poetic revolution of the mid-century poets, as some have called it, was an attempt to promote the "pure poetry" of feeling and emotion that figures like Edward Young, Joseph and Thomas Warton, and Thomas Gray saw as repressed by neo-classical principles. Theoretically, in critical works such as Young's *Conjectures on Original Composition*, Thomas Warton's *History of English Poetry*, and Joseph Warton's text on Pope, these poets attempted to promote Shakespeare's artful tragedies, Spenser's Gothic enchantments, and Milton's boundless sublimities at the expense of the classical Greek and Roman writers on which Augustan poetics was modeled. This experimentation in poetics was accomplished, according to Trevor Ross, "through a return to sources and to the purity of origins."[19] Several critics have recognized this poetic revolution with its concomitant flight from reality as a result of the increasing over-commodification of cultural life in mid-century England. Poetic activity and genius began to be viewed as a separate activity from the common world: "[P]oetic uniqueness was to be measured by its contrast to society."[20] The subject of poetic interest markedly moves away from social life and into the internal musings and self-reflections of the poet and the emotional and affective impact on the reader, those aspects believed repressed by the social interests of neo-classical poetry. The graveyard poets were developing a line of thought about the disconnect between poetry and the reality principle, as we see reflected in Gray's assertions that the "still small voice of Poetry was not to be heard in a crowd"[21] and that "the language of the age is never the language of poetry,"[22] and in Young's claim that poetic experience should be opposed to "this busy, and idle world."[23]

The mid-century poets felt that the affective power of poetry "was inevitably repressed or enervated when subordinated to the norms of a broadly social discursivity."[24] In addition to the thematic withdrawal into personal feeling, the graveyard poets also sponsored a temporal withdrawal through their attachment to the aesthetic barbarism of the gothic past. While Young and Joseph Warton theorized the original, non-repressed, genius of poetic introspection, Thomas Warton, Richard Hurd, and others looked to the gothic sensibilities inherent in English verse from its national past, thereby eschewing the desire for classical balance and precision promoted by the previous generation of poets. The withdrawal to the gothic was viewed as an attempt to re-capture the original genius and sublimity of poetry before it was corralled into what Young critically refers to as Pope's confining "petticoats." The desire for a phylogenetic return to primitive unenlightened poetry ultimately gets figured as an ontogenetic return to a period before the advent of the signifier and before the emergence of the lost object created by this advent.

Mid-century graveyard poetry circulates around darkness and pensive solitude because withdrawal is a necessary condition for pure poetry to reveal the beyond of the reality principle. It further relies on the Gothic paraphernalia of churchyard cemeteries, aged yew trees, charnel houses, hooting owls, midnight bells, worm-ravaged corpses, ruined tombs, misty vaults, scattered bones, wandering ghosts, and other elements of supernumerary horror to draw its speaker and reader alike into the more obscure but also more solitary realm beyond the socio-symbolic network—into a sort of living death. Graveyard poetry implies that the poetic subject has become separated from the Other, free from customary signification. Generically speaking, graveyard poetry can be understood as a subgenre of the elegy. The elegy, however, is a mourning poem, focusing on detaching from the dead, signifying the Thing, reinstating the object, registering loss, reinscribing the chain of desire, and, in short, reintegrating into the social sphere. Graveyard poetry, on the other hand, follows suit with melancholia by attaching to the dead, retreating with the Thing, making loss itself the object, leaving the signifying chain in disarray, and, to put it briefly, withdrawing from the Symbolic. The elegy, therefore, cannot sublimate because it is, ultimately, about rejoining the existing symbolic coordinates. Graveyard poetry, on the other hand, promotes the type of withdrawal away from the Other and a recognition and articulation of the real entombed within. As Lacan asks in *Seminar XXIV*, "Why shouldn't we invent a new signifier? For instance, a signifier that would have no sense at all, just like the Real?"[25] The graveyard poets' obsession with withdrawal demonstrates their dissatisfaction with the existing modes of poetic symbolization.

In "Night the First" of *Night Thoughts*, Edward Young pronounces:

> let heav'nly pity fall
> On me, more justly number'd with the dead.
> *This* is the desert, *this* is the solitude:
> How populous! how vital is the grave!
> *This* is creation's melancholy vault,
>
> . . .
>
> All, all on earth is shadow, all beyond
> Is substance; the reverse is Folly's creed:
>
> How solid all, where change shall be no more. (ll. 112–21)[26]

He is not only expressing the lack of satisfaction with what is, which is a commonplace with melancholia, but, following the long-established connection between melancholia and creativity that spans back to Aristotle, also attempting to establish Melancholia as the tenth Muse.[27] For Young, the ultimate withdrawal that is afforded only by death is metaphorically aligned to the fount of creativity. Only when every desire of the material world is forsaken can the poetic spirit find its true "substance." Late in "Night the First," Young will echo this sentiment by pointing to the futility of waking dreams by affirming his affinity with "night visions (ll. 162–63). The poetic spirit thrives, Young indicates, in isolation from the social or material world. Young sublimates his mourning of his lost loved ones and his desire for reunion into the mood necessary for the elevation of the poetic craft. By spiritually placing one foot beyond the grave, his poetic fancies are given free reign. In "Night the First," Young is still lamenting the three arrows Death used to take away his wife, stepdaughter, and son-in-law (ll. 204–13). But, by "Night the Fifth," his mourning has begun to chill into a melancholic joy: "What awful joy! what mental liberty! / (If not too bold,) in darkness in darkness I'm embow'r'd / Delightful gloom! The clust'ring thoughts around / Spontaneous rise (ll. 202–6). Halfway through his nine night mourning period, Young's speaker has grown accustombed [*sic*] to his isolation from the common poetic spirit. By "Night the Ninth and Last" of his meditation, Young's speaker, in mourning, has devolved into a full-fledged melancholia, admitting that only death can save one from the death of life "and turn the tide of souls another way" (l. 383). The disinterest in reality exhibited by Young's speaker—and in much graveyard poetry—reflects the change in object that characterizes sublimation. The melancholic subject loses interest in the objects of reality, except insofar as the feelings he or she suffers from the loss of the object become objects of desire themselves.

This same desire for withdrawal is articulated in Thomas Warton's "The Pleasures of Melancholy," when the speaker pleads:

> O lead me, queen sublime, to solemn glooms
> Congenial with my soul; to cheerless shades,
> To ruin'd seats, or twilight cells and bow'rs
> Where thoughtful Melancholy loves to muse,
> Her fav'rite midnight haunts. (ll. 17–21)

Through personification, the speaker articulates the affinity between personal withdrawal and the true spirit of poesie. The speaker here is not attempting to withdraw or escape from reality; rather, he is asking the sublime to transport him away from the given and toward a more poetic reality. Encountering the sublime evacuates the poet from the given, from the existing coordinates of the symbolic order and allows the poet to create *ex nihilo*, a mode of creation that reflects Jacques Lacan's famous characterization of sublimation.[28] This mode of aesthetic disinterestedness does not stem from a desire to withdraw so much as it is itself the cause of the withdrawal. It would be an involuntary withdrawal. A reader desires withdrawal from reality in the form of escapism and therefore seeks aesthetic disinterestedness, but poetry possesses the capacity to transport the reader beyond the reality principle by highlighting the limitations of the signifier and the symbolic order in which it operates.[29]

Pure poetry, according to the graveyard poets, must reach to the furthest ends of the symbolic order. When, in his poem "The Grave," Robert Blair claims that "the task be mine / To paint the gloomy horrors of the tomb" (ll. 4–5), he is attempting to do more than just titillate his potential readers with the ghastly gothic sensationalism of the macabre. He is illustrating the melancholic "withdrawal of libido into the tomb of the ego" away from the perceived inadequacy of the world of the living, "as if the melancholic were buried in the tomb."[30] As he later asks, "What is this world? / What? But a spacious burial-field unwall'd" (ll. 483–84), he illustrates the melancholic loss of the object cause of desire and concomitant attachment to the Thing. The Thing is not to be found in our collective socio-symbolic order, but rather, is itself that which "does not lend itself to signification."[31] If all graveyard poetry can be, at least partially, understood as an attempt to indirectly signify the Thing, to signify an impasse in signification, then it can also be understood as a poetic attempt to articulate the impossible and, therefore, as a form of sublimation, which Lacan specifically argues is about elevating the object to the dignity of the Thing.[32] The turn to the grave, to the tomb, is an attempt to articulate that which cannot be articulated. It is a melancholic attempt, attached to the death drive, to articulate that which precedes articulation and resists signification. In this manner, graveyard poetry points to the inadequacy of signification by either pointing to a beyond or by circumscribing signification's inherent lack. Because of the inability to demarcate loss, the melancholic lives in a world of symbolic disorder. But, according to Elizabeth Wright, "both aesthetic creation and religious discourse in its mythical dimension can work as remedies against symbolic disarray."[33] Both can, in a word, produce sublimations. Graveyard poetry displays two distinct modes of melancholic sublimation: one that emerges from religious dissenting circles, and one that emerges from dissenting poetic taste.

Recognizing that two visionary veins run through eighteenth-century British graveyard poetry leads to the critical observation that these two aesthetic veins can be psychoanalytically delineated through an examination of their respective melancholic figuration of the dead and through their particular modes of sublimation. Melancholia and sublimation are here linked as they share an affinity with the Thing, especially since melancholia attaches to and sublimation aims toward the Thing. Sublimation pays tribute to what lies beyond the pleasure principle, and melancholia expresses a painful pleasure in its attachment to what the reality principle/Symbolic order mourns. In *Seminar VII*, Lacan articulates the three human discourses' sublimatory signifying of the unknown (*das Ding*)— the "emptiness" of our knowledge. In this articulation, Lacan maintains that the Thing plays a "mediating function between the real and the signifier."[34] Lacan also argues that the Thing is introduced through sublimation and represented by emptiness because, ultimately, it cannot be represented by anything else, "or, more exactly, because it can only be represented by something else."[35] In other words, the Thing hovers at the very outer limit of symbolic representation because it designates that to which the signifier is inadequate in signifying, except negatively. Human discourse, within this argument, actually creates the Thing as that which it is incapable of signifying, and, in this manner, the real is introduced into the Symbolic order through sublimation.

Further in *Seminar VII*, Lacan lays out the three dominant human discourses (science, religion, art) that articulate this emptiness and, therefore, the Thing through their specific and respective sublimatory aims.[36] Science, according to Lacan, forecloses this emptiness by articulating the unknown in its discourse as not only immanent but as accessible. With more time, effort, and technology, science believes it can uncover the unknown and make it known, transforming the Thing into mere things yet unknown. Religion avoids this emptiness by articulating the unknown as transcendental and, therefore, inaccessible. For religion, the unknown that emerges with emptiness can be encountered only in the eternal realm, making the Thing divine. Art, however, organizes itself around this emptiness by articulating the unknown as paradoxically immanent yet inaccessible. In this manner, art is able to expose the Thing negatively through the very lack it produces.[37] The inability to mourn, which characterizes melancholia in graveyard poetry, functions as a means to sublimate the lacking lost object by elevating it to the level of the Thing. Following this logic, the poetry of the early graveyard poets (Carter, Blair, Young, Hervey) remains tied to a religious mode of sublimation as they posit the existence of the Thing in the transcendental realm of eternity, while the poetry of the later graveyard poets (Collins, the Warton Brothers, Gray) develops an aesthetic sublimation, outlined in Lacan's schema, as they attempt to transform poetic discourse into an end in itself.

Ultimately, the graveyard poets' melancholic musings attempt to create value where little was found before through a change in the lost object—another configuration of Lacan's definition of sublimation. Depending on the mode, sublimation either attempts to elevate the primordially repressed object mourned by the melancholic above the Symbolic order or to condescend it by forcing it directly into the signifier. Lacan himself formulates two different modes of sublimation "that attract our attention to the possibility of formulating, in the form of a question, a different criterion of another, or even the same, morality, in opposition to the reality principle."[38] One of these modes of sublimation is characterized by the activity that most readers of Lacan's *Seminar VII* are familiar with: "[S]ublimation is the following: it raises an object [. . .] to the dignity of the Thing."[39] As Alenka Zupančič has pointed out, this mode of sublimation is based on an ascending movement; the object is raised up or elevated to a higher level.[40] This mode of sublimation, of course, seems to come very close to the traditional eighteenth-century definition of the sublime: an elevation above the limit.[41] The other modality of sublimation is mentioned by Lacan three years later, in *Seminar X*, where he offers the possibility that, through love, sublimation can also allow jouissance to condescend to the level of desire.[42] Within the Lacanian psychoanalytic schema, jouissance not only points to what is beyond the pleasure principle but also, like the sublime sentiment of melancholia itself, expresses the paradoxical satisfaction that one derives from suffering the loss of a loved object. Just as the sentiment of the sublime absurdly and paradoxically provides a degree of pleasure through the evocation of terror or horror, the term *jouissance* also expresses the pleasure derived from the painful or traumatic loss that is inexorably associated with melancholia. This second mode of sublimation is based on a movement in the opposite direction. Rather than the object ascending to a higher level, *jouissance* (enjoyment) *descends* to a lower level. Etymologically, *sub-limin* can actually mean both *above the limit* or *below the threshold*. One's soul is elevated to the transcendental realm, or one's body is buried in a tomb, which functions as a signifier of loss.

The later, more secular, graveyard poets promote a poetic act of sublimation that encircles a lack of recompense in a melancholic world, characterized by an unstable master signifier where meaninglessness dominates. Contra the religious mode of graveyard poetry, the later, more secular graveyard verse attempts "to gain secular immortality as a substitute for an uncertain religious afterlife."[43] Writing from beyond the grave becomes, in the hands of these poets of sensibility, a trope for writing for poetic posterity. William Collins's "haunted cell" is not inhabited by decomposing corpses, but rather by the tragedies of Aeshylus, Sophocles's "incestuous queen," and the "divine emotions" of "Shakespeare's breast" ("Ode to Fear" ll. 48, 38, 68, 65). When Joseph Warton tunes his "alter'd strings to woe," he does so to spend his melancholic musings alongside "Spenser's moving verse" and "Sidney's hearse" ("Ode XII" ll. 4, 23, 24), and when he goes to "meet the matron Melancholy," it is from "thy lamented Shakespeare's tomb" ("To Fancy" ll. 62, 126). Here the lost object, figured as inspired poetry itself, is incorporated into the melancholic's verse as the lost object and as meta-textually demarcating poetry as an end in itself. Likewise, his brother Thomas Warton discovers the "mystic visions" of the "cloyster'd brothers" Spenser and Milton in "the gloomy void" of melancholy ("The Pleasures of Melancholy" ll. 63, 39). This poetic movement reaches its apotheosis in the most famous of all graveyard poems, Thomas Gray's "Elegy Written in a Country Churchyard," which concludes with the poet's own epitaph, cementing himself amongst the dead and toward poetic posterity. Through this approach, only the later graveyard poets circle around the foundational loss and thus promote a poetic edification.

In this later-developed mode of sublimation—that of condescending—the sublime object is revealed as just an object maintaining the illusion that there is something or some higher realm beyond it.[44] The sublime object is revealed as a deception. These later graveyard poets attach to the dead not in order to forsake the material world in favor of reclaiming the attachment to the Thing that can now be resuscitated only in the transcendental realm; rather, they do so to recall the lost poetic spirit itself as an aesthetic means to indicate the limitations of the reality principle. Apostrophizing metrical fancy as the "queen of numbers," Joseph Warton solicits:

> O hear our prayer, O hither come
> From thy lamented Shakespeare's tomb,
> On which thou lov'st to sit at eve,

> Musing o'er thy darling's grave;
> O queen of numbers, once again
> Animate some chosen swain,
> Who fill'd with unexhausted fire,
> May boldly smite the sounding lyre,
> Who with some new, unequall'd song,
> May rise above the rising throng,
> O'er all our list'ning passions reign,
> O'erwhelm our souls with joy and pain. ("To Fancy" ll. 125–28)

With Warton's speaker recalling proper poetic meter from Shakespeare's tomb, the reader realizes that true poesis has taken a leave of absence from contemporary poetry. The pure poetic spirit that inspired the Bard seems to have died with him, leaving contemporary poetry to fend for itself and flounder into spiritless satire and the like (e.g., the "throng"). Warton asks the queen of numbers to return to the living in order to revitalize contemporary poetry. She is to infuse some of the passion and jouissance ("joy and pain") from Shakespeare's versification into contemporary poetry. Modern poetry, according to the speaker, needs a new "unequaled song" to rise above the uninspired, lackluster verse of the current age. Pure poetic spirit, therefore, is for Warton the lost object, the thing that the melancholic poet cannot stop mourning and that has been forsaken by Augustan verse, steeped, as it is, in artificiality, decorum, and craft. Unlike James Hervey, who ridicules poetry and the poetic spirit as the spiritless limitations of terrestrial life, Thomas Warton invokes dramatic references in "The Pleasures of Melancholy" as if the fictitious events and characters depicted by the "tragic Muse" are real, in the sense that they possess the power to transport one beyond the reality principle: "The gay description palls upon the sense, / And coldly strikes the mind with feeble bliss" (ll. 164–65). Even when William Mason sounds as if he aligns himself sentimentally with the earlier graveyard poets, his rhetoric betrays his true alliance with the later, aesthetically inclined poets: "You know (what more can earthly science know?) / That all must die; by Revelation's ray / illumin'd, you trust the ashes placed below / These flow'ry tufts, shall rise again to day" ("Elegy VI" ll. 89–92). Here the placement of burial "below" begins to signify the condescension associated with Lacan's second, less popular, notion of sublimation as the "flowery tufts" start to metaphorically signify the flowery nature of pure poetic language that shall rise in the wake of Popean realism.

The condescension to the primordial dialect of pure poetry that is implied here reaches its definitive expression in Thomas Gray's *Elegy Written in a Country*

Churchyard. Similar to the melancholic stance, all graveyard poetry implies the elegist's position between two deaths: not yet dead but eliminating oneself from the world of the living.[45] Gray takes this position one step further by explicitly situating the elegist between two deaths. First off, the elegist is grammatically positioned as object in the first stanza: "The plowman homeward plods his weary way, / And leaves the world to darkness and to me" (ll. 3–4). Unlike the speaker in the poems of Carter, Blair, Young, Collins, Warton, and the rest, Gray's elegist never embodies the subjective pronominal position, instead only ever embodying the objective pronominal position and only in the opening stanza. Second, Gray's unstable and confusing Latinate syntax that was always noted by Joseph Warton, Oliver Goldsmith, and William Shenstone, has, more recently, been noted by critic W. Hutchings as creating a confusing or blending of the grammatically subjective and objective. In the line "Hands that the rod of empire might have swayed," for example, "hands" seems to morph from grammatical subject to grammatical object.[46] This movement from subject to object figures, of course, the morphing from living subject to object corpse. The elegist created by Gray as speaker for the *Elegy* occupies this very unstable place between two deaths. He witnesses his own funeral procession and a third-party rumination over his epitaph. In Gray's *Elegy*, therefore, the elegist itself condescends to the level of an object, the lost object of melancholia around which the poem circulates and evokes the Thing by bringing signification itself to rest.

Instead of endorsing an aesthetic mode of sublimation, the earlier group of graveyard poets promote an essentially religious sentiment of an afterlife as recompense, offering an idealization of loss and withdrawal from the world. The solitude promoted in the poetry of Elizabeth Carter, Robert Blair, Edward Young, and James Hervey copies the solitude of Protestant communion with the divine, a seclusion creating the ceding of desire that is necessary for an encounter with the Thing. As Eric Parisot points out, "Graveyard poetry duplicates closeted reading conditions *within* the poem, reproduced by the combination of two central tropes: night and solitude."[47] From Carter's "Melancholy! Silent Pow'r / Companion of my lonely hour" ("Ode to Melancholy" ll. 1–2) to Young's "Night / E'en in the zenith of her dark domain, / Is sunshine to the colour of my fate" (*Night Thoughts*, "Night the First" ll. 15–17), these religiously oriented graveyard apostrophes and anthropomorphisms attempt to teach the reader how to "master the art of dying"[48]; they attempt to change the object of desire from the meaninglessness of life on earth to the divine Thing that can be encountered only as an impossibility within the confines of the given reality principle. They indulge the silent power of melancholia in a poetic attempt to approximate existence in the afterlife. It is an approximation that can be figured only through a poetic alliance with melancholia. Parisot explains: "As a poetic mode intently focused upon the Christian experience of death, the graveyard poet must attempt to articulate this experience irrespective of the impossibility of knowledge and the incapacities of language."[49] The limitations of the symbolic order cannot be the limitations of poetry. The attempt to situate the speaker between two deaths—still biologically alive but symbolically dead—and the attempt to communicate with the dead are related as an attempt to indirectly communicate with the divine since the departed possess a symbolic connection to the eternal realm. Inspired by union with the dead, this mode of graveyard poetry inevitably closes upon a new transcendental vision. In Carter's "Ode to Melancholy," for example, the speaker expresses this vision:

> Sublim'd by thee, the soul aspires
> Beyond the range of low desires,
> In nobler views elate:
>
> [...]
>
> In Death's soft slumber lull'd to rest,
> She sleeps, by smiling visions blest,
> That gently whisper peace:
> 'Till the last mourn's fair op'ning ray
> Unfolds the bright eternal day
> Of active life and bliss. (ll. 67–78)

Carter's reference to sublime transport indicates the graveyard poet's pursuit of the unknown, for that which lies beyond symbolic parameters. Here also, Carter articulates the earlier, more religiously minded graveyard poets' drive for elevation: the soul, not the mind, aspires beyond the range of reality. Only in "death's soft slumber" can the lost object be elevated to the level of the Thing: "[T]he objects that inspire / Thy philosophic dream" (ll. 11–12). The pun on the "last mourn" and the reference to "bliss" indicate that Eros for these graveyard poets is essentially connected with the drive of infinite mourning associated with melancholia and death. The last morning of life on earth aligns with the end of the mourning period as it is poetically elevated into the first morning of the everlasting reunion with the lost object and the bliss of the eternal reward. Carter, resorting to paronomasia, effectively illustrates the wobbliness of the signifier. We are figuratively beyond the domain of stable signification. This vein of graveyard poetry promotes a specifically religious edification and dramatizes what Giorgio Agamben calls "the greedy desire to see the supreme good . . . as one of the causes of melancholy of the religious." This is, as Agamben says, "the perverse Eros of the slothful, who keeps his or her own desire fixed on the inaccessible."[50]

In this initial mode of sublimation—that of elevating the object to the level of the Thing—the sublime Thing points to something beyond, to which poetry can only fail to point because it is in excess of the signifier. This is the type of sublimation attempted by the early, more religiously inclined graveyard poets. The conjuring of the Thing can be heard in Carter's melancholic mood and her attention to the voice of God that underlies her inability to morn:

> When sunk by guilt in sad despair,
> Repentance breathes her humble pray'r,
> And owns thy threat'nings just:
> Thy voice the shudd'ring suppliant chears,
> With Mercy calms her tort'ring fears,
> And lifts her from the dust. ("Ode to Melancholy," ll. 61–66)

The speaker begins in a sunken state aspiring toward elevation and moves to a lifted condition through repentance. But this elevation can take place only after death, when the speaker's melancholic living-as-the-dead existence can be elevated "from the dust." Likewise, Carter ends her poem "Thoughts at Midnight" through a punning reference to the transcendental realm, illustrating the heights to which a melancholic musing can elevate thought:

> Calm let me slumber in that dark repose,
> 'Till the last morn its orient beam disclose:
> Then, when the great Archangel's potent sound,
> Shall echo thro' Creation's ample round,
> Wak'd from the sleep of Death, with joy survey
> The op'ning splendors of eternal day. (ll. 47–52)

While still alive and trapped on earth, Carter's speaker wants to remain isolated from the social sphere in "dark repose, / 'Till the last morn," the final awakening in the eternal realm and the end of the speaker's mourning period. The eternal realm is signaled by "orient beam" (the sunrise), the east being the customary direction of heaven, and by Gabriel's Judgment Day trumpet blast. Carter utilizes Judgment Day imagery to figure the eternal realm that is, from earth, both inaccessible and transcendental, as it can be brought forth only poetically.

Early graveyard poets likewise figuratively present the eternal realm as a means to elevate the purpose of poetry. They do so to signify that which inaccessible to signification. Robert Blair references the higher realm, "the aerial height," of the afterlife as the new day rising while chastising Death, that "great man-eater":

> But know! That thou must render up thy dead,
> And with high int'rest too! They are not thine;
> But only in thy keeping for a season,
> 'Till the great promis'd day of restitution;
> When loud diffusive sound from brazen trump
> Of strong-lung'd cherub shall alarm thy captives,
> And rouse the long, long sleepers into life,
> Day-light, and liberty. ("The Grave," ll. 654–61)

Also utilizing a reference to Gabriel and apostrophizing death, Blair attempts to articulate the eternal as that which can be represented only by something else, figuratively. The "sleepers" of Blair's allusion figure the dead waiting for Judgment Day and the living melancholic poet who has already withdrawn from this world. Similarly, Edward Young evokes the transcendental realm as a return to the homeostasis of union with the primordial Thing through his telling metaphor for terrestrial existence: "Embryos we must be, till we burst the shell, / Yon ambient azure shell, and spring to life, / The life of gods, O transport!" (*Night Thoughts*, "Night One," ll. 131–33). Young anticipates the breaking of the embryonic condition that characterizes the life on earth of the melancholic awaiting the afterlife. He also curiously alludes to the reunion with the lost object that was to be found only in the embryonic relationship with the Other. Also, James Hervey invokes the transcendental awakening achieved through an obsession with death: "Let me employ the little uncertain interval of respite from execution in preparing for a happier state and a better life. That, when the fatal moment comes, and I am commanded to shut my eyes upon all things here below, I may open them again, to see my Saviour in the mansions above."[51] The metonym "mansions above" draws attention to the eternal home, presenting it as that which remains inaccessible in life except through the poetic process of indirection.

In the end, it would seem that this earlier religious modality of sublimation is more akin to a form of idealization because it sets up an immanently inaccessible object, a Thing that cannot be expressed with a signifier of this world. The later aesthetic mode, however, appears more like a form of de-idealization because it exposes the fantasy behind the idealizing process. Where the early graveyard poetry produces a mode of perceiving an object that is beyond our experience because it belongs to the transcendental realm, the later graveyard poetry appears to produce the possibility of perceiving something that is also not an object of experience, without being the Thing in itself, paradoxically of this world but not accessible to signification, except indirectly, poetically. The early graveyard poets envision poetry as a means to transcendence; whereas, the later graveyard poets recognize poetry as an end in itself. Where the former points to the Thing beyond the pleasure principle, the latter points to, or reconfigures, the Thing as the very inconsistency of the pleasure and reality principles themselves, as a Thing that can be figured only through poetic indirection. While the former locates the real beyond reality, the latter illustrates how the real is nothing other than reality's own stumbling block, that which prevents it from ever coinciding with itself.

The early graveyard poets create through a religious mode of sublimation by elevating the gloomy fear of death into an ecstatic object cause of desire and by demarcating the afterlife as a recompense for the loss of the pre-Symbolic primordial Thing that results from the advent of signification. In this manner, this mode of melancholic sublimation attempts Lacan's earlier and more recognizable definition of sublimation: elevating the object to the dignity of the Thing. The later graveyard poets, on the other hand, rely on an artistic mode of sublimation in order to condescend the dead poetic voice itself as an object of drive, marking the Thing as that which suffers from, and yet is situated at the core of, the symbolic. In this manner, these more aesthetic graveyard poets attempt Lacan's lesser known notion of sublimation as a desublimation, where *jouissance* is allowed to condescend to the level of desire. Either way, the poetic sublimation enacted by graveyard poetry frees poetic signification from the restrictive "petticoats" of the reality principle and displays the enigmatic poetic force of an incomplete mourning.

Notes

1. Michael John Kooy, "Coleridge and Melancholy: The Case of the Wedding Guest," *E-rea* 4, no. 1 (2006). <http://erea.revues.org/264>.

2. In their definitive historical study of melancholia, Klibansky, Panofsky, and Saxl claim that, through his position as the highest of the planets, Saturn produces the "most spirited people," such as religious contemplatives, who are also "withdrawn from all worldly life." They also claim that historically Saturn was the only planet possessing "antithetical characteristics," registered in the coupling of a "self-affirmation, sometimes rising to hubris, and a self-doubt, sometimes sinking to despair." Raymond Klibansky, Erwin Panofsky, and Fritz Saxl, *Saturn and Melancholy: Studies in the History of Natural Philosophy, Religion, and Art* (London: Nelson and Sons, 1964), 253, 186, 247.

3. Jacques Lacan, *The Seminar of Jacques Lacan, Book VII: The Ethics of Psychoanalysis, 1959–1960*, trans. Dennis Porter (New York: Norton, 1992), 112.

4. Jacques Lacan, *The Seminar of Jacques Lacan, Book X: Anxiety*, trans. A. R. Price (Malden: Polity, 2014), 179.

5. Melancholia has long been and still is associated with poetic genius because, as Elizabeth Wright has noted, melancholic subjects "persist in denying" the socio-symbolic structure and, therefore, require the poetic to deliver them." This poetic delivery is itself the product of sublimation. Through the poetic, the melancholic is able to give form to the structurally unformed—what Lacan called *creatio ex nihilo*. Elizabeth Wright, *Speaking Desires Can Be Dangerous: The Poetics of the Unconscious* (Malden: Polity 1999), 40.

6. John F. Sena, "Melancholy in Anne Finch and Elizabeth Carter: The Ambivalence of an Idea," *The Yearbook of English Studies* 1 (1971): 119.

7. Ibid.

8. Minus, of course, the Bard's trademark humor. However, in *Seminar VI*, Jacques Lacan recognizes the connection between Hamlet's particular mode of humor, word play, and insufficient mourning. He claims that "the hole in the real that results from loss, sets the signifier in motion. This hole provides the place for the projection of the missing signifier" and that "the work of mourning is first of all performed to satisfy the disorder that is produced by the inadequacy of signifying elements to cope with the hole that has been created in existence." Hamlet's insistent punning and *Hamlet*'s concentrated wordplay results from the freeing of signification due to a breakdown of the symbolic coordinates caused by the loss of the king, the embodiment of the Master signifier. Hamlet's melancholia stems from the loss he suffers at the murder of the Symbolic father and this father's ghost ordering Hamlet not to "let thy soul contrive against thy mother" (1.5. 85–86) in his quest for revenge, essentially eliminating Hamlet's subjective desire by soldering it to the lost maternal object and removing the lack necessary for proper symbolic signification. In melancholia, signification is tenuous at best for this reason. The mid-eighteenth-century poetry of the graveyard school likewise maintains a loose tethering to meaning, often creating a confusion even noticed by Wordsworth. The resulting semantic ambiguity and the placing of meaning "somewhere between the subjective one and the objective one," as we will see, reaches its epitome in Gray's *Elegy*. See Jacques Lacan, "Desire and the Interpretation of Desire in Hamlet," trans. James Hulbert, in *Literature and Psychoanalysis: The Question of Reading: Otherwise*, ed. Shoshana Felman (Baltimore: Johns Hopkins University Press, 1982), 38, 45.

9. Robert Griffin, "The Eighteenth-Century Construction of Romanticism: Thomas Warton and the Pleasures of Melancholy," *ELH* 59, no. 4 (1992): 800–01;

Marlon B. Ross, *The Contours of Masculine Desire: Romanticism and the Rise of Women's Poetry* (Oxford: Oxford University Press, 1989).

10. "Petticoats" is actually Edward Young's metaphor used in his critique of Pope's decision to translate the *Iliad* into heroic couplets. Young was, of course, a huge champion of blank verse. Edward Young, *Conjectures on Original Composition: In a Letter to the Author of Sir Charles Grandison*, 2nd ed. (London: Dodsley, 1759), 59.

11. Griffin, "The Eighteenth-Century Construction of Romanticism," 804.

12. Joseph Warton, *On the Writings and Genius of Pope* (London: Cooper, 1756), iv.

13. Ibid., x.

14. Joan Pittock, *The Ascendancy of Taste: The Achievement of Joseph and Thomas Warton* (New York: Routledge, 1973), 118.

15. Ibid., 120.

16. Sigmund Freud, *The Standard Edition of the Complete Psychological Works of Sigmund Freud*, vol. 14, *On the History of the Psycho-analytic Movement and Other Works*, trans. James Strachey (London: Hogarth, 1957), 244.

17. Charles Shepardson, *Lacan and the Limits of Language* (New York: Fordham University Press, 2008), 86.

18. Freud, *The Standard Edition*, vol. 14, 249.

19. Trevor Ross, " 'Pure Poetry': Cultural Capital and the Rejection of Classicism," *Modern Language Quarterly* 58, no. 4 (1997): 438.

20. Ibid., 447–48. See also John Sitter, *Literary Loneliness in Mid-Eighteenth-Century England* (Ithaca: Cornell University Press, 1982) and William C. Dowling, "Ideology and the Flight from History in Eighteenth-Century Poetry," in *The Profession of Eighteenth-Century Literature: Reflections on an Institution*, ed. Leo Damrosch (Madison: University of Wisconsin Press, 1992), 135–53.

21. Ross, " 'Pure Poetry,' " 451.

22. Pittock, *The Ascendancy of Taste*, 110.

23. Ross, " 'Pure Poetry,' " 450.

24. Ibid., 448.

25. This is essentially what Lacan means by *creation ex nihilo*. Creation built without the already established guarantee of the Other, without the benefit of the existing coordinates of received signification. See Paul Verhaeghe and Frédéric Declercq, "Lacan's Analytic Goal: *Le sinthome* or the Feminine Way," in *Re-Inventing the Symptom: Essays on the Final Lacan*, ed. Luke Thurston (New York: Other Press, 2002), 74.

26. For sake of convenience, all poetry citations can be found in Jack G. Voller, ed., *The Graveyard School: An Anthology* (Richmond: Valancourt, 2015).

27. John Baker, "'Strange Contrarys': Figures of Melancholy in Eighteenth-Century Poetry," in *Melancholy Experience in the Literature of the Long Eighteenth Century: Before Depression, 1660–1800*, eds. Allan Ingram, et al. (New York, 2011): 85.

28. Lacan, *Seminar VII*, 122.

29. The secondary processes in Freud's account (or the Symbolic in Lacan's account) are regulated by the reality principle. The primary processes in Freud (or the Imaginary in Lacan) are regulated by the pleasure principle. The Imaginary and Symbolic are inextricable, existing simultaneously and in a dialectical relationship, and so to eschew the reality principle as the Graveyard poets do would signal the beyond of the pleasure principle as well.

30. Shepardson, *Lacan and the Limits of Language*, 86.

31. Julia Kristeva, *Black Sun: Depression and Melancholia*, trans. Leon S. Roudiez (New York: Columbia University Press, 1989), 13.

32. Lacan, *Seminar VII*, 112.

33. Elizabeth Wright, *Speaking Desires*, 45.

34. Lacan, *Seminar VII*, 129.

35. Ibid., 129–30.

36. For a full elaboration, see Lacan, *Seminar VII*, 128–38, and Zupančič, "Splendor."

37. Lacan makes this distinction between the "scientific point of view" and "artistic creation" again in *Seminar X*, 145.

38. Lacan, *Seminar VII*, 109.

39. Ibid., 112.

40. Alenka Zupančič, *The Shortest Shadow: Nietzsche's Philosophy of the Two* (Cambridge: The MIT Press, 2003), 165.

41. Lacan recognizes this affinity between sublimation and a specific eighteenth-century notion of the sublime. See *Seminar VII*, 301.

42. Lacan, *Seminar X*, 179. See also Zupančič, *The Shortest Shadow*, 165.

43. Eric Parisot, *Graveyard Poetry: Religion, Aesthetics and the Mid-Eighteenth-Century Poetic Condition* (Burlington: Ashgate, 2013), 141.

44. Lacan maintains that, while religion is an illusion because neurosis is involved, artistic sublimation does not produce illusions. Jacques Lacan, *Television: A Challenge to the Psychoanalytic Establishment*, trans. Jeffrey Mehlman (New York: Norton, 1990), 113.

45. Lacan, *Seminar VII*, 280.

46. W. Hutchings, "Syntax of Death: Instability in Gray's 'Elegy Written in a Country Churchyard,'" *Studies in Philology* 81, no. 4 (1984): 504.

47. Parisot, *Graveyard Poetry*, 14.

48. Ibid., 15.
49. Ibid., 73.
50. Georgio Agamben, *Stanzas: Word and Phantasm in Western Culture*, trans. Ronald L. Martinez (Minneapolis: University of Minnesota Press, 1993), 14.
51. Voller, *The Graveyard School*, 109.

Chapter Seven

Toric Tropes Are Stolen Boats
Reading Wordsworth's *The Prelude* Topologically, with Lacan

DAVID SIGLER

A TORUS IS A DECEPTIVELY SIMPLE SHAPE: a hollow tube with a hole in the middle. Inner tubes are tori, as are the surfaces of donuts. It is also a wonderfully poetic figure, holding in tension two emptinesses that cannot meet, but can be variously configured. Its internal space (e.g., the air in the inner tube) is kept separate (by the wall of the inner tube) from the external space interior to it (e.g., the hole in the middle). Paradoxically, then, a torus confounds the distinction between inside and outside by vigilantly maintaining that distinction.

If at first a torus may seem more mathematical than literary, one might consider how William Wordsworth's *The Prelude* offers us a speaker beset by his own unspeakable thoughts and feelings, which retroactively and only technically become his "own" in a play of incorporation and expulsion. In Book I of the 1850 version of that *magnum opus*, the speaker explains how he came to "endue some airy phantasies / That had been floating loose about for years, / And to such beings temperately deal forth / The many feelings that oppressed my heart."[1] His feelings are thus imposed upon him from the outside—which is something that Adela Pinch has observed about affect in Wordsworth and Romanticism more broadly—much as his "phantasies" were just "floating loose" in the wider world before he internalized them and experienced them as regulatory.[2] They can then be re-externalized, "dealt forth." Yet Wordsworth nevertheless asserts that "a dark / Inscrutable workmanship . . . reconciles / Discordant elements, makes them cling together / In one society" (1.34–44). Alien components, collated, make a poet—something singular and unique—but then, as they remain discordant, they dialectically allow him to perceive a larger "society" into which he might integrate, so as to glimpse a "universal earth" as surface. Both processes are experienced as radically exterior to the subject, the product of someone's "workmanship." Their inscrutability suggests their alienness. The subject is made out of his lack of access to himself, such that his own internal processes act upon him as if from outside: "[A] strong desire / O'erpowered my better reason" (1.318–19). I am suggesting that Wordsworth's relationship to his thoughts and memories—the shape of that relationship or the space in which it is imagined to take place—is actually a torus. A torus maintains a boundary between internal and external space but traverses that boundary as a single surface, much as the speaker's own feelings can be understood to "oppress" his heart.

Wordsworth's account of himself plays out at the levels of form and content, creating a structure that could be accounted for topologically because its strands, even as they are held in tension, are not really separate or separable. That is one way that Wordsworth can maintain what Joel Faflak has identified as Wordsworth's "double consciousness of imagination" in *The Prelude*, meaning precisely a gap maintained between the poem's form (i.e., Wordsworth's account of self) and its content (i.e., analysis interminable).[3] In Book I of *The Prelude*, such a process, seen topologically, reveals the function of fantasy in subject formation: fantasy ties the Real to the Imaginary to create, however provisionally, the structural conditions that could accommodate and support the subject's arrival as an "individual" and socially. The elaboration of this fantasy occurs, in this poem, through sexual pleasure and the way it disrupts the signifying systems of poetry. The subject must "endue" the "airy phantasies" topologically, within the space of the poem and through its literary language. When "subject formation intertwines with fantasy and the narrative structure that derives from it," as Paul A. Vatalaro has explained in relation to Shelley's poetry, we are left with a "dynamic, open-ended process."[4] Such processes are what topology was devised to track.

Jacques Lacan spoke exhaustively about topology, insisting that human subjectivity was shaped as a torus: "this is not a metaphor, . . . what we are dealing with exists,"[5] he would say, later reemphasizing that the torus was "not a metaphor but a structure."[6] I have no similar dread of metaphor, but want to note, at the outset, how Lacan's toplogical work was often staged through the renunciation of poetic language. It was, as Jeanne Lafont explains, Lacan's effort "to think the psychical apparatus as a topological space," via "a center that remains exterior."[7] The subject is toric because its lack in being is exterior to itself, but produces desire as a "central void" that "hollows itself within."[8] Lacan notes with admiration that "the inside that is at stake here and the outside, are exactly the same thing. There is only one inside, the one that we imagine as being the interior of the torus. But precisely, the introduction of the figure of the torus consists, in not taking account of this inside of the torus."[9] A torus, then, ignores its own construction. Yet one can trace a trajectory of desire—an itinerary of subjectivity—around the torus in a looping shape. When one traces a spiral around the tube, as if to track the progress of desire as it pursues its causes, or slices the tube to produce a Möbius strip, or bends or stretches it to test its logical limits, one discloses the structure of human sexuality in the defiles of the signifier.[10] Topology can track the human subject dynamically, through various lines of flight: as Lacan observed, "[T]he torus has two holes, the internal hole with its gyre and the hole that one can call external, thanks to which the torus is demonstrated as participating in the figure of the cylinder which ... materialises for us the figure of the straight line at infinity."[11] Lacan became interested in tori as early as the mid-1950s, dating at least back to his Rome Discourse, but intensified his attention to them through the 1960s and into the 70s, collaborating with mathematicians such as Pierre Soury and Georges-Th. Guillbaud. He would regularly task his mathematician friends with urgent and complicated analyses of figures.[12]

Lacan was attracted to the torus, in part, because it confounds its own dimensionality. In one of his earliest meditations on the subject, he explains that

> a torus's peripheral exteriority and central exteriority constitute but one single region. This schema represents the endless circularity of the dialectical process that occurs when the subject achieves his solitude, whether in the vital ambiguity of immediate desire or in the full immersion of his being-toward-death.[13]

This is Lacan being Hegelian: he is suggesting that being-for-self (and any individualism that would seem to result from such an achievement) is actually the outcome of a "dialectical process" that confronts the subject with the other, and thus with death. Hence "solitude" is a phase in a cycle of "endless circularity." This is a toric structure, in the sense that a torus, a three-dimensional figure of such circularity, shows us the inseparability of inside and outside, of the individual subject and the dyad, and from the dyad out to society broadly. Even as it accounts for the "solitude" of the individual, "we can simultaneously see that the dialectic is not individual," pointed as it is toward "the satisfaction of all."[14]

Lacan's comments on the torus map closely onto fantasmatic dialectic from *The Prelude* that I was outlining above, according to which Wordsworth accounts for his individual artistic consciousness in order to make himself "cling together" as a participant in something "universal." Wordsworth, as I have suggested, imagines that he contains an external void, something held separate from his own internal space, and he presents that as the pivotal aspect of his mature subjectivity and even as his reason for being. Yet he emphasizes how he holds that space apart from other externalities. Lacan's discussions of tori can help us understand this disjunction, for, as Pierre Skriabine asserts, "there is no subject... who is not a topologist, even without knowing it."[15]

The stolen boat episode in *The Prelude* authorizes the speaker to observe how "the surface of the universal earth" can "work like a sea," how it sometimes "rolled" or would manage to "stretch" (1.459–75). Wordsworth is, in such passages, thinking topologically, in the sense that topology is the study of how surfaces can change their shape while still retaining their properties. To build (at the level of fantasy) constancy in the face of fluidity, he implies, provides the ground on which lyric or epic subjectivity can arise. The language of topology, and specifically the figure of a torus, enables the poet, first, to account for the constant changes he perceives in himself while also claiming to be something abiding, or in the process of becoming; it enables him, second, to account for the enduring presence of something foreign-feeling inside himself while enabling it to remain alien.

The stolen boat scene has, since Robert Young's pioneering work in the 1970s, been a touchstone for Lacanian Romanticists, from Laura Claridge to David Collings to Gary Farnell, and for those interested in Wordsworth and psychoanalysis more broadly, such as Faflak and J. Douglas Kneale.[16] For Collings, who discusses the 1799 version of *The Prelude*, the implied masturbatory eroticism of the stolen boat episode reflects the poet's masochistic desire to be punished, castrated, and anally penetrated by his father, and so marks a new phase in Wordsworth's career, where the poet need not any longer represent himself as exempt from traumatic experience.[17] For Patricia Waugh, the scene reveals the big Other to be a "retroactive illusion," because Wordsworth "outlines the matrix of the oral fantasy which nurtures narratives of conquest (whether territorial or amorous)" once "the enigma of the Other's desire is transformed into an actual living Thing."[18] Joseph Sitterson sees the stolen boat episode as an exploration of "the child's metaphoric power and mastery of its own subjectivity," such that the passage illustrates the moment when "desire becomes human," per Lacan.[19] And Kneale, tracing the poem's "topos of symptom and scene," sees Wordsworth's epic "not as a journal of discovery that seeks the goal or ground of interpretation, but rather as a tour, all surface and no depth, where one term or event or sign displaces the next only for it to be displaced in turn."[20]

Without mentioning this body of criticism or even Lacan, Slavoj Žižek revitalized this critical conversation with his own somewhat recent discussion of the 1850 *Prelude*.[21] Žižek reads the stolen boat scene as an account of an "optical illusion": the speaker remembers having seen, in a trick of perspective, a mountain bearing ever closer on him as he paddled away, terrified. Noting how Wordsworth's speaker gets "caught between two vectors, two non-overlapping axes"—namely "subject–truth" and "ego–id"—Žižek sets out to explore how this parallax gap might offer a way of thinking about epistemology, consciousness, and perception.[22] The episode illustrates, for Žižek, how Truth emerges as a formal feature of a structure, rather than as something pertaining to the substance of one's statements.[23] Wordsworth would appear, then, to be providing Žižek with an example of how form overrides content. Yet Žižek focuses exclusively on the plot, leaving aside questions of poetic form and literary language.

Lacan specifically warns, in "Variations on the Standard Treatment," against any psychoanalysis that does not attend specifically to language and syntax, or that would focus merely on *what is happening*.[24] Although the scene definitely involves an illusion of a looming mountain, I want to suggest that the figural level is where a more fundamental and significant trick of perspective takes place in the stolen boat scene. Looking to Lacan directly, instead of always to Žižek as a Lacanian guide, I argue, can help us make sense of the literary language of the passage—its metaphors, similes, and metonymies, and figures for literary reading enjoyed, naturally, "by the margin of the trembling lake," as a way to rethink the perspectival illusion of the scene topologically (1.420). The gaps between language and event—two absences that are mediated and held together (but apart) by fantasy—which constructs the speaker's perspective as such. A focus on the literary language of the text, and closer contact with Lacan's ideas, can reveal topological aspects of the poetry crucial to its rhetorical acts of subject formation.

The speaker-poet, in narrating "the story of my life" as a form of self-analysis, and especially in offering a history of his own pleasures, pursues an endeavor that he knows to be impossible: he carries on despite not knowing "how the heart was framed": "Yet should these hopes / Prove vain, and thus should neither I be taught / To understand myself" (1.640, 1.626–29). This passage is a quintessentially Lacanian mediation, the Lacanian subject being, as Daniela Garofalo notes, "a subject aware of its fundamental unknowability."[25] Wordsworth waxes topological in an effort to "almost make remotest infancy / A visible scene" (1.635–36). The "almost" marks the speaker's acknowledgment of the impossibility of that project, which would seek to account for the apparent alienness of his feelings, and to situate the poet within and around them, and thus could account for his artistic and sexual development. To think about Wordsworth's poetry topologically is to focus not on the nascent subjectivity in the poem *per se* and its relation to language—as previous Lacanian approaches to *The Prelude* have done—but to consider the conditions in which such subjectivity can emerge.

For Žižek, the stolen boat scene is primarily a story. He emphasizes how the boy "fixed [his] view / Upon the summit" and then grew afraid, while backing away, as the more distant peak became visible. Yet the interesting part of that sentence is actually the preceding part, which figures this act of fixed looking: "But now, like one who rows, / Proud of his skill, to reach a chosen point / With an unswerving line, I fixed my view / Upon the summit" (1.367–70). This is a peculiar simile: our speaker, a proud boy rowing toward a chosen point, is comparing himself to "one who rows, / proud of his skill, to reach a chosen point." The vehicle and tenor are strangely indistinguishable, and so, given nothing that would separate the "his" from the "I," the simile itself is forced to create the movement that makes the perspectival illusion with the mountain possible. The simile, at the level of its content, insists that the rowing boy is "like" the boy who rows, and yet, because it is a simile, we can see it backhandedly insisting that there is a gap between these figures that must be traversed figuratively. The resulting web of signification produces assonance as a kind of excess jouissance, as the speaker cycles through letters to produce near-anagrams—"now," "one," "who," "rows"—as the letter begins to assert its own agency in the unconscious. We are witnessing what Lacan would call "castration": the boy turns to figural language to find himself externally, through a baffling simile that aggressively opens a gap between a "him" (who is me) and the me who rows.

Just as soon as *the I rowing* breaks apart from the *one who rows*, that *I* gets separated, syntactically, from the boat being rowed, and so the self-referential simile immediately stimulates the production of more: "[A]s I rose upon the stroke, my boat / Went heaving through the water like a swan," the speaker continues (1.375–76). The boat is "like a swan." Although here we have found adequate space between vehicle and tenor of the simile, still the vehicle somehow misfires: while it would be perfectly reasonable to compare a boat to a swan for the way it glides across the water, the "heaving" suggests that its motion is completely unlike the graceful paddling of a swan. The figural misfire is acknowledged through the line break, which is likewise askew: instead of separating the "I" who rose upon the stroke from the heaving boat, the line break arrives one metrical foot too late, separating the boat from its heaving motion. It appears that the boat, which is like a swan to the extent that it "heaves" like a swan, is no longer the subject of its own heaving—and thus no longer like a heaving swan in any case. This sets up further examples of wayward figuration, as the speaker describes himself as:

> Proud and exulting like an untired horse
> That cares not for his home. All shod with steel,
> We hissed along the polished ice in games
> . . . imitative of the chase
> And woodland pleasures,—the resounding horn,
> The pack loud chiming, and the hunted hare. (1.432–38)

There, "Every ice crag / Tinkled like iron" (1.441–42). What these similes share is how they effectively misfire. In the equine example, the speaker compares himself to a horse chasing a hunted hare, making no mention of a human rider or hound. We are left with the image of the horse and its inexplicable prey drive, or at best a horse along for the ride, as it were, chasing someone else's desires as a matter of custom. And yet the desires of that horse, his "cares," his refusal of nostalgia, are our focal point. Either interpretation is unsustainable. The simile figures pursuit in a peculiar or impossible way, with the speaker (through the simile) effectively chasing the wrong thing, harboring unnatural desires, or refusing to acknowledge his longings. Being the desires of someone who was like "one who rows," these similes cover over the gaps in the process of subjectivization, enabling the narrative to proceed even when no one, except for the force of figuration itself, is holding the reins.

What we are observing is how language "manifests a structure" with the center outside of itself, constantly pointing elsewhere—that is, how it creates a torus.[26] I was like a rower; my boat was like a heaving swan; I was hunting like a horse; the ice tinkled like iron. The figural mishaps interfere with the sexual pleasure so blatantly claimed in the scene—the stroking of the elfin pinnace and its consequent heaving—which themselves play out metaphorically. It is a recursive structure, and everything depends on the gaps that get sustained between each level: the content being sexual pleasure, but as displaced into a series of signifiers (boat, mountain), which are illustrated through form (epic, lyric, *bildung*), but break down through the misfiring of the figural language. The stolen boat episode reveals "the imperative of the Word as the law that has shaped him in its image," as Lacan would say, because it "exploits the poetic function of language to give his desire its symbolic mediation."[27] As the "I" of "I fixed my view" becomes detached from the "one" who is rowing, it is assured that "a chosen point" can never be reached. Hence the mountain, looming over the speaker, celebrates its primacy *qua* phallic signifier.

The phallic mountain is serving as a substitute for another phallic signifier. The boat had been heaving, and now this is heaving; the boat was moving, but now the mountain is moving. Wordsworth displaces the boy's jouissance onto first his act of rowing and then this terrifying sublime shape, *das Ding*. The substitution is significant because it turns, as Lacan would say, S1 into S2, making the phallus simply part of a chain of signification instead of the anchor of meaning or instrument of jouissance. Wordsworth presents a similar set of substitutions in "Strange Fits of Passion," in which the motion of the car in the context of sexual desire turns the moon into a sublime and horrifying object standing in for the speaker's jouissance and assuring its deferral. The substitutions in this stolen boat scene thus enact a poetic repetition for Wordsworth, making the substitution happen at the level of oeuvre as well. Moreover, it is important to note how caesura separates the boy from this wellspring of phallic jouissance: "a huge peak, black and huge... Upreared its head. I struck and struck again" (1.378–80). The commas, slowing the pace of the lines down and giving them a measured tone, prepare us to be stuck in the thick of enjoyment for a while; yet the caesura of the period separating "its head" from "I" provides a measure of protection from the Thing. The I is held at a remove from the Thing, suggesting the operations of the fundamental fantasy and the inaccessibility of sexual enjoyment to the boy. His pleasure is now "like a bee among the flowers" (1.580), not the "vulgar joy" and "giddy bliss" from before (1.581–83, 597). The misfirings are, I would suggest, symptoms of the toric nature of these acts of sexual pleasure: "[I]ts writing or drawing is very difficult, because [with a torus] the conventional lines of the curves disappear."[28] As Lacan explains, a torus is effectively "a distortion which is defined by encountering what creates an obstacle," in this case, sexual enjoyment: "[T]his is what makes the torus" and "that is what topology is."[29] "We are incapable of transmitting it in a message," he says.[30]

The *bildung* implicit in Book I of *The Prelude* trains us to expect the poet to emerge, from "Childhood and School-Time," into poetic self-consciousness, and so there is a concomitant temptation to read the stolen boat episode as a key moment in the speaker's sexual development and maturity. One must, however, resist that temptation, because nothing of the kind is happening. The child, terrified of the posterior mountain, paddles back to the tree to return the boat and to seek safety, but the poet reports these events with an air of irony: he "through the silent water stole my way / Back to the covert of the willow tree; / There in her mooring-place I left my bark" (1.386–88). With diction such as "stole" (meaning to move swiftly, but redolent of theft), "bark" (meaning boat, but redolent of a guard dog, or a surface membrane that covers up an interior) and "covert" (meaning clandestine, but here pressed into service as a noun, as if syntactically to hide an unmentionable thing), the speaker insinuates that the larceny occurs in returning the boat rather than in stealing it. This complicates the swan-and-rower tropes from earlier in the passage, because it marks the speaker's identification with the stolen boat—as if he himself were the thing stolen, rowed, returned home, and in this way confirms what had been obvious: that the rowing of the boat had been a kind of masturbation for the boy, because he was the boat, or was like a boat. It is an act of identification, a mechanism which marks, says Lafont, the torus turning inside-out as it is cut: "Identification is an answer to a question: how does something from the exterior become interior, exterior, and still central?"³¹ The result, she explains, is that the circles of demand and desire exchange positions. Consider the speaker's willingness "to cut across the reflex of a star / That fled" (1.450–51): reflex, here, meaning reflection, a mirror-effect taking place at the level of the imaginary. He marks a "cut across" that vector, slicing the torus to create a Möbius strip, and thus apprehends the scene from the other side: again we have a fixed point in the sky that appears to be moving, but here the star, rather than the boy, is the one fleeing, and the boy is the one chasing. Even still, the speaker says that "yet still the solitary cliffs / Wheeled by me" (1.458–59), registering a kind of traumatic aftereffect of the encounter with the mountain as the two sides of the Möbius strip—the subject and his lost enjoyment—converge and apprehend each other warily.

The boy speaks of having found "her mooring-place" in new habits of thought, "call it solitude / Or blank desertion," which become "unknown modes of being" (1.393–95). Why "her"? The boy is becoming aware that these "unknown modes of being" are, in effect, traps, or alibis for what he calls "a more subtle selfishness," "that now / Locks every function up in blank reserve, / Now dupes me, trusting to an anxious eye / That with intrusive restlessness beats off / Simplicity and self-presented truth" (1.245–49). Truth, then, far from coming into being as a formal structure, as Žižek would have it, is held at bay here perpetually: "A timorous capacity, from prudence, / From circumspection, infinite delay" (1.241–42). The subject, eschewing truth as a position from which to speak, agrees to be duped by his own "blank reserve," his own feelings—which never quite seem his own, in the toric manner—and yet comes to accept that "this is my lot" (1.261).

There is of course irony in finding one's home, one's "mooring-place," in the surplus, because in no sense could such a place be familiar. "Home," a term which names where one resides, cannot help but be familiar, and so it would be paradoxical to locate one's "home" in "unknown modes of being." Lacan would call this paradox *extimité*, which, as Mladen Dolar explains, is Lacan's preferred term for the uncanny. The extimate object, being at once an intimate kernel and a foreign body, becomes the point where inside coincides with outside, confounding any division between the familiar and the strange, and thus becoming, through its own impossible structure, "the pivotal point upon which psychoanalytic concepts revolve."³² The extimate object—the *objet petit a*—constructs the subject into a torus: an external gap is being held internally, apart from the other material "inside" the subject. The enjoyment written through the partial object is radically both inside and outside of the subject, because the Real can never be integrated into the Symbolic.³³ Subjectivity has a toric shape when the Real is retained inside, and yet maintained outside, the symbolic experience of the subject: "[F]or something to ek-sist, there must be a hole somewhere," Lacan says.[34] The term "ex-sistence" indicates how the inner workings of subjectivity are often held outside of one's body, and yet, in being thus held, marks the limit of "the body proper": "If there were not the Symbolic and the ek-sistence of the Real," Lacan explains, "this body would simply have no aesthetics at all, because it would have no tube-torus. The tube-torus . . . is a mathematical construction, namely, made of this inek-sistent relationship, qua ek-sistent, that there is between the Symbolic and the Real."[35]

Consider how Wordsworth's speaker describes his confrontation with the mountain. He takes the horrifying Thing into himself, so he can (and must) encounter it internally: "Huge and mighty forms, that do not live / Like living men, moved slowly through the mind / By day, and were a trouble to my dreams" (1.395–400). He discovers that he has a void on the inside ("blank desertion"), and that "no familiar shapes / Remained" (1.395–96). Wordsworth is speaking, then, of how a lack can be retained. Although the 1799 and 1805 versions of *The Prelude* said "*the* trouble *of* my dreams," the 1850 *Prelude* says "*a* trouble *to* my dreams," a revision which is subtle but important.[36] The earlier versions, with their genitive "of," imagine trouble as a property of the dreams, while the 1850 version imagines dreams being troubled variously and constantly. The revision reorients the word "trouble," which, as Judith Butler notes, can refer either to a disruption *per se* (i.e., something that interferes with the *status quo*) or the punitive response to a disruption (i.e., getting in trouble), such that "the rebellion and the reprimand seem to be caught up in the same terms."[37] Wordsworth's original formulation emphasizes the singularity of the "trouble," making the mountain seem like a specific horror that had haunted the speaker as a punishment: one trouble repeatedly haunts a myriad of dreams. The trouble belongs to the dreams, but the dreams belong to the subject. But in the 1850 version, the dreams themselves trouble the subject, who, being thus disrupted, is no longer even quite in possession of his own dreams. (Perhaps this is why the readings of the stolen boat scene that have emphasized how the boy seems desirous of punishment tend to use the 1799 *Prelude* as their textual object.[38]) In the earlier versions, the speaker has emerged into subjectivity despite prior traumatic events, which would periodically disrupt his sleep; in the later version, the speaker has actually been constructed around these traumatic events, with repressed material shaping subjectivity extimately. The earlier *Prelude*s imagine dreams as a separate state from waking life, imagine that dreams possess their trouble, and imagine that admonishment might actually be wished for, in the idiomatic manner of *the girl of my dreams*[39]; the revised line understands dreams as a constant state of being—more akin to what Lacan would call "fantasy"—forming a psychic matrix that can be continually disrupted, or troubled, by the looming mountain.

Young has read these lines as Wordsworth's acknowledgement of "the primary process that Freud identified in the dreamwork" and "the distinguishing moment of the unconscious" apart from signification.[40] But we can also understand them topologically: Wordsworth is marking how an extimate object, which "do[es] not live," moved through his thoughts as an internal deadness in an uncanny approximation of life. The disruption happens especially at the level of enjambment, building traumatic rupture into the substance of the literary language itself: the line break between "shapes" and "Remained" typographically signals a cut between the familiar and the new realities, just as the line break between "live" and "Like living men" violently separates the act of living on from the figural plane of language upon which a simile can emerge. The enjambment in the latter example produces a simile out of the disavowal of one, separating the "do not" from the "Like" in much the same way that the unconscious cannot entertain negation. The "forms" are thus marked for repression, and we have a simile that fashions a vehicle out of its tenor: to live "like living men" requires that one have inhuman stuff roaming "through the mind." The speaker reports that "my brain / Worked" as if it were a separate entity: his brain, rather than he himself, thinks things. The subject is thus de-subjectified into ex-sistence, encountering their own thoughts as alien and unfamiliar. The movement of the mountain, then, is not exactly an optical illusion caused by a perspective trick, as Žižek would have it—it is alien matter that continues to "move" "through the mind" day and night, forming the constitutive "trouble" of the speaker's preconscious as "trouble," and the manifest content of his dreams.

In Young's reading of this passage, Wordsworth is reckoning with lack as the speaker accepts the cut of the signifier.[41] I would supplement that insight by pointing out that Wordsworth is not merely coping with, but actively embracing his own position as the "dupe" of his own knowledge. It is the "non-dupes" who "err" in *The Prelude*. Yet even if the homophones *les non-dupes errent* and *les noms du père* don't have the same meaning, Lacan admits, "they [still] show the same knowledge"—namely, that "the unconscious is a knowledge from which the subject can decipher himself."[42] Acts of partial self-decipherment through the names of the father provide, he says, the "supplementary function of an extra torus."[43] These acts of self-decipherment demand to be read topologically. "Man goes round in circles," Lacan suggests, "because the structure, the structure of man is toric."[44] Consider how Wordsworth offers praise for "high objects" directly after the stolen boat episode:

> Not with the mean and vulgar works of man,
> But with high objects, with enduring things—
> With life and nature—purifying thus
> The elements of feeling and of thought,
> And sanctifying, by such discipline,
> Both pain and fear, until we recognize
> A grandeur in the beatings of the heart. (1.408–14)

These high objects, in their "purifying" action, depend upon the messy horror of sexual enjoyment but also enable one to establish one's desire. One might ask: Does the mountain from the previous verse paragraph get to be memorialized as a "high object," and if not, why not? Is it not a towering emblem of "life and nature"? Yet *The Prelude* seems to understand it as the alternative to, the opposite of, such a structure. Specifically, high objects allow one to "recognize" a structure inside of oneself, such that the "beatings of the heart" become something an index of the "pain and fear" that one encounters. The stolen boat scene reminds us that these acts of recognition are always acts of *méconnaissance*. They ask us to accept, as a matter of "sanctifying... discipline," that external encounters were matters of our perspective; they ask us to imagine that the horizon can be observed as an external phenomenon, which we merely watch without becoming implicated into it. That this disavowal, this gap in perspective, becomes invisible or occluded is exactly the point: "Even the hole in the middle of the torus, you must not believe that a purely toric being would even notice its function!," Lacan once shouted.[45] Thus subject formation happens neither inside nor outside of the subject's psyche. It is a topological matter, in the sense that objects with no edge, which hold their externalities inside as a way of keeping them at bay ("by such discipline"), are by definition tori and can be considered as such.[46]

Zak Watson has asked: "How are we to apply topology to literature? This is no easy question."[47] Wordsworth offers us a case study in that regard. For Watson, topology offers a way to get beyond "this sham infinity of the symbolic order," which proves to be an artificially "closed set" which "bears only ex-sistence."[48] Yet *The Prelude* counterintuitively shows how the symbolic order itself functions like a torus: the poem's symbolic systems of figuration, and especially tropes, such as metaphor and simile, provide the substance of a surface that can then be manipulated. Far from allowing us to get beyond that structure, topological thinking allows us to see how this symbolic set comes to rest uneasily alongside the Imaginary and Real. The mountain, for example, as we have seen, is both (at the level of the Real) a traumatic remainder haunting the speaker's dreams and (at the level of the Imaginary) an ego ideal in which he once located himself; yet it can function this way only by serving as a signifier that stands in for another signifier (at the level of the Symbolic). Reading topologically enables us to read across these vectors to see how they are all aspects of the same surface—a surface which would hold these different gaps apart from each other and maintain them in tension. For instance, the "work" in the aforementioned phrase "work like a sea" functions both as part of a maritime simile (i.e., nature makes the surface of the earth work like the sea is made to work, or like the way the sea makes us work), and as an account of that simile (the figural work of which is "like a sea"). The simile is performative in that sense, calling itself into being through self-description. The malleability of Wordsworth's tropes in Book I is what enables them to dip into the unconscious, into the invisible and unsayable material from which we are normally barred. Wordsworth's figural language holds externalities separate from internalities but while maintaining each, in different senses, inside—hence, "into a silent bay," or "Into the tumult" (1.448, 1.443). It is this inscription and its topological character which "Impressed, upon all forms, the characters / Of danger or desire" (1.471–72), as if danger or desire could be exchanged for each other so readily. (Desire and danger become interchangeable because the latter is functioning a metonym for the former, such that, as Lacan says, "desire is tied to prohibition."[49]) Perhaps because desire is something that gets "impressed" in and through "characters" in Wordsworth's text, the first book of the 1850 *The Prelude* is filled with tropes about writing, and even cryptography: "[W]ith pencil, and smooth slate / In square divisions parcelled out and all / With crosses and with cyphers scribbled o'er" (1.509–11). Wordsworth wants "to trace / How Nature . . . first / Peopled the mind with forms . . . And made me love them" (1.545–47). This "trace," by which love becomes, like other affects, a function of writing or drawing—procedures of repetition which, when they "people[] the mind," "people" it with "forms" instead of people. Love becomes the effect, rather than the cause, of the poem's psychic procedures, which are experienced as involuntary and even oppressive. Hence Nature, understood to be fantasmatic, "made me" in both senses: I am compelled to desire because I am produced as a surface for the Other's manipulation.

Lacan, like Wordsworth, is interested in the excess to this dangerous procedure, its untidiness in the face of its "workmanship." He reminds us that

> desire is . . . an illusory affirmation of synthesis. While it's always me who desires, this can only be grasped in me in the diversity of these desires. Behind this phenomenological diversity, behind the contradiction, the anomaly and the aporia of desire, . . . there exists a deeper relationship, which is the subject's relationship to life and, as one says, to the instincts.[50]

By understanding desire as an "aporia" that is internalized, synthetically, as "me," Lacan suggests a toric structure similar in shape to the internalized externalities that Wordsworth is exploring in the stolen boat scene. Hence the significance of Wordsworth's observation that the reconciliation of "discordant elements" remains "dark" to the subject, and that "airy phantasies," despite their necessary work in stabilizing the subject, still "oppress" by perpetually "floating loose." The synthesis that Wordsworth is tracking is illusory—the only coherent subject that emerges receives this apparent coherence by becoming subject to "the diversity of these desires." Yet that "phenomenological diversity" becomes the organizing principle of the subject, who has become, per the illusion, the subject of those desires. Subjectivity is an optical illusion, an "illusory affirmation," which makes possible the consequent illusion of figurative language, such as trope, which in turn necessitates the splitting of the "me" from the "I," a third illusion. All of this occurring before the subject moves around in the world in pursuit of lost enjoyment.

It is easy to be suspicious of Lacan's topological interests. Often, this final phase of Lacan's career is seen as a dead end, or a deliberate obscurantism. His biographer Elisabeth Roudinesco, for instance, suggests that "his entry into the world of knots led him to the destruction of what the matheme claimed to build," and that his investigations of topology were a "pact with the devil," according to which Lacan, fearing his declining powers, "sought the secret of the absolute" but "dissolved into the silent stupor of a Nietzschean aphasia" "in the heart of a community of irredentist mathematicians."[51] I think this overstates the break between the earlier Lacan of, say, the Rome Discourse—the talk in which, let us remember, Lacan began seriously to outline his interest in the torus—and the supposedly desperate and self-referential Lacan of the 1970s with his beleaguered team of irredentist mathematicians. I am arguing that the topological phase of Lacan's career can be seen as an outgrowth of his theories of fantasy and fantasy's role in delineating, and yet overlaying and tying together, the Imaginary, Symbolic, and Real. Lacan's topological thinking, far from abstracting us from exegetical analyses of texts, is what has enabled us to grasp how fantasy in *The Prelude* plays out at the level of the signifier—that is, at the level of literary language. In this sense, topology isn't a sustained diversion for Lacan, nor his ascension into the world of metaphor—and yet its facility for tracking dynamic situations and reading across levels enables us, in particular, to actually *analyze* metaphor. This attribute links Lacan's topological thought to the practice of literary criticism as much as to mathematics.

This is where a Lacanian approach to optical illusion most sharply diverges from Žižek's. "Perspective is not optics," Lacan says flatly in *Seminar XIII*:

It is not at all a matter in perspective of visual properties but, precisely, of this correspondence of what is established concerning the figures which are inscribed on one surface with those which, on another surface, are produced from the simple consistency established of the function of a point starting from which straight lines join this point to the articulations of the first figure, to find themselves, by crossing another surface, making another figure appear. We rediscover here the function of the screen.... The screen, here, functions as what is interposed between the subject and the world. It is not an object like any other. Something is painted on it. Before defining what is involved in representation, the screen already announces to us, at the horizon, the dimension of the representative of the representation. Before the world becomes representation, its representative—I mean the representative of the representation—emerges.[52]

This passage offers what is obviously a very complicated theory of mediation, one that will take some unpacking. Lacan is employing a very Shelleyan metaphor: the subject comes into the experience of perspective by learning to peer at and through a painted veil, which in turn screens off the subject's perception of the other forms of mediation—namely, writing, "interposed between the subject and the world." The discourse of writing is everywhere here: Lacan highlights a "correspondence" between "figures" which are "inscribed" over here, and the figures which appear as a "point" connecting the "lines" over there. The subject perceives not the object directly, but a reality constructed, extremely laboriously, through acts of language and writing that become co-implicated. He speaks of a "horizon" indicating an unreachable point between two screens, one of which is written upon by the other and whose sides, as with a Möbius strip, are conjoined. This "horizon" indicates a point of convergence between what is ultimately only a representation of a representation. The emphasis, then, is on the multiple and complementary ways that one's access to this "horizon" is multiply and densely mediated by writing or by language. To understand perspective, Lacan explains, we need to be able to think topologically, to think about perception as an act sustained by fantasy, which operates as lines cross from one surface to another to converge as a painted veil. The lines signal our distance from the Thing, at "the horizon." This is Lacan being proto-Deleuzian: we have here a surface upon which writing and recording transpires—lines are drawn and figures articulated—and that surface (which Deleuze and Guattari would call the body without organs) is produced by and through the machinery of desire.[53] Yet, unlike Deleuze and Guattari, Lacan is emphasizing how this process produces an individualized point of view, by affixing the subject within the visual field formed at the level of their own fantasy. The co-implication of the two surfaces at the horizon suggests a kind of Möbius strip: what had appeared to be two surfaces is revealed, through "the function of the screen," to be a single surface. A Möbius strip is derived from a particular way of cutting a torus: indeed for Lacan, "the subject begins with the cut" in the torus, which ushers the subject out of the imaginary."[54] Hence perspective is a topological problem rather than an optical one.

At the beginning of Book I, in a passage unmentioned by Žižek, Wordsworth implicitly beseeches us to read the upcoming stolen boat scene symbolically rather than literally. The speaker yearns for a place of Truth and invites us to track the psychodynamics of the later scene: "A discontented sojourner... Free as a bird to settle where I will. / What dwelling shall receive me?" (1.8–10). The speaker presents himself as an unmoored vessel adrift in the world, in search of a place of Truth, in a way that anticipates the way that the tree will be said to be the "usual home" of the stolen boat. And the speaker acknowledges that "mountings of the mind / Come fast upon me" (1.19–21), lines which prepare us, through the homophony between "mountings" and "mountains," for the famous scene shortly to follow, in which a mountain *comes fast upon me*. Wordsworth is training the reader to see the stolen boat episode not, primarily, as a trick of perspective but as an exploration of metaphor and its role in cognition. As Kneale has observed, Wordsworth stages "the symptom *as a repetition* of the scene" in a way that is "thoroughly rhetorical and semiotic."[55] That rhetorical symptom holds the subject together as a knot. It has sometimes been asserted that Lacan turned to topology to find "the Real of structure itself, structure with grammar peeled off it,"[56] meaning as a way to locate and describe psychic formations that might defy grammatical or syntactical rules. Wordsworth is showing the impossibility of that Lacanian endeavor: the structure as Real emerges, paradoxically, only in and through figural language.

The optical illusion that Žižek analyzes occurs once "the summit of [the] craggy ridge," upon which the speaker "fixed [his] view," is acknowledged to be "the horizon's utmost boundary" (1.370–71). This is a strange formulation for a number of reasons, all of which destabilize Žižek's discussion of this horizon as optical illusion. First, as the horizon is the name for an unimpeded view of where the land seems to meet the sky, it doesn't compute that a craggy ridge could begin to function as a horizon—it would, rather, prevent one from perceiving a horizon. Second, the term "horizon" names an optical illusion to start with, as the very term requires an eye to be built in to its structure and deceived. As the *OED* indicates, the horizon exists only in "a given point of view," because it is "the circle of contact with the earth's surface of a cone whose vertex is at the observer's eye."[57] So one cannot easily "fix one's view" upon the horizon, as "horizon" is the name for one's view—the poem is treating an internal feature of the visual scene as if it were the object of an independent gaze, which is misleading. It is an eye viewing itself, as if from outside—a toric structure if ever there were one. This becomes a descriptor of the gazing subject, in a sense: the mountain is an extimate object, which dramatizes a process internal to the gazing subject. And thus a second, figurative, meaning of "horizon" comes into play here: a "horizon" is also, according to the *OED*, "the boundary or limit of any 'circle' or 'sphere' of view, thought, action, etc. (often with reference to sense 1); that which bounds one's mental vision or perception."[58] The horizon, then, is all at once the boundary or limit of the subject's perception, the name for the delimitation of sense; meanwhile, paradoxically, it names the space obscured by the mountain and thus beyond one's perception. It is a limit to perception that, in taking itself as its own object, encompasses the zone beyond its own boundaries. It is a void that exists within the subject that holds at a remove a void that exists beyond the subject, and in that sense literally makes a torus of the speaker. It names the process by which that predicament is disavowed so that it can appear to be an external phenomenon, the object upon which one can fix one's gaze, so the "boundary" appears to be part of the "horizon" instead of "horizon" being the name for the boundary itself. To identify the "boundary" as part of a "horizon," or a property of the horizon, is to forget that the horizon is the name for the boundary to vision itself. We might call this fantasy. As the subject becomes retrofitted to accept the loss of sexual enjoyment at the level of the symbolic, that enjoyment, now perpetually deferred, appears as "an ideal point" of one's belief: "[E]njoying, as one might say, is at the horizon."[59] A horizon *is* the boundary to vision; it doesn't *have* a boundary. But Wordsworth's sentence attempts (impossibly) to disarticulate the horizon from the boundary. The mountain begins to function as the limit and anchoring point of meaning in this passage, and thus it is the phallus, not simply a figure for the phallus, and thus the distinction between its being and having a limit point is of the utmost importance, as we have already seen. There is a slippage, then, between the mountain's being a boundary and having a boundary that we can see as a displacement of the masturbatory experience the speaker has just been having in his boat.

What Žižek presumed to be an optical illusion, then, is the result of a topological and semantic confusion. Topology is capacitating these displaced perceptions, not the other way around. Faflak finds that Wordsworth is attempting, in Book I of *The Prelude*, to "work-through this ambivalence" of writing the uncontainable, in a failed attempt to contain the task of self-analysis, such that the poem presents a "symptomology," which "demands psychoanalysis."[60] In *Seminar XIII*, Lacan explains that

> this is what ought to reveal, materialize for us, the topology from which it results that something is produced in the construction of vision which is nothing other than what gives us the basis and the support of the phantasy, namely, a loss which is none other than the one that I call the loss of the [*objet petit a*], and which is none other than the look and, on the other hand, a division of the subject. What, in effect, does perspective teach us? Perspective teaches us that all the ocular lines which are parallel to the ground plane are going to determine on the figure plane a line which is none other than the horizon line. This horizon line is, as you know, the major reference point for any construction of perspective.[61]

As the subject forfeits the *objet petit a*—a fragment of enjoyment—through "the construction of vision," and constructs phantasy as a compensatory measure to help them accept this loss, the splitting of the subject becomes a topological event. Lacan's question, then, is slyer than it might first appear: in asking "[W]hat, in effect, does perspective teach us?" he subtly indicates that perspective is *itself* the effect of the splitting of the subject—that the orientation of the subject is created in relation to a "horizon line" which is constructed as a way of managing the loss of jouissance that created by any topological experimentation with subjectivity.

Lacan uses the metaphor of horizon to indicate how the subject, heading in search of the *objet petit a*, arrives into fantasy: "[W]hat I will have to develop then in the next seminars on the function of the [*objet petit a*], a certain value—I would not say of anticipation—but of horizon... it allows us, in a certain type of structure which has no other name than that of phantasy, to comprehend the determining function, determining in the manner of a support or of a mounting, I have said, which the [*objet petit a*] has in determining the splitting of the subject."[62] In *The Prelude*, a mountain—a "grim shape"—is the occasion for such a mounting. In reacting to the mounting/mountain, the subject

>   struck and struck again,
> And growing still in stature the grim shape
> Towered up between me and the stars, and still,
> For so it seemed, with purpose of its own
> And measured motion like a living thing,
> Strode after me. (1.380–85)

The poet is encountering his own abandoned jouissance. Because the subject has become caught in a chain of signification, the repressed jouissance returns as *das Ding* ("the grim shape"). The terror is not in the proximity of this towering object but in its distance: the diction emphasizes the experience of being blockaded, of experiencing things in a strangely delimited way—of "between me and the stars" and "so it seemed," or the way its motion seems "measured." The terror is that one's sexual enjoyment moves "with a purpose of its own"—its autonomy, its separation from the subject, is the horrifying part. The subject has come into a new fantasmatic structure that will sustain his desire as such, instead of fulfilling his needs or demands: hence "still," here, means the opposite of "still"—it means still more, still coming, as opposed to motionlessness. And yet its mobility, this unending longing, is becoming part of a repeated process: the repetition of "struck and struck again" finds its corollary in the repetition of "still." The repetition changes the meaning of "still" yet again: now "growing still" becomes something which "and still... strode after me." The stillness of the striding—quintessentially an act of motion rather than stillness—is a supplement ("and") superadded to its "growing still."

The Prelude, then, teaches its reader a significant Lacanian lesson: in a traumatic encounter such as is narrated in the stolen boat episode, the Real doesn't return as a horrifying interruption to one's desire, but serves as the support for one's fantasy. Fantasy and the Real work together to offer support to the subject and, indeed, each other: "The real supports the phantasy, the phantasy protects the real," as Lacan explains.[63] Indeed, the poet's "first encounter" with the Real, such as Wordsworth narrates it, "lies behind the phantasy" and supports it.[64] The subject is thus, as Wordsworth says, "fostered alike by beauty and by fear" (1.302), so that the looming mountain actually enables the speaker to emerge in his phallic jouissance, just as (conversely) the cloak of language, including the poet's uses of trope, shields the speaker from the all-consuming terror of that encounter. The subject can step into the "defiles of the signifier" because his losses appear to be offset by the fundamental fantasy, which assures him that he was once in possession of the now-debarred Thing and might get it back.[65] It is the story of how the subject becomes enmeshed within fantasy through the procedures of figural language. This is obviously not a straightforward process in the poem. Even if, for Lacan, in reading literature one "encounters the very structure of the subject that psychoanalysis sketches out," still it appears "that something retains its value in the very difficulty that these things present by being decanted."[66]

Notes

1. William Wordsworth, *The Prelude: 1799, 1805, 1850*, ed. Jonathan Wordsworth, M. H. Abrams, and Stephen Gill (New York: Norton, 1979), l. 1850: 1.120–23. Further citations to *The Prelude* given parenthetically.

2. Adela Pinch, *Strange Fits of Passion: Epistemologies of Emotion, Hume to Austen* (Stanford: Stanford University Press, 1996).

3. Joel Faflak, *Romantic Psychoanalysis: The Burden of the Mystery* (Albany: State University of New York Press, 2008), 80.

4. Paul A. Vatalaro, *Shelley's Music: Fantasy, Authority, and the Object Voice* (Farnham: Ashgate, 2009), 23, 21.

5. Jacques Lacan, "The Seminar of Jacques Lacan, Book XIV: The Logic of Phantasy, 1966–1967," trans. Cormac Gallagher n.d., sec. 1.2.1967.

6. Jacques Lacan, "The Seminar of Jacques Lacan, Book XXIV: *L'insu Que Sait de L'une-Bévue S'aile À Mourre*, 1976–1977," trans. Cormac Gallagher n.d., sec. Seminar 8: March 8, 1977.

7. Jeanne Lafont, "Topology and Efficiency," in *Lacan: Topologically Speaking*, ed. Ellie Ragland and Dragan Milovanovic, trans. Jeanne Lafont (New York: Other Press, 2004), 12, 22.

8. Jeanne Lafont, "The Ordinary Topology of Jacques Lacan," trans. Jack W. Stone, 1986, 26.

9. Jacques Lacan, "The Seminar of Jacques Lacan, Book XXII: R. S. I., 1974–1975," trans. Cormac Gallagher n.d., sec. 10.02.75.

10. Alexandre Leupin, *Lacan Today: Psychoanalysis, Science, Religion* (Other Press, LLC, 2004), 25–26.

11. Lacan, "Seminar XXII," 13.05.75.

12. Elisabeth Roudinesco, *Jacques Lacan: Outline of a Life, History of a System of Thought*, trans. Barbara Bray (New York: Columbia University Press, 1997), 363–67.

13. Jacques Lacan, *Écrits: The First Complete Edition in English*, trans. Bruce Fink (New York: Norton, 2006), 264.

14. Ibid.

15. Pierre Skriabine, "Clinic and Topology: The Flaw in the Universe," in *Lacan: Topologically Speaking*, ed. Ellie Ragland and Dragan Milovanovic, trans. Ellie Ragland and Véronique Voruz (New York: Other Press, 2004), 74.

16. Laura Claridge, *Romantic Potency: The Paradox of Desire* (Ithaca: Cornell University Press, 1992), 98–99; David Collings, *Wordsworthian Errancies: The Poetics of Cultural Dismemberment* (Baltimore: Johns Hopkins University Press, 1994), 135–38; Gary Farnell, "Wordsworth's The Prelude as Autobiography of An Orphan," *Romanticism on the Net*, no. 13 (1999): paras. 10–22, http://id.erudit.org/iderudit/005847ar; J. Douglas Kneale, "Symptom and Scene in Freud and Wordsworth," in *New Romanticisms: Theory and Critical Practice*, ed. David L. Clark and Donald C. Goellnicht (Toronto: University of Toronto Press, 1994), 135–63; Faflak, *Romantic Psychoanalysis*, 101–2.

17. Collings, *Wordsworthian Errancies*, 118–39.

18. Patricia Waugh, *Literary Theory and Criticism: An Oxford Guide* (Oxford: Oxford University Press, 2006), 285.

19. Joseph C. Sitterson, *Romantic Poems, Poets, and Narrators* (Kent: Kent State University Press, 2000), 71.

20. Kneale, "Symptom and Scene," 146, 143–44.

21. Slavoj Žižek, *The Parallax View* (Cambridge: MIT Press, 2006), 152–55; Slavoj Žižek, "Burned by the Sun," in *Lacan: The Silent Partners*, ed. Slavoj Žižek (London: Verso, 2006), 217–30.

22. Žižek, *Parallax*, 150.

23. Ibid.

24. Lacan, *Écrits*, 278–81.

25. Daniela Garofalo, "The Uses of Lacan in Recent British Romantic Studies," *Literature Compass* 10, no. 7 (2013): 569.

26. Lacan, *Écrits*, 263.

27. Ibid., 264.

28. Lafont, "Ordinary Topology," 28.

29. Lacan, "Seminar XXII," sec. 18.03.1975.

30. Ibid., sec. 8.4.1975.

31. Lafont, "Ordinary Topology," 24.

32. Mladen Dolar, "'I Shall Be With You On Your Wedding-Night': Lacan and the Uncanny," *October* 58 (Fall 1991): 6.

33. Jacques-Alain Miller, "Lacan's Later Teaching," trans. Barbara P. Fulks, *Lacanian Ink*, no. 21 (Spring 2003), http://www.lacan.com/frameXXI2.htm.

34. Lacan, "Seminar XXII," sec. 17.12.1974.

35. Ibid., 18.03.75.

36. Wordsworth, *The Prelude* 1.129 (1799 version) and 1.400 (1805), emphasis mine.

37. Judith Butler, *Gender Trouble: Feminism and the Subversion of Identity*, 10th Anniversary Edition (New York: Routledge, 1999), xxvii.

38. Judith W. Page, *Wordsworth and the Cultivation of Women* (Berkeley: University of California Press, 1994), 15–18; Collings, *Wordsworthian Errancies*, 137–39.

39. The *OED* gives J. Fellowes's *Reminiscences* (1824) as the earliest use of the phrase "the—of one's dreams," but finds usages for phrases such as "dream come true" for a cherished outcome as early as 1803. See *OED*, "dream, n.2 and adj," P4 and P2.

40. Robert Young, "The Eye and Progress of His Song: A Lacanian Reading of 'The Prelude,'" *Oxford Literary Review* 3, no. 3 (1979): 88.

41. Ibid., 84.

42. Jacques Lacan, "The Seminar of Jacques Lacan, Book XXI: Les Non-Dupes Errent, 1973–1974," trans. Cormac Gallagher n.d., 13.11.1973.
43. Lacan, "Seminar XXII," sec. 11.02.75.
44. Lacan, "Seminar XXIV," sec. Seminar 2: December 14, 1976.
45. Lacan, "Seminar XIV," sec. 16.11.1966.
46. Ellie Ragland, *The Logic of Sexuation: From Aristotle to Lacan* (Albany: State University of New York Press, 2004), 171.
47. Zak Watson, "Floating between Original and Semblance," in *Lacan: Topologically Speaking*, ed. Ellie Ragland and Dragan Milovanovic (New York: Other Press, 2004), 117.
48. Ibid., 120.
49. Lacan, *Écrits*, 723.
50. Jacques Lacan, *The Seminar of Jacques Lacan, Book V: Formations of the Unconscious*, ed. Jacques-Alain Miller, trans. Russell Grigg (Cambridge: Polity, 2017), 301.
51. Roudinesco, *Jacques Lacan*, 359.
52. Jacques Lacan, "The Seminar of Jacques Lacan, Book XIII: The Object of Psychoanalysis, 1965–1966," trans. Cormac Gallagher n.d., sec. 4.5.1966.
53. Gilles Deleuze and Félix Guattari, *Anti-Oedipus: Capitalism and Schizophrenia*, trans. Robert Hurley, Mark Seem, and Helen R. Lane (Minneapolis: University of Minnesota Press, 1983), 3–32.
54. Lacan, "Seminar XIV," sec. 16.11.1966.
55. Kneale, "Symptom and Scene," 149.
56. Ellie Ragland and Dragan Milovanovic, "Introduction: Topologically Speaking," in *Lacan: Topologically Speaking*, ed. Ellie Ragland and Dragan Milovanovic (New York: Other Press, 2004), xix.
57. "Horizon, N.," *OED Online* (Oxford University Press), sec. 1.a., accessed February 11, 2017, http://www.oed.com.
58. Ibid., sec. 2.b.
59. Lacan, "Seminar XXII," sec. 11.03.1975.
60. Faflak, *Romantic Psychoanalysis*, 77.
61. Lacan, "Seminar XIII," sec. 4.5.1966.
62. Ibid., sec. 27.4.1966.
63. Jacques Lacan, *The Seminar of Jacques Lacan, Book XI: The Four Fundamental Concepts of Psychoanalysis*, ed. Jacques-Alain Miller, trans. Alan Sheridan (New York: Norton, 1978), 41.
64. Ibid., 54.
65. Ibid., 149.
66. Lacan, *Écrits*, 630; Lacan, "Seminar XIII," sec. 15.12.1965.

Chapter Eight

TYRANNY AS DEMAND
Lacan Reading the Dreams of the Gothic Romance

MATT FOLEY

AMID THE ACOUSTICS of the Gothic romance, what do the polyphony of commanding voices that express often perverse or taboo desires tell us about demand? We should consider that, from a Lacanian perspective, the tyrant tends to conflate need with demand. That is, it is not only the desire of the Other that locates and typifies the perverse desire of the tyrannical subject but, too, their misrecognition (*méconnaissance*) of need itself as something constructed by the Other. Take, for instance, the symbolic law of primogeniture—the rights of the eldest son to inheritance as illuminated by the writings of Michel Foucault—that fuels the monomania of Manfred in *The Castle of Otranto* (1764). After losing his sickly heir, Manfred pursues his daughter-in-law-to-be Isabella as his bride and the future mother to another heir. As well as representing a cautionary critique of the powers of George III's royal prerogative, the tyrant's demand seems always to carry the force of a need to his subjects. The immediacy of such insatiable want is understood often by critics as a change in register from desire to drive. This view, however, eschews a more nuanced—and Lacanian—understanding of desire as emerging in *the space between* need and demand.[1] It is not that the tyrants of the Gothic simply have unquenchable needs—reflecting the registers of psychosis and of the drives—but that their demands are misrecognized as needs.

Often, this conflation gives rise to an overpowering—perhaps even taboo and incestuous—sense of sexual desire. As Lionel Bailly states, "[D]esire grows around objects that fulfil a psychological need, rather than a physical one: it grows most strongly around the objects around which the Subject is constructed."[2] Sexual discourse is a particularly desirous space because sex is a demand that, itself, often masquerades as a need: we must procreate for the continuation of the species, certainly, but, at least for Lacan, sex acts more as a recognition of love than a biological imperative such as the need for water. Summarizing Lacan's understanding of sex as essentially unrelated to need, Bailly suggests that, "as a drive with an object but no need, the sex drive therefore provides fertile ground for the seeds of desire, as there can be no demand that arises from it that is justifiable with a physical need."[3] The demand for sex is always already excessive and, as a result, desire proliferates in the subsequent gap that opens between a demand and the need from which it is alienated. Derived from the perceived desire of the Other for his lineage to come to an end, Manfred not only misrecognizes his demands as needs but his desire, as a consequence, becomes increasingly excessive, and clearly symbolic of incest. This "too much" of desire is a central preoccupation of the horror Gothic's many subsequent forms that can, at least in part, be traced back to the more transgressive imaginings of the Gothic romance. In the Gothic more broadly, the supposedly rational subject may be "over-whelmed by feeling and passion," in a series of encounters with tyranny that are "paralysing" in their incitement of "an excess of feeling... too intense for words."[4] Yet, the tyrant aspires to command as if he himself is the big Other (that is, the state or the crown) and, in so doing, he seeks to harness the power of language in order to force his demands upon the little others—his subjects—that surround him. The tyrant must ventriloquize the power and rhetorical force that once belonged to the prophecy that structures his desire.

This Gothicizing of demand as need is evident, too, in one of the last major iterations of the Gothic romance, Charles Maturin's *Melmoth the Wanderer* (1820).[5] Recalling and extending the storytelling techniques of Mary Shelley's *Frankenstein; or The Modern Prometheus* (1818), Maturin's novel consists of a series of frame and embedded narratives that intertwine to tell the story of the infernally damned Melmoth, who, as a Faustian figure, is condemned to roam the earth for more than a century to find another soul to take his place in his pact. Both Melmoth's gaze and his voice convey that he is no longer merely a mortal man but, through torment, possesses something of the supernatural demon. Seemingly embodying pure drive, he warns Stanton that "[m]y voice shall ring in your ears... the glance of these eyes shall be reflected from every object, animate or inanimate."[6] In "The Subversion of the Subject and the Dialectic of Desire in the Freudian Unconscious" (1966), Lacan argues that "the drive is what becomes of demand when the subject vanishes from it,"[7] and we can observe this disappearance of the subject at work in the monomania of the infernal Melmoth, as well as in Manfred's lust for Isabella in *The Castle of Otranto*. The Gothic tyrant *becomes* his demand and promises of certain death or symbolic downfall from the Other underpin the monomaniac dispositions of both Manfred and Melmoth. Yet, where the prophecy against the House of Manfred is writ large in *The Castle of Otranto*, the origin of the pact that binds Melmoth's soul to the devil remains hidden, off stage and seemingly censored from the story itself. Viewed from the perspective of the Lacanian future anterior, the Gothic tyrant is always already the fallen, doomed antihero that he becomes.[8] It is in turning to read *The Castle of Otranto* that this dynamic becomes most obvious.

The ethical power of the supernatural in *Otranto* is tied to its author's reverence for the dreamscape. As in much of the Gothic, to dream in *Otranto* is to experience truthful revelation, but importantly the textual dreams in the novel mirror the powerful symbolism of Walpole's inspirational dream for the story. Isabella's father, Frederic, is led by the imagery of a dream to discover a giant sabre in the wood at Joppa, upon which a prophecy is inscribed:

> Where'er a casque that suits this sword is found,
> With perils is thy daughter compass'd round:
> Alfonso's blood alone can save the maid,
> And quiet a long-restless prince's shade.[9]

Events are preordained and Manfred's downfall is inevitable: the "blood" of Alfonso, we discover with Frederic at Otranto, runs through Theodore's veins. If the supernatural and giant "casque" signifies the power of the Other that supersedes the tyrant's rule of perverse law then we should regard this being, too, as a conscious agent that may guide and manipulate the future. The giant knight in armour is symbolic of a power that lauds chivalry and rejects tyranny. Walpole's dream inspired a story in which dreaming itself forms part of a higher and just power. In turn, the true and ethically sound demand, for Walpole, comes through encountering a dream imagery that—from a psychoanalytic perspective—can be read as the first marker of an unexpressed and presumably prohibited desire.

Often intertwined, dreaming and prophecy are at the heart of the Gothic romance's narrative forms. The temporal register of prophecy in the Gothic resonates, from a Lacanian perspective, with the logic of the future anterior. Lacan reflects that "what is realized in my history is . . . what I will have been, given what I am in the process of becoming."[10] In this conceptual model of the self, there is "a retroversion effect by which the subject, at each stage, becomes what he was (to be) [*était*] before that, and 'he will have been' is announced in the future perfect tense."[11] In his translation, Bruce Fink highlights Lacan's original word choice for "was (to be):" "était." Fink's note draws attention to the lexical similarity of *était* to *état* (the state). Louis VIX's (in)famous proclamation of absolute sovereign power—"L'état, c'est moi" (I am the state)—sits in pronounced juxtaposition with the late-eighteenth-century Whiggish sense of statehood to which the father of Gothic literature Horace Walpole subscribed. Walpole and his fellow parliamentarians argued that the power of the sovereign should be delineated. As I suggest below in my reading of *The Castle of Otranto*, the tyrant's relationship to prophecy situates the future anterior as the temporal register of both the Gothic state and the self. Reading his essay "The Subversion of the Subject," I draw from Lacan's understanding of desire as emerging in the gap between demand and need to explore the Gothic tyrant's attempts to reclaim his desire from the Other in the face of his prophesized downfall.[12] In this conflict between the tyrant and the big Other two distinct models of symbolic law emerge that compete for rule: the perverse law of tyranny and a more chivalrous (and powerful) divine law of the Other. If, as Lacan puts it, "the Other... defines the parameters of the subject's demand" then the tyrant's conflation of need with demand in the Gothic seems to place this relationship in crisis until, through supernatural means, the big Other as an agent of justice reasserts order and its prophecy is fulfilled. The supernatural machinery that arrives from the big Other in *Otranto* is inextricably linked to the dream symbolism that inspired Walpole's writing of the Gothic text; while the prophetic dream within the text itself acts as a divine demand for justice that usurps tyrannical power.

The Gothic's status as a dream literature is a particularly important context for reading its representations of excessive desire. As Fink puts it, "in both hysteria and obsession, obstacles are placed in the way of any possible realization of desire (except, of course, in dreams, fantasies, or daydreams—the wish fulfilment *they* stage does not lead to the fading of desire)."[13] The liberating aesthetic of the Gothic was lauded by André Breton, the leader of those avant-garde dreamers the surrealists, as a literature free from the totalizing tendencies of realism and, in turn, as potentially revolutionary in its symbolism.[14] Invoking the powerful dream that inspired his Gothic romance in a letter to his friend the Reverend Cole, Walpole provides an account of the genesis of *Otranto*:

> I waked one morning in the beginning of last June from a dream, of which all I could recover was, that I had thought myself in an ancient castle (a very natural dream for a head filled like mine with Gothic story) and that on the uppermost staircase I saw a gigantic hand in armour. In the evening I sat down and began to write, without knowing in the least what I intended to say or relate.... I was so engrossed with my tale, which I completed in less than two months, that one evening I wrote from the time I had drunk my tea, about six o'clock, till half an hour after one in the morning.[15]

The parallels that we may draw between Walpole's moment of creation, which in many ways marks the beginning of the Gothic aesthetic in literature and its broader, often troubling responses to modernity, and the surrealist preference for automatic writing—a variation upon Freudian free association—are significant.

Some time ago now, in her account of gendered dreaming in the eighteenth-century novel, which includes a reading of the Gothic as a space in which masculine nightmares could proliferate, Margaret Ann Doody recognized that in *Otranto*, "Walpole refuses to give way to belief in the reality, at any level, of what he was writing." Doody then goes on to criticize *Otranto*'s "silly machinery" and "ridiculous images"—that is, she draws attention to its surrealist and dream-inspired imagery.[16] The symbolic power of *Otranto*'s strange giant casque, which I read below, may lie partly in Walpole's deference to the original imagery of his dream. For psychoanalysts, the dreamwork is a rebus to be read: a coiling of desire later unravelled through the process of analysis. In *The Interpretation of Dreams* (1899), Freud notes that "[d]reams are brief, meagre and laconic in comparison with the range and wealth of the dream-thoughts."[17] Freud believed primarily in *listening* to speech, and he would often take only the briefest of written notes after a therapeutic session. It is in the sliding of the signifier—that is, the ways in which other words or homophones cluster around the magic word that appears and reappears in a patient's case notes—that the truth of desire may be found.[18] Like the dreamscape, the Gothic is a space in which normally prohibited desires may find their expression. In the dream, for instance, desire is evident in the extravagance of what we wish for: our hunger and thirst may be satiated by bread and water but we dream of a lavish buffet and bottles of champagne. In his essay "Creative Writers and Day Dreaming" (1908), Freud draws a connection between the waking "phantasies" of creative writers and dreaming with the important caveat that dreams symbolize desires of which "we are ashamed" and that "repressed wishes of this sort and their derivatives are only allowed to come to expression in a very distorted form."[19]

Intuitively, we may read the striking symbol of Walpole's dream—that "gigantic hand in armour"—as evident of the author's desire for a return to pre-modernity—that is, those medieval and chivalric codes that were so characteristic of the "Gothic story" or romance of which Walpole's head was so "full" (i.e., the castles and armory of a gallant past, the heroine and her courtly beloved, and all of the other trappings of the Gothic Romance). Yet, the novel's "gigantic" supernatural machinery is also imbued with the illogical and primary power of dream symbolism. Although absent from Walpole's account of his dream, in the published version of *Otranto* threat is embodied in the form of its tyrant, Manfred, whose actions provide this Gothic romance with its transgressive moments—a side to the genre that would be accentuated in Matthew Lewis's *The Monk* (1796). In the preamble to her brother John's satire of the Gothic, "Sir Bertrand: A Fragment," Anna Laetitia Aikin (later Barbauld) recognises the paradox of the readerly enjoyment of scenes of pain and fright:

> The pain of suspense, and the irresistible desire of satisfying curiosity, when once raised, for our eagerness to go quite through an adventure, though we suffer actual pain during the whole course of it. We rather chuse [*sic*] to suffer the smart pang of a violent emotion than the uneasy craving of an unsatisfied desire.[20]

Aikin's suggestion that desire may be resolutely satisfied goes against the Lacanian understanding of desire as indicative of lack. Nevertheless, this privileging of a desire for knowledge over artistry suggests that the tyrant's refusal to give up on his own desire is mirrored in the voracious appetite for the resolution of terror and mystery that characterized representations of the quixotic readership of the Gothic romance. Aikin's account of the aesthetic appeal or pleasure of Gothic horrors, though, does little to address *why* the compulsion to satisfy desire should supersede those feelings of disgust—or, less spectacularly, boredom, as Aikin later points out—that are the typical affects associated with Gothic readerly encounters. For Lacan, when there is a gap in knowledge or, more specifically, "truth," it may indicate the sexual encounter's resistance to signification: "[W]hen I talk about a hole in truth... it is the negative aspect that appears in anything to do with the sexual, namely its inability to aver. That is what a psychoanalysis is all about."[21] In the Gothic, the gap in knowledge of the protagonist or heroine (which is rendered, for instance, by Ann Radcliffe in her novels often as a paternal secret) is juxtaposed elsewhere with the sense that the Other knows too much—such as in the prophecies and supernatural machinery of *Otranto* that I read below.

Before I turn to reading Manfred's desire at more length, it seems pertinent to ask: why is this phantasmatic screen of nostalgia and chivalry—that is, the Gothic romance—so frequently preoccupied with tyranny?[22] Certainly, the tyrant in these tales does not only perform an ideological or political function, as drawn from by Whig politicians like Walpole or later Matthew Gregory "Monk" Lewis, who used the trope to promote a democratic check upon sovereign power.[23] Their textual positioning and characteristics in this literature of dreams can also be read as metaphoric (or as a condensation) of the *anxiety* that comes with one's desire, as Lacan puts it, being the desire of the other/Other. The tyrant's excessive desire for mastery over the other/Other produces much of the subjective violence of the plot—those sexual or personal assaults acted out against the entrapped heroine, for instance. These more baroque sorts of violence should not distract attention away from the underlying and disturbing interruptions to the symbolic order in the Gothic, which are so central to its stagings of entrapped and troubled subjectivities. The most prominent and horrifying encounter with desire and alterity for the tyrant themselves is that they conceive of the big Other—the structuring higher power of the text—as desiring their downfall.²⁴ That is, for all the sadistic desires that the tyrant shows for little others (the heroine, the hero)—where such obscenities are pronounced in the male Gothic mode and inferred, too, in those female Gothic fictions that are patterned as Bluebeard tales—it is their fear of the desire of the big Other that propels their monomaniac or obsessive behaviors.²⁵ Manfred is doomed as his downfall is prophesized, albeit elliptically, in an ancient saying *"that the castle and lordship of Otranto should pass from the present family, whenever the real owner should be grown too large to inhabit it."*²⁶ That it is "difficult to make any sense of this prophecy" does not stop us, Manfred, or, indeed the "populace" of Otranto in attempting to decipher it.²⁷ From the very first page of the first Gothic novel, then, the narrator implies that a praxis of close reading, and perhaps even cryptography, provides some of the suspense of the genre. It is the exact economies that convert this fear of the desire of the Other into tyrannical action that I now explore, where such a consideration relies upon making a clearer distinction between Lacan's categories of demand, need, and desire.

Even if Lacan did not directly read the early, at times surreal, Gothic aesthetic, his understandings of dreaming and desire can illuminate the genre's powerful imagery. An influential text for Lacan's return to Freud, *The Interpretation of Dreams* could be described too, however playfully, as the first Gothic text of the twentieth century.²⁸ While the late-eighteenth century Gothic romance marks the beginning of a modern discourse of interpreting dream logic by providing a hermeneutics of the desire of the other/Other. David Sigler has pointed out that there is "nothing necessarily psychoanalytic about the presence of dreams in gothic novels; usually, though, these dreams foretell the future ... as was a common assumption about dreams in the medical and medico-literary discourses of the early nineteenth century."²⁹ Reading closely Victoria's response to dreaming in Charlotte Dacre's *Zofloya, or The Moor* (1806), however, Sigler also argues convincingly that she displays an exceptional astuteness for interpreting her dreams in terms of desire. In this sense, at the beginning of the nineteenth century the Gothic starts to prefigure later psychoanalytic thought even if dream-reading in Walpole's mid-eighteenth century novel is less evolved and aligned more closely with portentous interpretation.

Lacan's work touches only tangentially upon the Gothic aesthetic in his discussions of the work of Edgar Allan Poe, ghostliness, the dead and Freud's famous essay on the uncanny. His most extended response to the Freudian uncanny is found in his seminar *Anxiety* (1962–1963) in which he describes Freud's essay on the *unheimlich* as "indispensable for broaching the question of anxiety."³⁰ During this seminar, Lacan demonstrates a knowledge of E. T. A. Hoffmann's writing that extends beyond Freud's reading if only to reiterate it. In particular,

Lacan echoes and paraphrases Freud's reference to Hoffmann's *The Devil's Elixirs* (1815) as a novel in which "*all the occasions when the reaction of the* unheimlich *may occur are clarified.*"[31] Although both Freud and Lacan emphasize the linguistic play of the signifier in their readings of the uncanny, Lacan's visual metaphor for the *unheimlich* object is useful to conceptualizing Walpole's dream. Lacan argues that "*the dreadful, the shady, the disturbing,* everything by which we translate, as best we can in French, the magisterial German *Unheimlich,* presents itself through little windows. The field of anxiety is situated as something framed."[32] The spatial frame in Walpole's dream is the "upper staircase" of "an ancient castle" and the *unheimlich* object is the "gigantic hand in armour." Thus, while the Gothic Romance as a genre reiterates the framing of Walpole's dream in its many figurations of labyrinthine castles, the original *unheimlich* and anxiety-inducing "gigantic" object of the genre has been ridiculed and often overlooked. A Lacanian reading brings the novel's unique supernatural machinery and its relationship to desire back into focus.

Receiving a lukewarm reception upon the publication of its second edition, *Otranto* went from being heralded as an object of antiquarian intrigue upon its first release—when Walpole masqueraded it as an old translation of an ancient found manuscript—to being understood as a strangely unmodern and uncivilized hybrid of—as Walpole himself puts it in his 1765 "Preface"—the novel and the medieval Romance. In her dialogue *The Progress of Romance* (1785), Clara Reeve outlines a definition of the romance and novel that resonates closely with Walpole's understanding: "The Romance is an heroic fable, which treats of fabulous persons and things.—The Novel is a picture of real life and manners, and of the times in which it is written."[33] As Fred Botting puts it, the inter-generic designation "'Gothic romance' is more applicable than 'Gothic novel' as it highlights the link between medieval narratives of love, chivalry and adventure."[34] If we consider the plot of *Otranto* in classical or even novelistic terms it seems more farce than romance novel. For instance, Manfred's expression of guilt in the story's closing section is entirely incongruous with his previously frenzied and monomaniacal character. As the narrative reaches its end, and the prophecy against his house becomes fulfilled, he gives an extraordinary declaration of contrition as he fears that he has offended the divine authority of the big Other: "To heap shame upon my own head is all the satisfaction I have left to offer the offended heaven! . . . may this bloody record be a warning to future tyrants!"[35] The "record" to which Manfred refers is surely his murdering of his daughter Matilda in the "consecrated place" of the Church.[36] The novel's imagery, particularly the supernatural machinery that haunt, pursue, and ultimately delegitimize Manfred, seems as absurd as the plot. Recognized by even those writers Walpole would influence, such as Clara Reeve and Anna Aikin, *Otranto*'s aesthetic flaws are stark. Yet, the tyrant imagined by Walpole had a profound impact upon the imagery of the Gothic romance as it emerged in the latter half of the eighteenth century. Clara Reeve's *The Old English Baron* (1778) and Ann Radcliffe's *A Sicilian Romance* (1791), to give but two examples, show Walpole's influence but refrain from the lavish investment in supernatural machinery that characterizes *Otranto*'s aesthetic. *Otranto* is a cautionary tale and the message that it sends to sovereign power is clear: authority must be delineated.

The Gothic tyrant is typically an obsessive whose demands are misrecognized as needs and for whom the maintenance of a familial lineage is the principal *raison d'être* of being. Yet, there are more subtle contours to consider from a Lacanian perspective. The fight that *Otranto* stages between the tyrant and divined fate creates an ethics of demand—which we may even read as hierarchical—in which the demand of the big Other supersedes and seeks to uncouple the conflation of demand with need by the monomaniacal tyrant. One of the central instruments that Manfred uses to command those whom he encounters is the authority of his voice, which imbues even his most outrageous of commands with the authority of the sovereign or father. Like its visual counterpart the gaze, for Lacan the voice is a part object—that is, a structuring part of the subject that they themselves can never fully grasp. As Mladen Dolar has noted, Lacan emphasizes the extra-symbolic side to the voice and he sees it as a carrier of language that is "against *logos*"—it is "the voice as the other of *logos*, its radical alterity."[37] The voice in the Gothic is an instrument of power: the sovereign or father's speech may imbue in his subjects revere and terror. The content of his speech may be obscene, but the voice is the medium through which Manfred delivers his demand as need. For instance, he explicitly disavows the power of the supernatural to undermine his plans when he interrupts Theodore and Isabella's first encounter, saying that "I will find her [Isabella] in spite of enchantment."[38] Intriguingly, this voice of (perverse) authority brings with it a certain element of rationality: the law is reliable, it grounds us, it is sceptical of supernatural means. In other words, the commanding voice of the tyrant seems to normalize even his taboo desires, such as Manfred's demand to marry Isabella and undertake symbolic incest. Theodore's power to resist Manfred's command seems to be gained in collaboration with the supernatural apparitions: "[T]he cheeks of the enchanted casque," at first thought to have crushed Theodore, actually broke through the rafters of the floor and provide him with an escape route to Isabella.[39] The supernatural, then, not only revenges the transgenerational secret that underpins Manfred's usurpation of the crown. In this dream-like novel, it acts as a more powerful arbiter of law than Manfred's illegitimate commands.

Theodore is able to challenge the authority of Manfred's voice as he is a stranger to Otranto and to its tyrannical power. Not only does the tyrant's voice interrupt Theodore's saving of Isabella, it also later disrupts the life-affirming and romantic bond that forms between Theodore and Matilda.[40] Her speculation over the uncanny similarity that Theodore's features bear to the visage of Alfonso's portrait—that so haunts her father—is cut short by a voice that "grew louder at every word" on Manfred's approach.[41] As a stranger, Theodore bemoans and names "the injustice" that Manfred has subjected him to and states defiantly that he has "done a good deed in delivering the princess from thy tyranny."[42] In Ann Radcliffe's *A Sicilian Romance* the heroine, Julia, is, too, "thrilled . . . with a universal tremour; the dread of discovery so strongly operated upon her mind" after hearing her father's voice approach.[43] Julia fears detection as she has trespassed upon the forbidden wing of the castle Mazzini in which she discovers that her mother has been secretly imprisoned for years. Like Manfred's, the Marquis de Mazzini's voice imbues terror in the subject—in both cases, the daughter—who has discovered a secret that threatens tyrannical authority. The tyrant does not merely conflate their need with demand but his subjects and his family internalize this fusion as law itself. In the dark recesses of the Gothic's medieval setting, the voice becomes the bearer of rule, since, as Foucault has noted, in premodern times the power of the gaze was less pervasive in controlling and demarcating the subject than it became after the invention of modern systemic surveillance.[44]

Manfred is driven to villainy in order to protect a transgenerational secret that only the big Other knows. Ricardo, the grandfather of Manfred, was lord chamberlain to Alfonso when he poisoned the king and then fashioned a counterfeit will that named himself as heir to the throne. Thus, the sins of the grandfather foreshadow the fall of the grandchild. Yet, at the end of the novel, Manfred demonstrates unexpected contrition. In so doing, he signs his papers of abdication and adopts "the habit of religion" in a nearby convent once the revelation of his illegitimacy, which the omnipotent big Other always knew, comes to light.[45] The confession of his sins and his willingness to do penance for them seem entirely out of step with Manfred's earlier monomaniacal demands to maintain his bloodline through the most perverse and murderous of means. A generous reading of this radical change of character would not consider it merely an absurd change in register but take into account the effects of this transformation more closely. Manfred is not disposed of as the typical tyrant should be: he is not murdered by a chivalrous knight with claims to his land, poisoned by a revengeful wife, or imprisoned after being brought to justice through trial. This first Gothic tyrant is, instead, silenced, and delegitimized through public confession. There is a certain irony, then, that the supposed anti-Catholic attitude of the Gothic is handled ambivalently in Walpole's foundational text. Religious habit provides sanctity in *Otranto* and the central religious character—Father Jerome—holds the knowledge that allows Theodore to inherit his rightful lands. Yet, if we consider Manfred's confession in terms solely of *Otranto*'s staging of the tyrannical voice as the agent of perverse law then it becomes necessary to his disempowerment that he should vocalize his contrition before taking to the monastic life. That is, the strain of the voice that is a threat to life-affirming subjectivity—including the imaginary fantasy of love between heroine and hero—must be defused through public shaming before a new order of rule can assert itself.

Scholars of the Gothic romance have drawn from Lacanian models of critical inquiry for many years. Dale Townshend, for instance, notes that a number of the foundational studies of Gothic from the 1970s and '80s rely upon psychoanalysis "often in its crudest and most diffuse terms" for their "critical language."[46] In true psychoanalytic fashion, this critical zeitgeist of the Gothic academy returned in the late 1990s and early 2000s as critics came to "fuse together psychoanalytic and historicist modes of enquiry."[47] More recently established studies in the field tend to draw from Lacanian understandings of law and the symbolic order to account for Gothic tyranny and perversity. In her predominantly Žižekian reading of the genre, Sue Chaplin recognizes that "Gothic fictions bring to the fore the law's obscene dimension."[48] The word or *logos* may be understood to represent law as constituted by the paternal metaphor and the emergence of the symbolic order for the subject. Yet it is sustained by a dangerous surplus that speaks to Gothic registers: an excess of jouissance that is persecutory both to the self and the other.

The demand/need/desire triad complicates such readings. As I argue above, tyrannical law relies upon the timbral voice to assert itself and to dominate or command not only feminine or tortured subjects, but also to approach an impossible jouissance that comes to sustain the subject at a time at which their symbolic power is under threat. This is the point at which tyrannical command most forcefully fuses need with demand. Paying close attention to Lacan's formulation of demand in "The Subversion of the Subject," I argue that in constructing their own desire the tyrant "imagines he is the Other in order to ensure his own jouissance"—that is, in order to maintain his familial lineage and privileges.[49] This misrecognition indicates a lack in the tyrant's power that means their domineering commands will always already fall short of their aim; and, in turn, a fatalistic sense of ever-impending defeat leads them to view and present their demands (for satisfaction) as absolute needs (for their survival). It is in the process of this final conflation that desire takes on its excessive forms—incestuous, sadistic, torturous, etc.—so as to draw attention to the widening gap between demand and need that seems to become starker the more strongly the tyrant presents their demands for survival.

What are the ramifications for Lacanian thought of such a reading? Considered in light of current psychoanalytic understandings, *Otranto*'s supernatural machinery suspends—even transcends—the Lacanian idea that the big Other, which is inscribed in language, has no other itself. The divine machinery in *Otranto* is intent on undermining its other: the tyranny of Manfred. In his reading of its relationship to need and desire in Lacan's work, Philippe Van Haute argues that demand

> pertains fundamentally to linguistically articulated need. It is enacted in the order of language. The subject that articulates the demand is thereby directed to another subject—I ask you for an object that can satisfy my need—and in this sense, demand implies an essentially intersubjective relationship.[50]

Otranto, though, delegitimizes a certain kind of demand that is linguistically articulated—that is, the tyrant's desperate pleas to maintain his status as the principal agent of law. Indeed, even extrasymbolic demand—delivered in imagery through dreams and associated with the big Other—takes primacy over the dominant voice in the text. Evident in the deep hollow groan that emanates from the vaults of John Aikin's "Sir Bertrand, a fragment" (1773), for instance, or in "the low hollow" moaning of the incarcerated mother of Radcliffe's *A Sicilian Romance*, the Gothic consistently returns to a formulation of demand as being beyond the signifier.[51] In *Otranto*, too, a "deep and hollow groan, which seemed to come from above" is ludicrously explained away by Matilda and Theodore as "the effect of pent-up vapours."[52] Emanating from the inscrutable big Other, the groan performs the same function as portentous dreams or supernatural machinery: it demands that its prophecy, at a moment at which Theodore declares he can forget his injuries at the hands of Manfred, be heeded above all other laws of courtship, reconciliation, or tyranny. In reading the linguistics of Ferdinand de Saussure, Mladen Dolar once wrote that "the voice is the impending element that one has to be rid of in order to initiate a new science of language."[53] What *Otranto* suggests is that the voice of the tyrant, as the primary object of law in premodern times, must be muted or vocalize an unexpected confession for a new political order to establish itself. *Otranto* ends with the confirmation of a new epoch. Theodore will marry Isabella *in memoriam* of his murdered love Matilda so that "he could forever indulge the melancholy that had taken possession of his soul" since her death.[54] The transgenerational secret is revealed, certainly, but we should not overlook the disempowering of Manfred's voice and command—the dissociation of his demands with need—that allows for this smooth transition of power. This changing of the guard has been initiated by a big Other that regards tyrannical law as its absolute alterity and demands its subversion through dreams and prophecy.

Notes

1. Lionel Bailly, *Lacan: A Beginner's Guide* (Oxford: Oneworld, 2009), 113. As Lacan puts it in "The Subversion of the Subject and the Dialectic of Desire in the Freudian Unconscious": "Desire begins to take shape in the margin in which demand rips away from need, this margin being the one that demanded—whose appeal can be unconditional only with respect to the Other—opens up in the guise of the possible gap need may give rise to here, because it has no universal satisfaction (this is called 'anxiety')" (Lacan, *Écrits*, 689).

2. Ibid., 113.

3. Ibid., 116.

4. Fred Botting, *Gothic*, 2nd ed. (New York: Routledge, 2013), 6.

5. Referring to the genre of the Gothic romance, Chris Baldick suggests that "Maturin's achievement in *Melmoth the Wanderer*... was to have breathed some belated vitality—albeit of a strangely nervous and galvanic sort—into what seemed an exhausted convention" ("Introduction," in Charles Maturin, *Melmoth the Wanderer* (Oxford: Oxford University Press, 1998), vii-xix, ix.)

6. Charles Maturin, *Melmoth the Wanderer* (Oxford: Oxford University Press, 1998), 44, original emphasis.

7. Lacan, *Écrits*, trans. Bruce Fink (New York: Norton, 2006), 692.

8. Underpinning these issues is the sense that enjoyment or jouissance is, ultimately, barred to the speaking subject. As Lacan puts it,

> We must keep in mind that jouissance is prohibited [*interdite*] to whoever speaks, as such—or, put differently, it can only be said [*dite*] between the lines by whoever is a subject of the Law, since the Law is founded on that very prohibition. Indeed, were the Law to give the order, "*Jouis!*" ["Enjoy!" or "Come!"] the subject could only reply '*J'ouïs*' ['I hear']. (Lacan, *Écrits*, 696)

9. Horace Walpole, *The Castle of Otranto* (Oxford: Oxford University Press, 2014), 76.

10. Lacan, *Écrits*, 247.

11. Ibid., 684.

12. Bailly, *Lacan*, 111.

13. Bruce Fink, *A Clinical Introduction to Lacanian Psychoanalysis: Theory and Technique* (London: Harvard University Press, 1997), 51.

14. Initially adopting Freud's ideas to treat WWI veterans suffering from shell shock, Breton later adapted Freud's interest in the dreamwork for his own artistic and political purposes, and he saw in the Gothic novel a dream logic that beckoned towards the radical potential of the imagination. Breton referenced that "admirable" novel *The Monk* in his "First Manifesto of Surrealism" published in 1924 (André Breton, "From the First Manifesto of Surrealism," in *Modernism: An Anthology*, ed. Lawrence Rainey (Oxford: Blackwell, 2005), 718–41, 723).

15. Cited in Dale Townshend, *Terror and Wonder: The Gothic Imagination* (London: British Library, 2014), 10.

16. Margaret Anne Doody, "Deserts, Ruins and Troubled Waters: Female Dreams in Fiction and the Development of the Gothic Novel." In *The Eighteenth-Century English Novel*, ed. Harold Bloom (Philadelphia: Chelsea House, 2004), 71–112, 92.

17. Sigmund Freud, *The Penguin Freud Library*, eds. Angela Richards and Albert Dickson, trans. James Strachey, 14 vols. (Harmondsworth: Penguin, 1984), vol. 4, 383.

18. For a more detailed discussion see Bruce Fink's account of dream interpretation and psychoanalytic technique in his *Fundamentals of Psychoanalytic Technique: A Lacanian Approach for Practitioners* (New York: W. W. Norton and Company, 2007), 101–25.

19. Sigmund Freud, *The Penguin Freud Library*, eds. Angela Richards and Albert Dickson, trans. James Strachey, 14 vols. (Harmondsworth: Penguin Ltd, 1984), vol. 14, 136.

20. Anna Laetitia Aikin, "On the Pleasure Derived from Objects of Terror," in *Gothic Readings: The First Wave 1764–1840*, ed. Rictor Norton (London: Leicester University Press, 2000), 281–83, 282.

21. Jacques Lacan, *My Teaching*, trans. David Macey (London: Verso, 2008), 22.

22. An influential mediation upon chivalry of the time can be found in Bishop Richard Hurd's *Letters on Chivalry and Romance* (1762). These letters represent a cultural re-evaluation of literature of the past, which challenged the supremacy of the pope by critiquing neo-classical principles of art. Demonstrating a preference for Feudalism, Hurd uses the term 'Gothic' to mean old or medieval and applies it to Edmund Spenser's *The Faerie Queen* (1590). In Hurd's third letter, he defines chivalry as being related to prowess, gallantry, and the honour of knighthood. To

be chivalrous, then, is to demonstrate the courtesy and affability of the chivalric code that, at least from this perspective, venerated womanhood.

23. As Dale Townshend has summarized, before its generic application to literatures of terror and horror, the term "Goth" already carried certain connotations of democracy in the work of a series of British eighteenth-century historiographers. Townshend notes in particular that "the Gothic tribe that was said to originate in Germany or central and Northern Europe 'swarmed' through various parts of the known world, bringing with them the powers of civilization, democracy, Liberty and Enlightenment as they did so. Perhaps unsurprisingly, this sense of the past was especially popular amongst English historiographers of a Whiggish political affiliation in the eighteenth-century, in all their investments in teleological narratives of continuous progress and improvement'" (Dale Townshend, "Introduction," in *The Gothic World*, eds. Dale Townshend and Glennis Byron (New York: Routledge, 2013), xxiv–xlvi, xxix).

24. There is also a psychoanalytic reading to be made of these stories' tendencies to reiterate and repeat certain character types, particularly the triad of hero, heroine and tyrannical impediment to their love.

25. For useful overviews of the male and female Gothic modes, see Andrew Smith and Diana Wallace's "The Female Gothic: Then and Now" (*Gothic Studies* 6, no. 1 (May 2004): 1–7) and David Punter and Glennis Byron's chapter on "Female Gothic" in their book *The Gothic* (Oxford: Blackwell, 2004. 273–82).

26. Walpole, *Otranto*, 17, original emphases.

27. Ibid.

28. For a reading of Freud's letters to Wilhelm Fleiss undertaken from the perspective of Romantic Gothic masculinities, see Ellen Brinks's *Gothic Masculinity: Effeminacy and the Supernatural in English and German Romanticism* (London: Associated University Presses, 2003)

29. David Sigler, *Sexual Enjoyment in British Romanticism: Gender and Psychoanalysis, 1753–1835* (Montreal and Kingston: McGill-Queen's University Press, 2015), 159.

30. Jacques Lacan, *The Seminar of Jacques Lacan, Book X: Anxiety, 1962–1963*, edited by Jacques-Alain Miller, translated by A. R. Price (Cambridge: Polity Press, 2016), 41.

31. Ibid., 48, original emphases.

32. Ibid., 74–75, original emphases.

33. Clara Reeve, *The Progress of Romance* (New York: The Facsimile Text Society, 1930), 111.

34. Botting, *Gothic*, 23.

35. Walpole, *Otranto*, 103–04.

36. Ibid., 104.

37. Mladen Dolar, *A Voice and Nothing More* (Cambridge: MIT Press, 2006), 52, original emphasis.

38. Walpole, *Otranto*, 29.

39. Ibid., 29–30.

40. Ibid., 51.

41. Ibid.

42. Ibid.

43. Ann Radcliffe. *A Sicilian Romance* (Oxford: Oxford University Press, 2008), 175.

44. Foucault explicitly reads the genre of the Gothic Romance in his essay "The Eye of Power" (1974) and draws attention to its cavernous, occluded, and dark settings as particularly anxiety-inducing given, as Foucault reads it, modernity's contemporaneous turn towards a model of law that relies upon visuality and light as prerequisites for various authoritative gazes to enforce their power over the subject.

45. Walpole, *Otranto*, 105.

46. Dale Townshend, *The Orders of Gothic: Foucault, Lacan, and the Subject of Gothic Writing 1764–1820* (New York: AMS, 2007), 16.

47. Ibid., 13.

48. Sue Chaplin, *The Gothic and the Rule of Law, 1764-1820* (Basingstoke: Palgrave, 2007), 153.

49. Lacan, *Écrits*, 699.

50. Philippe Van Haute, *Against Adaptation: Lacan's 'Subversion' of the Subject* (New York: Other Press, 2002), 104.

51. Ann Radcliffe, *A Sicilian Romance* (Oxford: Oxford University Press, 2008), 35.

52. Walpole, *Otranto*, 68.

53. Mladen Dolar, "The Object Voice," in *Gaze and Voice as Love Objects*, eds. Renata Saleci and Slavoj Žižek (Durham: Duke University Press, 1996) 7–31, 7.

54. Walpole, *Otranto*, 105.

Chapter Nine

Jouissance, Obscene Undersides, and Utopian/Dystopian Formations in Sarah Scott's *Millenium Hall* and Mary Shelley's *The Last Man*

EVAN GOTTLIEB

TRADITIONALLY, psychoanalysis has not been kind to utopia. For Freud, after all, society is built upon the repression and sublimation of humanity's natural aggression, sexual and otherwise; since the "death instinct" from which this aggression springs is as innate to us as "the work of Eros... which shares world-dominion with it," there is no hope of putting an end to "this battle of the giants," as every utopian formation purports to accomplish.[1] If civilization threatens to render "the whole of mankind" neurotic, then this is the price of avoiding total chaos, as Freud's late allusion to the rise of Nazism at the end of *Civilization and its Discontents* (1930) makes clear.[2] Such Freudian pragmatism follows clearly the trajectory laid down in *The Future of an Illusion* (1927), with its withering condemnations of mass wishful thinking: although it "would be very nice if there were a God who created the world and was a benevolent Providence, and if there were a moral order in the universe and an after-life," for example, responsible adults must learn to live in the absence of all such childlike guarantees of future bliss.[3] Given that Freud's entire *oeuvre* is committed to demonstrating the extent to which humanity is driven by instinctual and unconscious dynamics rather than rationality, his skepticism regarding the quintessentially Enlightened project of utopia is not surprising.

Initially, Lacan's view on the prospects of realizing a utopian social formation appears to be equally dim. The word itself—derived, of course, from Thomas More's original coinage, which designates a "no place" (*u-topia*) that simultaneously, homophonically evokes a "good place" (*eu-topia*)—appears infrequently in Lacan's writings, and almost always pejoratively. In the "Seminar on 'The

Purloined Letter'" it's invoked twice: first, when Lacan dismisses Bishop Wilkins's seventeenth-century proposal for a universal language as a "semiological utopia," and then when he criticizes object-relations psychoanalysis for its tendency to "reduce analytic treatment to a utopian rectification of the imaginary couple"—a reduction achieved only by ignoring the symbolic identities that Lacanian psychoanalysis is committed to illuminating.[4] The only other invocation of utopian thinking in *Écrits* occurs in "Kant with Sade," when the "order of fantasy" is shown to "prop up the utopia of desire," again aligning utopianism with impossible, naïve dreams of satiety and fulfillment that fatally overlook the inevitable mediations through which desire must pass to be constituted as such.[5] The lone other published references to utopia in Lacan's oeuvre occur in a 1938 *Encyclopèdie française* article, "Les complexes familiaux dans la formation de l'individu," in which the neurotic's ambitions to be recognized as a subject are described as being enclosed ("enferment") by "l'impuissance et l'utopie": a characterization that Adrian Johnston likens to Hegel's diagnosis of the beautiful soul, who sees evil everywhere but in herself.[6] This is followed by a second, perhaps even more telling invocation of the utopian dynamic, in which Lacan likens individual nostalgia for "the maternal" to a "metaphysical mirage of universal harmony," which in turn is likened to an impossible desire for the "lost paradise" of "social utopia" that can be recovered only before birth or, perhaps, after death.[7]

Like his published writings, Lacan's seminars contain few references to utopian thinking, and those that appear sparsely over their course are predominantly pejorative. According to Johnston, there are only four mentions of the concept across those twenty-seven years: one each in Seminars Five and Seven, and two in Seminar Sixteen. As Johnston observes, the thread that links these invocations is Lacan's specification of utopian thinking's failure to account for the complexity of human psychology. Assuming that every utopia aims at instituting some form of "a revolutionary new political economy" that will satisfy everyone equally,[8] Lacan unsurprisingly sees this as quite literally impossible: not only does it ignore the distinctions between needs, demands, and desires that Lacan correlates with the respective orders of the Real, the Imaginary, and the Symbolic,[9] but perhaps more damningly, it fails to account for the innately excessive nature of *jouissance*, that enjoyment that goes beyond the pleasure principle.[10] This oversight is highly problematic because, as Chris McMillan observes, "[A]ny political intervention that is unable to take into account the role of enjoyment in politics is doomed to failure."[11] Of course, *jouissance* is a notoriously slippery term, which Lacan arguably defined differently at different stages of his career. Accordingly, in what follows I will be guided by McMillan's basic account of the production of *jouissance* in political life:

According to both Freud and Lacan (in different variants), ideological notions about what it means to live well, to match up to moral standards imposed by the collective, are nothing but the imposition of the superego upon the body. This imposition creates perverse forms of *jouissance* (enjoyment) that move the subject away from the kinds of behaviours notionally encouraged by these ideologies. Any notion of how we should live must tally with the dialectics of enjoyment that structure social life.[12]

To be perverse, for McMillan, means to be essentially non-normative with respect to the Symbolic Order/ superego which nonetheless produces such enjoyments. In a capitalist social formation, forms of competition and uneven material accumulation are frequently posited as the outlets into which jouissance is canalized and dispersed; lacking these, most utopian visions fail to account for the potentially destabilizing effects of "enjoying one's symptoms" (to paraphrase Žižek). This is the position adopted by Juliet Flower MacCannell, then, when she asserts that in "attempting to solve the insoluble puzzle of what to do with the surplus that comes from/ with the sacrifices (of enjoyment) imposed on us in the name of civilization," most utopian visions succeed only in delineating "a series of proposals for *administering* this excess—which is also its waste."[13]

As we've seen, Lacan may be technically correct in his assumption that utopian thought is profoundly anti-psychological; by the same token, Utopian Studies scholars such as Ruth Levitas may be narrowly justified in claiming that Lacanian psychoanalysis is fundamentally anti-utopian.[14] Nevertheless, Lacanian theory may still provide us with the tools to see utopian productions and especially utopian fictions anew, and for a simple reason: no imagined utopia is as straightforward as (Johnston's reconstruction of) Lacan's understanding of the concept would suggest. Indeed, most utopian fictions are demonstrably, inherently flawed. More's seminal text of 1516, for example, not only reeks of totalitarianism (as many critics have noted), but his island society is both founded on the displacement of its aboriginal population, and on maintaining a slave caste that serves its new citizens' basic needs. Subsequent early modern utopias, too, are notably imperfect: Henry Neville's *Isle of Pines* (1688) recreates a patriarchal paradise that reduces women nearly to the status of chattel, and the seemingly happy lands of Swift's *Gulliver's Travels* (1721) are each explicitly or implicitly flawed.

Once we dispense with the myth that utopias are perfectly harmonious, moreover, then we can mobilize Lacanian theory to probe the reasons for their problematic entailments. As Fredric Jameson observes, every utopian formation tends to be founded on a "persistent and obsessive search for a simple, a single-shot solution to all our ills":[15] the abolishment of private property in More's proto-communist Utopia, for example, or the prohibition on saying "the-thing-that-is-not" in Swift's Houyhnhnmland. But as MacCannell points out in the passage quoted above, due to their lack of psychoanalytic sophistication, utopias generally fail to account for the surplus of enjoyment (*jouissance*) that is produced precisely by obeying this central prohibition or restriction. Whereas MacCannell asserts that utopias "manage" this jouissance, their general failure to account for it in the first place suggests that they actually remain unaware of it. Instead, I want to suggest, it is precisely the unmanaged, unacknowledged jouissance produced by obeying the central, superego-like demand or prohibition of a given utopian formation that in turn produces those unsavory elements—genocide and slavery in More's Utopia, enlightened instrumentalism in Swift Houyhnhnmland—that seem to accompany even the best-intentioned utopia. Following Žižek, I propose we can identify such formations as utopia's "obscene underside": the "dirty" but entirely necessary counterpart to the official version of a given authority, entity, or social formation.[16] If the presence of an obscene underside to Power is universal, however, then the particular form it takes is historically specific, since it will reflect the nature of the prohibited pleasure, action, or mode of life that forms the basis of a given utopia's "solution" to the social ills of the day.

Romanticism has long been associated with a proclivity for utopian thinking. From William Blake's mytho-poetic world building to Percy Shelley's idealistic assertions of poetry's power to renew the senses and by extension the world, the link between Romanticism and utopian thought was forged not only by its practitioners but also by those mid-twentieth century literary critics who canonized them. Northrop Frye, among others, articulates this well-known perspective as follows: "There is a strongly conservative element at the core of realism, an acceptance of society in its present structure, an attitude of mind that helps to make Balzac typical of realism, just as the opposite revolutionary attitude helps to make Victor Hugo typical of romanticism."[17] Putting aside the questionable accuracy of this assertion, Frye clearly means to compliment Hugo and his fellow revolutionaries for their progressive optimism; critics or skeptics of Romanticism, by contrast, have long brandished the Romantic propensity to engage in utopianism as evidence of naïve idealism. More recently, Anahid Nersessian has sought to reconfigure Romanticism's relation to utopian thought in a way that "fetishizes neither apocalyptic ruin nor its redemption."[18] This is a valuable argument, to be sure, but one that risks acquiescing in advance to the logic of contemporary neoliberalism, which naturalizes precarity and loss as inevitable, albeit unevenly distributed, features of modern existence. Deploying the Lacanian insight that utopian formations become problematic insofar as they fail to account for the jouissance produced by obeying their strictures, by contrast, may allow us to develop accounts of Romantic utopianism that recognize its problematic features while refusing to preemptively foreclose its potential to imagine better worlds.

Sarah Scott's *Millenium Hall* was published in 1762—not quite four decades after *Gulliver's Travels*, but far enough removed from Swift and his fellow satirists to take the idea of utopia seriously once more. Published on the early side of "the Romantic century" (e.g., 1750–1850), Scott's text still resembles an eighteenth-century epistolary novel or picaresque as much as it anticipates the community-building national tales and historical novels of the era's later decades;[19] accordingly, it presents an exemplary opportunity to use Lacanian analysis to intervene at a moment of generic as well as socio-economic transition. Under cover of a domestic travel narrative, Scott presents a utopian community in which harmony has been achieved by eliminating not just money and private property but also their historically most virulent proponents: men. Nevertheless, perhaps to set (male) readers at ease, *Millenium Hall* purports to be authored by an anonymous "gentleman on his travels," whose purpose (stated on the book's title page) is to "excite in the Reader proper Sentiments of Humanity, and lead the Mind to the Love of Virtue."[20] Unlike More's presentation of *Utopia* as a political model to be copied or at least used to criticize currently existing conditions, *Millenium Hall* is presented as beneficial primarily for individual readers. In this sense, it is less a political book than a moral one; accordingly, its vision of a better world is both smaller in scale than More's and closer to hand. Indeed it is literally closer, since Scott's feminist community is located on the British mainland, albeit on its margins, somewhere near Cornwall in the southwest. But although it is not reached by crossing a channel, a border of sorts must be traversed in order to approach it, as the narrator's initial description suggests:

> Mr. Lamont and I walked towards an avenue of oaks, which we observed at a small distance. The thick shade they afforded us, the fragrance wafted from the woodbines with which they were encircled, was so delightful, and the beauty of the grounds so very attracting, that we strolled on, desirous of approaching the house to which this avenue led. It is a mile and a half in length, but the eye is so charmed with the remarkable verdure and neatness of the fields... that time steals away insensibly. (56)

Moments—or is it hours?—later, the narrator reports that "we began to think ourselves in the days of Theocritus, so sweetly did a flute come wafted through the air." The pastoral passageway, which the narrator and his traveling companion enter in order to reach the Hall, is like a kind of eighteenth-century cosmic wormhole, seeming to transport them back in time even as it robs time of its forward momentum. Little wonder, then, that the narrator's name for the estate, "Millenium Hall," is a ruse, a mask that supposedly protects its inhabitants' anonymity but also underscores its fantastical nature. It also gestures toward this intentional community's unusual relation to time and history, since in the mid-eighteenth century millennialism was associated both with Cromwell's past Commonwealth and with various messianic beliefs in the coming apocalypse.[21] As Jameson observes, moreover, untimeliness is a common characteristic of utopias, which usually present themselves as representing "the end of history" in their realization of human perfectibility, and thus exist in tension with the temporal plots and historical circumstances in which they're necessarily inscribed.[22]

In Millenium Hall's case, its particular history eventually comes to trouble its status as a place of day-to-day harmony.[23] From the talkative Mrs. Melvyn, readers eventually learn that the estate is owned by one of its female inhabitants, Mrs. Morgan, whose feckless and cruel husband recognized her true worth only shortly before his untimely death, leaving her Millenium Hall and a large annuity as a reward for her long-suffering "obedience" (157). Morgan subsequently took two of her female friends—whose woeful back stories we also learn over the novel's course—to live with her there, "in a way of life where all their satisfactions might be rational, and as conducive to eternal, as to temporal happiness" (159). With the assistance of a park steward (the only male resident of the estate) and an income generated by their labors as well as the rent paid by several boarders, by the time of our gentleman traveler's visit Millenium Hall has thirty or so permanent residents, and "the society now subsists with the utmost plenty and convenience." Accordingly, Millenium Hall is very much an "asylum"—the word used by the loquacious Melvyn when explaining its rules (116)—for women who have been (in Gary Kelly's apt phrasing) "oppressed and excluded by patriarchal and courtly gentry culture in the world outside [their] utopia."[24] It thus belongs to the class of idealized places that Jameson calls "enclaves": utopian spaces "separate from the dominant state, and [which] have their own geographical autonomy."[25] But although beneficial for their occupants, by definition enclaves cannot be scaled up. Thus despite Kelly's position that "the feminized economy of Millenium Hall . . . [functions] as a metonymy for the reformed economy of the state itself," there is little evidence for this assertion within the novel. The women neither actively promote their way of life nor seek to expand their estate. More, although the gentleman narrator closes his account by reflecting that "if what I have described, may tempt any one to go and do likewise, I shall think myself fortunate in communicating it" (249), such a sentiment is hardly a call for widespread socio-political change; as another resident puts it plainly, "We do not set up for reformers" (166).

Lacking both the ability and the desire to significantly expand their utopian operation, should the gentlewomen of Millenium Hall be considered utopians at all? To answer in the affirmative, we can certainly point to the set of rules by which the women must agree to be guided while in residence. These eleven "regulations," faithfully enumerated for the narrator's and readers' benefits, include giving all one's money to the Hall for the duration of one's residence, "the interest... being appropriated to the use of the community"; taking meals and most forms of indoor entertainment in common; abiding by a dress code that mandates "plain and neat" clothing; avoiding "behav[ing] with imprudence" and "disturb[ing] the society" of Millenium Hall "by turbulence or pettishness of temper" (116–17). When Lamont asks whether these rules have led to many expulsions, Maynard happily contradicts his assumption; after admitting that their life "is not without its difficulties" (117), she asserts that between voluntary dropouts and peer pressure to conform, "there has been but one [resident] expelled" (119) since the Hall's founding. Mrs. Maynard's explanations leave no doubt that it is precisely the demands on the women's comportment and morality that make their lives at Millenium Hall fulfilling, despite "being exposed to few temptations in this retired place" (120).

The concept of duty, in fact, is the master virtue on which Scott's vision of the good life depends. As Jacques-Alain Miller notes, the semiotic registers of "duty" also fascinated Lacan, whose (in)famous linking of Kant and Sade depends on recognizing how the latter transposes the former's invocation of duty as an ethical call heard by the subject into a merciless, punishing yet seductive master figure—which is to say, into a forerunner of the superego.[26] It should thus not escape our notice that "duty" is invoked more than thirty times in Scott's novel, almost always with regard to the proper behavior expected of the female characters. As we've already seen, it's the regulatory norm on which life at Millenium Hall operates; additionally, it's frequently deployed to characterize the women's lives *before* their residencies at the Hall begin. During Mrs. Morgan's backstory, for example, we learn she was told by her husband "that when it became her duty to love him, she would no longer remain indifferent" (126), as well as that she was prevented from abandoning him by the realization that in doing so "she would not be less guilty of a violation of her duty to society, since she must appear very culpable to those who knew her" (127). Likewise, before she comes to the Hall, Miss Mancel learns "that to suffer was her duty, and though she might grieve [at the death of a would-be husband], she must not repine" (154). The Hall was established precisely to provide women with a refuge from these kinds of disappointments and obligations. So what should we make of the fact that, once in residence, a series of duties and renunciations continues to define and regulate the women's daily lives? Superficially, the spirit in which duty is invoked at the Hall is novel: previously, the women's obligations were clearly enforced by patriarchal authority, whereas now they are willingly assumed for the community's greater good. As Giorgio Agamben has demonstrated, however, the modern notion of duty still owes much to the "liturgical tradition of *officium* [official duties]" from which it is descended;[27] accordingly, although the women of Millenium Hall are party to their own regulations, they continue to participate in an ethical economy that not only defines obedience to a set of norms as the highest good, but also ensures that complete fulfillment of those norms remains always just out of reach. When Lamont suggests that the women have done so much good that "were he a Roman Catholic, he should beg of them to confer on him the merit of some of their works of supererogation," for example, Mrs. Mancel replies without hesitation: "I do not know where you could find them . . . on the contrary, we are sensible of great deficiencies in the performance of our duty" (244). She goes on to explain that, since the women of Millenium Hall experience their obligations as an imitation of divine love and mercy, by definition they can never do enough.

In basic psychoanalytic terms, this is readily understood as the burden of constant guilt that the subject experiences due to its inevitable inability to fulfill dutifully the superego's demands, either for infinite renunciation and obedience or, in Žižek's updated version, for endlessly repeated consumption and enjoyment.[28] But there is an added element to the women's auto-subjection worth noting. Recapping Lamont's previous observation that "we live for others, without any regard to our own pleasure," Mrs. Trentham vigorously denies that they are therefore unhappy, first asking "What is there worth enjoying in this world that we do not possess?" (245) and then answering her own question with a nearly comprehensive list of the luxuries they "wisely" do without: "a large retinue," expensive clothes, "the greatest luxury of the table," and travel (246). The "infinite satisfaction" that Mrs. Trentham claims they enjoy from going without these middle-class feminine pleasures—now recoded as "superfluities" (246)—is a clear case of the production of jouissance via the pleasures of submission and renunciation, amplified by the fact that, as noted above, the inhabitants of Millenium Hall already exist in a liminal relation to the patriarchal status quo (which means, from a psychoanalytic perspective, a liminal relation to signification itself).[29]

The missing element of Mrs. Trentham's explanation, then, is an account of what happens to this jouissance: where does that "infinite satisfaction" find its release? The answer lies in the arena of their lives that necessarily spills over the physical boundaries of the Hall and its land and, in doing so, inevitably problematizes its utopian status. For the primary duties that the women of Millenium Hall have freed themselves from are, of course, marrying and bearing children—the two obligations most frequently expected and indeed required of middle-class eighteenth-century women. Instead, as part of the "charity" work that is an essential node in the web of duties that defines and regulates their lives, Millenium Hall's residences have effectively outsourced these burdensome obligations to the local village girls. Again, Mrs. Melvyn explains that

> when, among the lower sort, [the residents of the Hall] meet with an uncommon genius, they will admit her among their number... they are educated in such a manner as will render them acceptable, where accomplished women of an humble rank and behaviour are wanted, either for the care of a house or children. (160)

These actions are accompanied by a series of patronizing, disciplinary gestures: while at the Hall, the local "girls" are kept away from the gentlewomen after eight in the evening "lest their being always in our company should make them think their situation above a menial state" (160); after they have been returned to their villages, the women continue to keep tabs on them, portioning out "little presents," which "makes them vye with each other in endeavours to excel in sobriety, cleanliness, meekness, and industry" (168). When they succeed in marrying off one of their former charges, moreover, they shower her with gifts; in one case, we learn, "Mrs. Mancel gave the young bride a fortune, and that she might have her share of employment, and contribute to the provision of her family, had stocked her dairy, and furnished her with poultry" (163).

The impressive level of enthusiasm with which these human makeover and improvement projects are undertaken calls attention to their sublimative function: the training and management of these local girls is precisely what channels the Hall's women's jouissance, engendered by their submission to the duties and restrictions described above.[30] By the same token, however, their cadre of protégées clearly makes up the obscene underside of the Hall's "female Arcadia" (223). Initially, of course, Millenium Hall appears to represent a decisive break from the regular world in favor of a socially harmonious, proto-feminist alternative to patriarchal gentry capitalism. But the women's management of their "infinite satisfaction" by training the local village girls ultimately reinforces the very system it claims to oppose, as the following exchange—which takes place immediately after the above description of Mrs. Mancel's generosity to a former charge—reveals:

> As the ladies conduct in this particular was uncommon, I could not forbear telling them, that "I was surprised to find so great encouragement given to matrimony by persons, whose choice showed them little inclined in its favor."

> Does it surprise you, answered Mrs. Melvyn smiling, to see people promote that in others, which they themselves do not chuse to practice? We consider matrimony as absolutely necessary to the good of society; it is a general duty; but as, according to all antient tenures, those obliged to perform a knight's service, might, if they chose to enjoy their own firesides, be excused by sending deputies to supply their places; so we, using the same privilege substitute many others, and certainly much more promote wedlock, than we could do by entering into it ourselves. (163)

Here, the narrator's initial observation—that a whiff of hypocrisy surrounds the Hall's women's grooming of young village girls for roles (primarily, wives and mothers) they themselves have worked hard to escape—is met with a defensive rebuttal that gives away more than it intends. Once again invoking "duty" as the prime directive behind the obligation to marry, Mrs. Melvyn confirms its religious inheritance; in this vein, procreation is presumably the "promotion" that the young village girls can bring to wedlock more effectively than the generally older ladies of Millenium Hall. Furthermore, the allusion to feudalism ("antient tenures") truly discloses the retrograde, conservative character of this endeavor: by admitting and even welcoming a parallel between the knight errant who sends a lesser emissary in his place and their own training and insertion of local girls to take their places in the gentry economy, Mrs. Melvyn confirms that their utopia not only depends upon but also promotes the ongoing exploitation of female domestic labor in eighteenth-century Britain at large.

Ironically, the ladies' proudest achievement is the production of the obscene underside of their female Arcadia. Yet calling the exploitation of these young women the obscene underside of Scott's imagined female utopia is in some ways misleading, for like the presence of slavery in More's original Utopia, these exploitative arrangements are hardly hidden from their participants, much less from readers. As such, they might be better described along the lines of the "open secret," which Anne-Lise François calls "a trope for the implicit workings of ideology itself" in "post-Marxist, psychoanalytically informed ideology theory."[31] Either way, their consistent presence may do much to account for the well-known fact that utopias, both fictional and real (or at least attempted), have a disconcerting tendency to become—or reveal themselves to be—increasingly dystopian over time.

Instead of pursuing this well-known theme further, however, in what remains of this chapter I propose to investigate a related but distinct question: if utopias are inevitably shadowed by obscene undersides, might dystopias be found to have built-in features or aspects that are redeeming or at least compensatory? To begin to formulate an answer, I turn to a novel from the other end of

Romantic century from *Millenium Hall*, one that is also increasingly recognized as one of the first pure dystopian fictions: Mary Shelley's *The Last Man* (1826).

According to the *OED*, the adjective "dystopian" didn't enter the English language until the middle of the twentieth century (although J. S. Mill is quoted using it as a noun in the 1860s). Nevertheless, the genre clearly preceded the denomination thanks to texts such as *Gulliver's Travels*, with its depictions of societies that are much less happy than its famously gullible narrator generally realizes. Shelley also arguably follows Swift's lead insofar as her novel contains plenty of allusions to contemporary situations and personages; indeed, *The Last Man* has frequently been read allegorically, or at least as a kind of *roman à clef* in which the main male characters are not-so-thinly veiled versions of Shelley's husband, Percy Shelley, and their charismatic friend Lord Byron, both of whom had died only a few years earlier. Lionel Verney, the novel's narrator, has even been read as a gender-bending authorial self-portrait.[32] Shelley's text holds interest for us today on much broader grounds than mere biography, however, not least because its main conceit—in the 2090s, a deadly plague begins spreading across the planet—eerily anticipates our contemporary fascination with apocalyptic global pandemics.[33] In fact, so-called last man narratives were already popular when Shelley wrote her novel, although of course they reflected the anxieties of her era rather than ours: these include a futuristic vision of London reduced to rubble in Anna Laetitia Barbauld's poem *Eighteen Hundred and Eleven* (1812), published when the outcome of the Napoleonic Wars was still in doubt, and Byron's poem "Darkness," written in the "year without a summer" caused by the climatic aftereffects of Mount Tambora's massive 1815 eruption.[34] In addition to these traumatic events and the works they inspired, Shelley's particular choice of disaster was undoubtedly influenced by the real-life, massive cholera outbreak which began in 1817.[35] Accordingly, *The Last Man* is not only dystopian insofar as it seizes on a single problem—communicable disease—and extrapolates a future based on its unmitigated expansion, it's also classically nightmarish in the Freudian sense of being overdetermined by a multitude of anxieties, societal (war, environmental disaster) and personal.

Nevertheless, Shelley's dystopian narrative contains within itself and even facilitates moments of utopian possibility. To see how this happens, a degree of familiarity with the details of its plot and pacing is necessary. In Shelley's telling, the plague begins "on the shores of the Nile" before rapidly infecting "parts of Asia" and then Constantinople, where a battle against the Turks ends with a massive explosion that levels the city and spreads its pestilence as effectively as any volcanic ash cloud.[36] From that cosmopolitan city's destruction, the plague begins its inexorable movement across the globe, ultimately consuming every nation and society in its path. That path, moreover, is mostly airborne, suggesting that Shelley's plague is more atmospheric than viral (although there are moments in the book that suggest person-to-person infection too): a major focus for recent critics looking to take seriously Mary Shelley's literary productions beyond *Frankenstein* (1818).

It's entirely understandable that most interpretations of *The Last Man* focus on what happens after the plague begins to spread. Yet the mysteriously communicable disease for which the novel is best known starts to play a major role only about one-third of the way through; before that, Shelley keeps readers entirely absorbed in the political and romantic intrigues of her main characters. In this light, the greatest shock of the first volume arguably occurs at the start of chapter two, when Verney recalls that in the year 2073 Britain's last king voluntarily abdicated shortly before dying, thereby allowing Britain to become a republic (albeit one that still retains inheritable lands and ranks). As Verney tells us about his unusual childhood, we learn that he eventually befriended the ex-king's dreamy, intellectual son, Adrian, whose mother had hoped he would reclaim the family's throne. But Adrian—the novel's version of Percy Shelley—is deeply committed to reform and leads the "republican" party; the remnants of the royalist party are instead led by Lord Raymond, the book's charismatic Byron figure, who has just returned from helping the Greeks earn a truce with the Turks, a seemingly intractable conflict in Shelley's time. (There is also a third political party, even more iconoclastic than Adrian's, led by a commoner named Ryland whose real-life model is usually taken to be William Cobbett.)

So why should we pay attention to these early chapters when they primarily seem like a warm-up for the coming plague in volume two? From a modern perspective, volume one's pacing certainly leaves much to be desired, and its various romantic subplots can feel strained; although there is much talk of love and even passion, authentic jouissance mostly goes missing here. Nevertheless, the surprisingly conventional intrigues of the first volume are important insofar as they establish the baseline norms, both generic and socio-political, against which the mutations of the rest of the novel can be measured. In fact, the Shelley-like Adrian has long harbored idealistic plans for social improvement: against his mother's wishes, for example, we are told that he "published his intention of using his influence to diminish the power of the aristocracy, to effect a greater equalization of wealth and privilege, and to introduce a perfect system of republican government into England" (34). Furthermore, when Raymond is unexpectedly elected Lord Protector, he too embarks on a series of plans that sound quintessentially utopian:

> Canals, aqueducts, bridges, stately buildings, and various edifices for public utility, were entered upon; [Raymond] was continually surrounded

> by projectors and projects, which were to render England one scene of fertility and magnificence; the state of poverty was to be abolished... disease was to be banished; labour lightened of its heaviest burden. Nor did this seem extravagant.... Raymond was to inspire them with his beneficial will, and the mechanism of society, once systematised according to faultless rules, would never again swerve into disorder. (83–84)

Alongside its faith in society's perfectibility, this talk of "systematization" in accordance with "faultless rules" definitively marks this passage as a quintessential piece of Enlightened utopianism. If any "obstacles" to happiness yet remain, we are told, they are "self-raised" (83)—an apparent allusion to the distinctions of rank that cause interpersonal tensions in the novel's opening chapters, and on a larger scale keep British society hierarchically static and divided. Ultimately, Raymond is caught in a love triangle, abandons his office, and goes abroad once more to fight the Turks, where he is killed in the explosion that levels Constantinople and releases the festering plague into the global atmosphere.[37]

Yet as the human world implodes into dystopian chaos in volumes two and three of *The Last Man*, opportunities arise to realize the kind of utopian social harmony that proved impossible in volume one. In the brief lull after the destruction of Constantinople but before the plague spreads to Europe, for example, Adrian sees the potential for positive change:

> Let this last but twelve months... and earth will become a Paradise. The energies of man were before directed to the destruction of his species; they now aim at his liberation and preservation.... What may not the forces, never before united, of liberty and peace achieve in this dwelling of man? (172)

Adrian is wrong to predict peace and prosperity, of course—but he is not altogether wrong to see that the impending disaster of the plague activates a potential for equality and social harmony to spontaneously manifest themselves. The island of Britain temporarily begins to resemble More's original island Utopia. Along these lines, I'd like to present in some detail one more passage, a description of social life from Verney's perspective, as the plague draws ever nearer and refugees begin to pour across the English Channel:

> In this emergency, to feed the very people to whom we had given refuge, we were obliged to yield to the plough and the mattock our pleasure-grounds and parks.... Adrian did not rest only with the exertions he could make with regard to his own possessions. He addressed himself to the wealthy

of the land; he made proposals in parliament little adapted to please the rich; but his earnest pleadings and benevolent eloquence were irresistible... to the honor of the English be it recorded, that, although natural disinclination made them delay awhile, yet when the misery of their fellow-creatures became glaring, an enthusiastic generosity inspired their decrees. The most luxurious were often the first to part with their indulgencies.... It was more common, for all who possessed landed property to secede to their estates, attended by whole troops of the indigent, to cut down their woods to erect temporary dwellings, and to portion out their parks, parterres, and flower-gardens, to necessitous families. (187)

Once again, the utopian potential of a thoroughly dystopian scenario is unexpectedly invoked.

What does this mean for our understanding of the relation between these two apparently contradictory states? Historically speaking, this passage is infused with the optimistic proto-anarchism of Shelley's father, William Godwin. The irony that it takes a world-devouring plague to actualize Godwin's belief that (to quote Robert Mitchell) "social relations could be slowly perfected to the extent that legal and political 'institutions' were eliminated,"[38] however, cannot be missed; as Verney comments in the next paragraph, "It may be imagined that things were in a bad state indeed, before this spirit of benevolence could have struck such deep roots" (187). Nevertheless, as the plague surges forward—but before it has entirely overtaken everyone—the best instincts of human solidarity and altruism are on display, albeit temporarily; in this context, Mark Canuel notes, the plague has a positive function beyond its mere destructiveness insofar as it "powerfully and contradictorily reveals the extent to which individual associations are dependent upon group formations."[39] Group identities, irretrievably threatened by the plague, are at least momentarily revealed to be more important and indeed more personal than individual ones—a direct critique of Godwin's anarchistic philosophy.

Beyond this historical conjuncture, however, the momentary window of utopian possibility opened by the novel's generic transition from romance to tragedy can be understood productively in psychoanalytic terms as well. Here, we might begin with Eric Santer's insight that what is missing from most sociopolitical accounts of sovereignty is "the bareness, nakedness, and vulnerability" that pertain to both "the precariousness of our organic, mortal lives" and "the fact that the historical forms of life in which we dwell are susceptible to breakdown."[40] From this angle, the advancement of the plague in *The Last Man* may be understood as nothing other than the eruption of the Real into the novel's Symbolic order, an eruption that opens the potential for a rearrangement of the coordinates of that order. The "self-raised obstacles" of rank, in other words, are revealed to be the true fantasy structuring the novel's (and Shelley's) social reality: one that must be fully traversed before other, more egalitarian social arrangements can begin to be imagined and instituted.[41] Given the already destabilized state of the nation's socio-political frame, moreover, it is even possible to imagine that any excess jouissance produced by adherence to the new, more egalitarian norms of British social life may not need to be sublimated quite as insistently as in previous utopian formations, and therefore might prove less threatening to the new (dis)order. It even seems momentarily possible that a new kind of political economy could bring with it a new psycho-social regime—one in which, as Todd McGowan has suggested, the death drive rather than the pleasure principle could become the basis for a *socius* whose members might finally learn to "enjoy what we don't have."[42] Only several paragraphs after the passage quoted above, however, we hear the first rumors that the plague has reached London—and from this point on, more or less midway through the second volume, humanity begins to die out so quickly and thoroughly that all utopian planning becomes impossible.

Both for reasons of space and because the novel's second half has been discussed so thoroughly elsewhere, I leave off my reading of *The Last Man* here.[43] But despite the extraordinarily bleak trajectory of Shelley's novel, its frame tale—in which Shelley claims to have discovered Verney's manuscript in a seaside grotto near Naples reputed to be "the Sibyl's Cave" (1)—offers a potential note of redemption. After all, as Canuel observes, if Verney truly believes himself to be "the last man," then why write and hide the manuscript at all, if not in the belief that someone will eventually find and read it?[44] *The Last Man* thus shelters at its core the most basic utopian dynamic: a desire for something different than what presently exists. It does so, moreover, along precisely the lines indicated by Žižek when he observes that "utopia has nothing to do with idle dreaming about ideal society in total abstraction from real life: 'utopia' is a matter of innermost urgency, something we are pushed into as a matter of survival, when it is no longer possible to go on within the parameters of the 'possible.'"[45] Eventually, even mere survival proves to be elusive in *The Last Man*; nevertheless, the brief flowering of hope that opens in the midst of Shelley's depictions of society's dissolution embodies exactly what Žižek, thinking of the work of Ernst Bloch, names "the emancipatory imagination" that "haunt[s] [market reality] . . . as a dream waiting to be realized."[46]

At the time of its publication, Shelley's novel was met with a lukewarm reception at best; the *Monthly Review*, characteristically, complained that "[h]er imagination appears to delight in inventions which have no foundations in ordinary occurrences, and no charm for the common sympathies of mankind."[47]

Ironically, although the anonymous reviewer's overall condemnation of *The Last Man* is clearly misguided, the observation that neither "ordinary occurrences" nor "common sympathies" are feasible components of utopian and dystopian formations is remarkably accurate. As I've tried to show in this chapter, the excessive jouissance produced by acceding to the rigorous demands of utopian living tends to issue in obscene undersides that problematize or even nullify the beneficial dynamics of the original utopias; conversely, dystopian scenarios harbor the potential for utopian flowerings during those moments when the Symbolic order is most vulnerable to restructuring. The truth of the latter, however, should not lead us to embrace or even resign ourselves to dystopias as the only possible frame of the future, although their popularity in contemporary film, television, and literature clearly speaks to their current hold on our collective imagination. By the same token, neither should the obvious difficulties and attendant dangers of realizing more egalitarian relations dissuade us from at least attempting to keep certain utopian horizons in sight. To conclude with a well-worn Lacanian dictum, albeit slightly modified: "[T]he only thing of which one can be guilty is of having given ground relative to one's desire"[48]—for a better world.

Notes

1. Sigmund Freud, *Civilization and its Discontents*, ed. and trans. James Strachey (New York: Norton, 1961), 82.

2. Ibid., 110, 112.

3. Freud, *The Future of an Illusion*, trans. W. D. Robson-Scott, rev. and ed. James Strachey (Garden City: Anchor Books, 1964), 54. This orientation is given perhaps its fullest expression in David Bleich, *Utopia: The Psychology of a Cultural Fantasy* (Ann Arbor: UMI Research Press, 1984).

4. Jacques Lacan, "Seminar on 'The Purloined Letter,'" in *Écrits: The First Complete Edition in English*, trans. Bruce Fink (New York: Norton, 2006), 16, 41.

5. Lacan, "Kant with Sade," in *Écrits*, 653.

6. Lacan, "Les complexes familiaux dans la formation de l'individu," in *Autres Écrits* (Paris: Éditions du Seuil, 2001), 61; Adrian Johnston, "A Blast from the Future: Freud, Lacan, Marcuse, and Snapping the Threads of the Past," *Umbr(a): A Journal of the Unconscious* (2008): 73.

7. Lacan, "Les complexes familiaux," 36.

8. Johnston, 73.

9. I draw here on Elizabeth Grosz's explanation of these relations in her *Jacques Lacan: A Feminist Introduction* (New York: Routledge, 1990), 59–65.

10. Johnston, 74.

11. Chris McMillan, *Žižek and Communist Strategy: On the Disavowed Foundations of Global Capitalism* (Edinburgh: Edinburgh University Press, 2012), 62.

12. McMillan, 50.

13. Juliet Flower MacCannell, "Nowhere, Else: On Utopia," *Umbr(a): A Journal of the Unconscious* (2008): 44.

14. Ruth Levitas, *The Concept of Utopia*, 2nd ed. (Oxford: Peter Lang, 2010), xiv; quoted in "Varieties of Lacanian Anti-Utopianism," *Radical Desire* (blog), July 6, 2010, http://radicaldesire.blogspot.com/2010/07/varieties-of-lacanian-anti-utopianism.html.

15. Fredric Jameson, *Archaeologies of the Future: The Desire Called Utopia and Other Science Fictions* (New York: Verso, 2005), 11.

16. Slavoj Žižek, *Welcome to the Desert of the Real!: Five Essays on September 11th and Related Dates* (New York: Verso, 2002), 30.

17. Northrop Frye, *The Secular Scripture: A Study of the Structure of Romance* (Cambridge: Harvard University Press, 1976), 164.

18. Anahid Nersessian, *Utopia, Limited: Romanticism and Adjustment* (Cambridge: Harvard University Press, 2015), 2.

19. See (e.g., Katie Trumpener, *Bardic Nationalism: The Romantic Novel and the British Empire* (Princeton: Princeton University Press, 1997).

20. Sarah Scott, *Millenium Hall*, ed. Gary Kelly (Ontario: Broadview Press, 1995), 51. Subsequent citations will appear parenthetically. Scott's idiosyncratic spelling and punctuation are reproduced here as they appear in this edition.

21. James Bryant Reeves, "Untimely Old Age and Deformity in Sarah Scott's *Millenium Hall*," *Eighteenth Century Fiction* 27, no. 2 (Winter 2014–2015): 243–44.

22. See (e.g., Jameson's list of a number of "undecideable questions" raised by most fictional Utopias):

> [T]he formal dilemma of how works that posit the end of history can offer any usable historical impulses, how works which aim to resolve all political differences can continue to be in any sense political, how texts designed to overcome the needs of the body can remain materialistic, and how visions of the 'epoch of rest' (Morris) can energize and compel us to action. *Archaeologies of the Future*, xiv.

23. Jameson quotes Roland Barthes: "la marque de l'Utopie, c'est le quotidian" (quoted in *Archaeologies of the Future*, 7).

24. Gary Kelly, "Introduction: Sarah Scott, Bluestocking Feminism, and *Millenium Hall*," *Millenium Hall*, ed. Kelly, 29.

25. Jameson, *An American Utopia: Dual Power and the Universal Army* (New York: Verso, 2016), 4.

26. See Jacques-Alain Miller, "A Discussion of Lacan's 'Kant with Sade,'" in *Reading Seminars I and II: Lacan's Return to Freud*, eds. Richard Feldstein, Bruce Fink, and Maire Janaus (Albany: State University of New York Press, 1996), 221–22.

27. Giorgio Agamben, *Opus Dei: An Archaeology of Duty*, trans. Adam Kotsko (Stanford: Stanford University Press, 2013), 122.

28. See (e.g., Žižek, *The Metastases of Enjoyment: Six Essays on Women and Causality* (New York: Verso, 1994), 174.

29. For a brilliant reading of the liminal status of woman/the feminine in Lacan, and its relation to the Kantian sublime and thus to jouissance, see Joan Copjec, "Sex and the Euthanasia of Reading," in *Read My Desire: Lacan against the Historicists* (Cambridge: The MIT Press, 1994), 201–36. In a different but not unrelated context, John Kucich has analyzed the often empowering function of masochism in later nineteenth-century British novels; see his *Imperial Masochism: British Fiction, Fantasy, and Social Class* (Princeton: Princeton University Press, 2008).

30. There is, arguably, a similar dynamic at work in the ladies' relationship to the elderly and differently abled women whom they alternately employ and shelter on the grounds of the Hall itself; for a fuller account of this aspect of the novel, and one that is more sympathetic to Scott's project than I am here, see Reeves, "Untimely Old Age": 229–56. Crystal Lake also finds redemptive and progressive dynamics in the women's relation to the structures they inhabit and restore; see her "Redecorating the Ruin: Women and Antiquarianism in Sarah Scott's *Millenium Hall*," *ELH* 76, no. 3 (2009): 661–86.

31. Anne-Lise François, *Open Secrets: The Literature of Uncounted Experience* (Stanford: Stanford University Press, 2008), 5.

32. Not only does Verney speak with Shelley's authority, but in an 1824 journal entry—written after returning to England following Percy's untimely drowning in Italy—Shelley herself explains: "The Last man! Yes, I may well describe that solitary being's feelings, feeling myself as the last relic of a beloved race, my companions extinct before me." Quoted in Jonathan Elmer, "'Vaulted Over by the Present': Melancholy and Sovereignty in Mary Shelley's *The Last Man*," *Novel: A Forum on Fiction* 42, no. 2 (Summer 2009): 355.

33. For more on this generic trajectory, see Peter Y. Paik, *From Utopia to Apocalypse: Science Fiction and the Politics of Catastrophe* (Minneapolis: University of Minnesota Press, 2010). Recent Hollywood movies that play on fears of global pandemics include *Contagion* (dir. Soderbergh, 2011) and *World War Z* (dir.

Forster, 2013); the latter is based on a novel by Max Brooks, *World War Z: An Oral History of the Zombie War* (New York: Crown Books, 2006).

34. For an expanded reading of Barbauld's poem in its geopolitical context, see Gottlieb, *Romantic Globalism: British Literature and Modern World Order, 1750–1830* (Columbus: Ohio State University Press, 2014), 78–83; on Byron's "Darkness" and volcanism, see Gillen D'Arcy Wood, *Tambora: The Eruption That Changed the World* (Princeton: Princeton University Press, 2014), 64–69.

35. Alan Bewell, *Romanticism and Colonial Disease* (Baltimore: Johns Hopkins University Press, 1999), 296.

36. Mary Shelley, *The Last Man*, ed. Anne McWhir (Peterborough, ON: Broadview Press, 1996), 137. Subsequent citations will appear parenthetically.

37. Byron, of course, died in Greece two years before the publication of *The Last Man*. In killing off Raymond this way, Shelley may also have been thinking of Byron's depiction of a similarly apocalyptic explosion that concludes his narrative poem *The Siege of Corinth* (1816).

38. Robert Mitchell, "Population Aesthetics in Romantic and Post-Romantic Literature," in *Constellations of a Contemporary Romanticism*, eds. Jacques Khalip and Forest Pyle (New York: Fordham University Press, 2016), 267.

39. Mark Canuel, "Acts, Rules, and *The Last Man*," *Nineteenth-Century Literature* 53, no. 2 (Sept. 1998): 151.

40. Eric L. Santner, *The Royal Remains: The People's Two Bodies and the Endgames of Sovereignty* (Chicago: University of Chicago Press, 2011), 18. Santner's psychoanalytic rereadings of Ernst Kantorowicz's theory of the king's two bodies, and its historical transformation into popular sovereignty, provides another valuable account of how socio-political structures produce excess jouissance.

41. Cf. Žižek's foundational insight in *The Sublime Object of Ideology* that "ideology is not a dreamlike illusion that we build to escape insupportable reality; in its basic dimension it is a fantasy-construction which serves as a support for our 'reality' itself" (London: Verso, 1989), 45.

42. See Todd McGowan, *Enjoying What We Don't Have: The Political Project of Psychoanalysis* (Lincoln: University of Nebraska Press, 2013).

43. See, in addition to sources already cited (e.g., Ranita Chatterjee, "Our Bodies, Our Catastrophes: Biopolitics in Mary Shelley's *The Last Man*," *European Romantic Review* 25, no. 1 (2014): 35–49; Patricia Cove, "'The Earth's Deep Entrails': Gothic Landscapes and Grotesque Bodies in Mary Shelley's *The Last Man*," *Gothic Studies* 15, no. 2 (Nov. 2013): 19–36; Peter Melville, "The Problem of Immunity in *The Last Man*," *SEL 1500–1900* 47, no. 4 (2007): 825–46; Charlotte Sussman, "'Islanded in the World': Cultural Memory and Human Mobility in *The Last Man*," *PMLA* 118, no. 2 (March 2003): 286–301).

44. See (e.g., Canuel, 169–70).

45. Žižek, *Iraq: The Borrowed Kettle* (New York: Verso, 2005), 123–24.

46. Žižek, "Preface: Bloch's Ontology of Not-Yet-Being," in *The Privatization of Hope: Ernst Bloch and the Future of Utopia*, eds. Peter Thompson and Slavoj Žižek (Durham: Duke University Press, 2013), xix.

47. *Monthly Review* 1 (1826): 33–35, in Shelley, *Last Man*, 412.

48. Jacques Lacan, *The Seminar of Jacques Lacan, Book VII: The Ethics of Psychoanalysis,* ed. Jacques-Alain Miller, trans. Dennis Porter (New York: Norton, 1992), 319.

CONTRIBUTORS

ED CAMERON is professor of literary and film studies at the University of Texas, Rio Grande Valley. He is the author of *The Psychopathology of the Gothic Romance: Perversion, Neuroses and Psychosis in Early Works of the Genre* (McFarland, 2010), editor of Thomas de Quincey's Gothic novel *Klosterheim* (Valancourt, 2011), and the author of numerous articles on psychoanalysis, gothic literature, and film.

COLIN CARMAN is instructor of English at Colorado Mesa University, Grand Junction, Colorado. His work has appeared in such journals as *European Romantic Review*, *Nineteenth-Century Prose*, and *ISLE*. A contributing writer at *The Gay and Lesbian Review*, his essays have also appeared in two edited book collections, *Romantic Ecocriticism* and *The Brokeback Book*.

MATT FOLEY is lecturer in modern and contemporary literature at Manchester Metropolitan University. His most recent work on the Gothic has appeared in the *Routledge Handbook to the Ghost Story*, *Sound Effects: The Object Voice in Fiction*, and the journal *Horror Studies*. His monograph *Haunting Modernisms* (Palgrave) was published in 2017.

DANIELA GAROFALO is professor of English at University of Oklahoma. She is the author of *Manly Leaders in Nineteenth-Century British Literature* (SUNY 2008) and *Women, Love, and Commodity Culture in British Romanticism* (Ashgate, 2012).

EVAN GOTTLIEB is professor of English at Oregon State University. He is the author of four monographs, including *Romantic Globalism: British Literature and the Modern World Order* (Ohio State University Press, 2014) and *Romantic Realities: Speculative Realism and British Romanticism* (Edinburgh University Press, 2016). He has also edited three collections of essays and the Norton Critical Edition of Tobias Smollett's *The Expedition of Humphry Clinker*.

RITHIKA RAMAMURTHY is a graduate student in English at Brown University. Her research focuses on the Victorian and turn-of-the-century novel as the form in which discourses such as visual culture, psychoanalysis, and democracy are mediated and reimagined.

DAVID SIGLER is associate professor of English at University of Calgary. He is the author of *Sexual Enjoyment in British Romanticism: Gender and Psychoanalysis, 1757–1835* (McGill-Queen's University Press, 2015).

PAUL A. VATALARO is professor of English at Merrimack College. He is the author of *Shelley's Music: Fantasy, Authority, and the Object Voice* (Ashgate, 2009).

ZAK WATSON is associate professor and head of English and philosophy at Missouri Southern State University. He has published a number of articles on Lacan and Romanticism, including in *Re-Turn* and *Novel*, and contributed to *Lacan: Topologically Speaking* (Other, 2004).

INDEX

Addison, Joseph, 84, 85
Agamben, Giorgio, 111, 112, 164
Aiken, Anna Laetitia (Barbauld), 145, 146, 175n34
Aiken, John: "Sir Bertrand, a fragment," 145, 153
Akenside, Mark, 81, 91; and *The Pleasures of Imagination: A Poem*, 81
The Ambassadors (Holbein), 16
animal, 37–54; and studies, xviii, 40, 43; and jouissance, 37, 38, 39, 45–47, 49, 52; and imaginary, 43, 44; and animality, 44, 51; and phobia, 44; and rights, 44
anthropocentricism, 40, 53
anxiety, 3, 12, 13, 15, 21, 23, 26, 28, 40, 43, 100, 146, 147, 148, 153n1, 156n44; and anxiety-hysteria, 44; and castration anxiety, 12
Aristotle, 43, 56n27, 57n63, 104
Augustan, 100, 109; and poetics, 101, 102
Austen, Jane, xiii, xv, xvi, xix; and capitalism, 61; and Enlightenment feminism, 70; and *Persuasion*, 61–77; and romance, 62

Baillie, John: *An Essay on the Sublime* (1747), 81
Bailly, Lionel, 141, 142
Batten, Guin, xvii
Berlant, Lauren, 38
big Other, xx, 66, 70, 71, 74, 75, 76, 122, 142, 144, 146, 147, 148, 149, 150, 152, 153

bildung, 126, 125
Bion, Wilfred, xvi
Blair, Robert: "The Grave," 113
Blake, William, 160; and "The Fly," 39; and *The Four Zoas*, xvi
Boime, Alfred, 25, 26
biopower, 53
Botting, Fred, 148
Breton, André, 144, 154n14
Bronfen, Elizabeth, 13
Burke, Edmund, 84, 85
Butler, Judith, 128
Byron, George Gordon, xv, xvi, 1, 167, 175n37; Byronic figure, 168; and "Darkness," 167; and *Manfred*, xv; and *Mazeppa*, 1

Canuel, Mark, 171, 170
capitalism, xviii, 58n53, 61, 63, 68, 166
Carter, Elizabeth, xix, 110; and "Ode to Melancholy," 110–12; and "Thoughts at Midnight," 112
Cartesian, 40, 51
Chaplin, Sue, 151
Chiesa, Lorenzo, 37
Claridge, Laura, 122
Clark, David L., 21, 22
cognitive science, xvi
Coleridge, Samuel Taylor, xvi, 40; "Kubla Khan," xii; "To a Young Ass," 39; "The Rime of the Ancient Mariner," 39
Collings, David, xvi, xix, 4, 5, 122

179

Collins, William, xix, xx, 81–87, 90–94, 100, 108; and "Ode to Fear," 81, 85, 86; and "Ode on the Poetical Character," 81, 83, 90, 91
Cooney, Brian, xvii
Copjec, Joan, 83
Cowper, William, 100

Dacre, Charlotte: and *Zofloya, or The Moor*, 147
das Ding, xvi, 106, 125, 136
Deleuze, Gilles, 134; and Guattari, Felix, 134
Derrida, Jacques, 39, 42, 40, 44
Didi-Huberman, Georges, 26, 27
digital humanities (DH), xiii
Dolar, Mladen, 3, 127, 149, 152
Donne, John, 101
Doody, Margaret Ann, 145
drive, 114; and death drive, 26, 171; and demand, 142; and desire, 141; and melancholia, 111; and sex drive, 142

Ecrits, xi, xvi, 42, 87, 121, 123, 131, 132, 143, 151; and "Aggressivity in psychoanalysis," 10, 14; and "Kant with Sade," 158, 164; and "Logical Time and the Assertion of Anticipated Certainty," 87–90; and "The Seminar on the Purloined Letter," 157, 158; and "The Subversion of the Subject and the Dialectic of Desire," xviii, 142, 144, 151; and "Variations on the Standard Treatment," 123
Edelman, Lee, 38, 39, 53
Edwards, Peter, 39
Enlightenment, 3, 4, 155n23; faith in empirical knowledge, 5; feminism, 70; rationality, 39; Spanish Enlightenment, 26; subject of, 4; zero degree representations, 6
ex-sistence, 128, 129, 130

extimité, 3, 127

Fantasy, 13, 15–17, 26, 28, 46, 48, 51, 52, 63, 68–76, 100, 120, 122, 123, 126, 129, 132–37, 151, 158, 171
Faflak, Joel, xiv, 122,120, 135
Farnell, Gary, 122
feminine, 31, 49, 75, 76; and masks, 28; and sexuation, 62, 63, 83, 174n29
Fink, Bruce, 144; and desire, 144; and *Lacan On Love*, 44, 45; and phallus, 73
Foucault, Michel, 23, 24; and *Madness and Civilization*, 22
Fraistat, Neil, xvii
Freeman, Barbara Claire, 83
Freud, Sigmund, xii, xiv, 44, 45, 82, 84, 85, 94, 159, 167; and *Civilization and its Discontents*, 157; and Daniel Paul Schreber, xv; and *The Future of an Illusion*, 157; and *The Interpretation of Dreams*, 145, 147
Frye, Northrop, 160

Galperin, William, 67, 68
Gaze, xvi, xviii, xix, 3–7, 9–12, 16, 18, 19, 21, 22, 24, 27, 28, 31, 32, 33, 135, 142, 149, 150; of Apollonius, 50; and demand of, 22; and desire, 50; and Goya's gaze, 33; and mask, 21; and as object, 3, 12, 14, 15; and painting, 21; and paternal, 2, 8, 13, 14, 17
Gigante, Denise, xix, 3, 4, 5
Godwin, William, 18, 44, 170; and *St. Leon*, 5
Goldsmith, Oliver, 110
Gothic, xv, xviii, xx, 141–153, 154n14, 154n22,155n23, 156n44; and desire, 39, 101–03, 105, 141, 142, 143; and Gothicism, 101; and Gothic tyrant, 142–44, 149–51; and satire, 145; and symbolic order, 146

Goya, Francisco, 21–33, 35n38; and *Disasters of War*, 21, 22; and *Disparates, Desastres*, 24; and *Even thus he cannot make her out (Ni asi la distingue)*, 31; and *The Idiot*, 23; and *Nobody knows himself*, 31; and *Now I see what she is (Ya la percivo)*, 31; and *The sleep of reason produces monsters (El sueno de la razon produce monstrous)*, 23
Graveyard poetry, xx, 99–114, passim
Gray, Thomas, 100, 102; and "Elegy Written in a Country Churchyard," 108–10
Griffin, Robert, 100

Haggerty, George, xvii
Hazlitt, William, xvi
Heidegger, Martin, 42
Hegel, G. W., 82, 83, 88, 121
Hervey, James, 100, 109, 110, 113
historicism, xi, xiv, 25; and historicist, xii, 24, 25, 61, 151
Hoffmann, E. T. A., 147; and *The Devil's Elixirs*, 148
Hurd, Richard, 103, 154n22
Hurtz, Neil, 90
Hutchings, W., 110

Imago, 2, 7, 8, 10, 11

Jameson, Frederic, 159, 162, 173n22
Johnston, Adrian, 158, 159
Johnson, Claudia, L., 61
Johnson, Samuel, 91
Jouissance, 39, 45–47, 49, 51–54, 90, 99, 100, 107, 109, 114, 124, 125, 137, 151, 158–65, 171, 172; and phallic, 43, 61–63, 73, 126

Kant, Immanuel, xx, 82, 83, 84, 85; and dynamic sublime, 84
Keats, John, 37–54; and *Endymion*, xix; and *Lamia*, 37, 39, 42; and negative capability, 38; and animals, 39, 41, 45, 47–51, 53, 54; and "The Cap and Bells," 42; and "Ode to a Nightingale," 46; and "On the Grasshopper and Cricket," 46; and *The Eve of St. Agnes*, 51
Kelly, Gary, 163
Kneale, J. Douglas, 122, 134
Knox-Shaw, Peter, 69, 70
Kroeber, Karl, 38

Lacan, Jacques: and "Desire and the Interpretation of Desire in Hamlet," 100; and *My Teaching*, xvii. See also *Ecrits*; *Seminars*
Lafont, Jeanne, 120, 126
Leitch, Vincent, xi
Levinas, Emmanuel, 42
Levinson, Marjorie, xii, 52, 58n53
Levitas, Ruth, 159
Lewis, Matthew: and *The Monk*, 146
Longinus, 84, 85, 90
Lussier, Mark, xvi
Lyotard, Jean-Francois, 83

masculine, 28, 39, 71, 145; and jouissance, 43; and sexuation, 62, 76, 83
Mason, William, 109
Maturin, Charles: and *Melmoth the Wanderer*, 142, 153n5
MacCannell, Juliet Flower, 160
McGann, Jerome, xii
McGowan, Todd, xiii, 68, 75, 171
McMillan, Chris, 158, 159
meconnaissance, 52, 88, 141
melancholia, 99, 100, 102–4, 106, 107, 110, 111, 115n8
Menely, Tobias, 39
Miell, Sam Warren, xvii
Miller, Jacques-Alain, xvi, 163
Milton, John, 85, 92, 100, 101, 102; and *Paradise Lost*, 9, 94

Mirror stage, xi, xviii, 2, 5–9, 11, 14, 38, 44, 45, 51
Mitchell, Robert, 170
Möbius strip, 121, 127, 133, 134
More, Thomas, 157, 160–66
Moretti, Franco, xiii, xiv
Morton, Timothy, 39

Nancy, Jean-Luc, 43
Nandrea, Lorri G., 69, 75–77
Nersessian, Anahid, 160
Neville, Henry: and *Isle of Pines*, 159

Oedipus complex, 14, 48, 85, 90, 101

Parisot, Eric, 110
Parnell, Thomas, 100
Peeping Tom (Powell 1960), 13, 14, 17
Perversion, xvi, 14
phallic, 67, 71, 75, 85; and fantasy, 63, 67; and mother, 58n53; and objects, 62, 68; and power, 77; and signifier, 125; and women, 76
Pinch, Adela, 119
Pittock, Joan, 101
Poe, Edgar Allan, 147
Polidori, John, 1
Pope, Alexander, 116n10, 100–3, 109; and "Elegy to the Memory of an Unfortunate Lady," 101; and "Eloisa to Abelard," 101
providence, 61–77, passim

Radcliffe, Ann: and *A Sicilian Romance*, 149, 150, 152
Reeve, Clara, 149; and *The Old English Baron*, 149; and *The Progress of Romance*, 148
Richard, Jessica, 62, 63, 64, 66, 76
Ross, Marlon, B., 100
Ross, Trevor, 102
Roudinesco, Elizabeth, 132

Sandy, Mark, xvii

Sarup, Madan, 40
Saturn, 99, 114n2
Saussure, Ferdinand de, 42, 86, 87, 152
Schulz, Andrew, 26
Scott, Sarah, xix; and *Millenium Hall*, xx, 161–67
Scott, Walter, xiii
Seminars of Jacques Lacan: *Seminar V*, xv, xvii, xv, *Seminar VII*, xvi, 99, 106, 107, 158; and *Seminar VIII*, 135; and *Seminar X*, xvii, 10, 147; and *Seminar XI*, 21, 27; and *Seminar XX*, xvi, 37, 99; and *Seminar XXIII*, xvii, 52; and *Seminar XXVI*, 103
Sena, John, 100
sensibility, 100, 102, 108, 26, 39
sexuation, xix, 61–63, 76, 83
Sha, Richard, 53
Shakespeare, William, 82, 87, 102, 108, 109; and *Hamlet*, 115n8
Shelley, Mary, xix; and *The Last Man*, xx, 167–172
Shepardson, Charles, 102
signifier, 16, 59n66, 83, 84, 85, 86, 89–91, 92, 94, 103, 104, 105, 107, 108, 111, 112, 114, 115n8, 121, 131, 132, 137; and phallic, 79n11, 125; and Saussurean, 42, 87; and signified, 27, 49, 79n11, 84–87; and transcendental signifier, 40
Sitterson, Joseph, 122
Shinstone, William, 100, 110
Skriabine, Pierre, 122
Skorin-Kapov, Jadranka, 84
Smart, Christopher, 100
Spenser, Edmund, 85, 92, 94, 101, 102, 108; and *Faerie Queene*, 92, 93
Southcott, Joanna, xiii
Spivak, Gayatri Chakravorty, 40
sublime, 81–94, passim
sublimation, xx, 10, 99, 100, 105–110, 112–114, 115n5, 117n41, 117n44, 157

Swift, Jonathan, 101, 167; and *Gulliver's Travels*, 159, 160
symptomatic readings, xi, xii

Taylor, Charles, 40
Thomson, James, 100
topology, xviii, xx, 120–22, 126, 130, 132, 134–36
tropes, 126, 130, 131
torus, 119–22, 126–130, 132, 134, 135
Townshend, Dale, 155n23

uncanny (unheimlich), 2–5, 12, 13, 17, 127, 129, 147, 148
utopia, xviii, xx, 157–72, passim; and dystopia, xx, 166–72

Visual field, 2, 3, 11, 17, 28, 134; and desire, 24, 50; and pleasure, 49; and metaphor, 148
Voltaire, 41

Walpole, Horace, xix; and *Castle of Otranto*, xx, 141–53
Wang, N. C., xvii
Warton, Joseph, 91, 102, 103, 107–10; and *An Essay on the Writings and Genius of Pope*, 101; and "To Fancy," 108, 109
Warton, Thomas, 102, 103, 107–9; and *History of English Poetry*, 102; and "The Pleasures of Melancholy," 105
Waugh, Patricia, 122
Wecker, John, 41
Weiskel, Theodore: and *The Romantic Sublime*, 84–87, 90, 94
Wilberforce, William, 41
Wollstonecraft, Mary, xvi, 18, 44
Wordsworth, William, xv, xvi, xix, xx, 51, 116n8, 119–137 passim; and "Ode: intimations of Immortality," xv; and Dorothy, 42; and *The Prelude*, 42, 119–137 passim; and leech gatherers, 49; and Mount Snowdon, 87; and egotistical sublime, 91; and "Strange Fits of Passion," 125, and St Bartholomew's Fair, 42
Wright, Elizabeth, 106, 115n5

Young, Edward, 100, 104, 110, 113; and *Conjectures on Original Composition*, 102; and *Night Thoughts*, 104
Young, Robert, 122

Zizek, Slavoj, xvii, 39, 48, 151, 159, 160, 164; and the sexual relation, 49; and *objet petit a*, 51; and sublime, 58; and *The Prelude*, 122, 123, 129, 132, 134, 135; and utopia, 171

www.ingramcontent.com/pod-product-compliance
Lightning Source LLC
Chambersburg PA
CBHW070805230426
43665CB00017B/2500